Home-Grown Vegetable Manual

Steve Ott

CONTENTS

INTRODUCTION

Why Grow Your Own?

Producing home-grown fresh vegetables hasn't been this popular since the Dig for Victory campaign in the Second World War when growing food was a necessity. At that time many of the great gardens in the UK, such as the Queen's residence at Sandringham, were literally turned over to producing food for the war effort. Thankfully we no longer have to worry about shortages, so why the sudden rediscovery of the delights of growing our own? Well, there are lots of reasons why people who have never grown food before are taking up the spade.

Thanks to the way that modern transport has 'shrunk' the world and the way that clever storage techniques have allowed producers to maintain the quality of the most fragile of food items, we have become used to buying fruit and vegetables on demand, at times when they would never normally be available to us. It sounds great, but there are serious drawbacks.

Rather than eating local produce when it would naturally be available in our climate, we are used to eating all kinds of foods whenever we wish, most of which have travelled halfway round the world to reach our plate. In order to satisfy our demand for unseasonal fare, food has to be frozen, chilled or stored, often in very unnatural ways, and frequently harvested when unripe, all of which affects the flavour and nutritional value.

Growing your own veg means that you will be harvesting your produce when it should be harvested – at its freshest and most nutritious. And the shorter the journey from harvest to plate, the more the naturally occurring vitamins and minerals within the food survive to feed us.

There is another factor: professional growers are under great pressure to produce maximum yields of blemish-free food. To do this, crops are often fed on a diet of man-made fertilisers and sprayed with pesticides to prevent damage from bugs and diseases. Pressure on supply and prices is forcing supermarkets to consider the use of genetically modified ingredients. Reacting against this, more and more consumers are deciding to grow their own in order to know exactly what treatment their food has had before it reaches the table.

Commercial growers choose the most profitable varieties – those with natural vigour and the longest shelf-life. They are

not necessarily the tastiest. If you grow your own, you can select which types to plant and they can provide you with a far greater range of flavours. Tomatoes are a good example; there are hundreds of varieties available, yet go to any supermarket and you are likely to have to choose from the same half-dozen. And the same goes for all other fruit and veg. Taste home-grown sweetcorn, for example, and you will never want to eat the shop-bought version again, and home-grown peas and new potatoes have to be eaten to be believed.

Growing your own can be cheaper, especially if you concentrate on foods that are always expensive in the shops, such as asparagus, globe artichokes, beans and more exotic items such as sweet potatoes. Finally, there is the serious moral consideration: can it be good that produce has had to be flown halfway round the world to get to our plate? More and more consumers say no.

If you have a hankering to join the ever-swelling ranks of people who wish to grow their own then this book is for you. In the first sections we give you all the information and tools you need to get you started, whether you plan to grow a few vegetables in a tub on the patio or balcony or to take on a full-sized allotment. In addition, we provide you with a handy reference to all the most common vegetables you are likely to grow. Start with a few easy vegetables in your first season and then, once you have a feel for it, move on to broaden your repertoire.

And should you get bitten by the growing bug, as we are sure you will, we also teach you some of the more advanced skills required to extend your growing season and improve your success year after year, gradually reducing your dependence on the supermarket. You may never be able to grow all your needs, but given a little time, you could be growing significant amounts and what you do produce will taste so much better than vegetables have ever tasted before.

PART 1 Home-grown Vegetable Manual

SELECTING YOUR SITE

Siting Your Plot

Left: Victorian kitchen garden designers appreciated the importance of shelter. The wonderful walled gardens they constructed are still very much in use today

Below: When looking for a suitable spot to grow vegetables at home, you may have to settle for somewhere less than perfect, but don't let that put you off

Having decided to take the plunge and to create a veg patch in your garden, where should you put it? Keep in mind that most vegetables need:

■ **Sun** for much, if not all, the day. Some leafy vegetables and salads will tolerate a shady spot where they receive sunshine for less than half the day, but they are the exception.
■ **Shelter** from strong winds and the cold; this may be provided by nearby buildings, fences, walls or trees.
■ **Reasonably fertile and free-draining soil**; most soils can be slowly improved as described in Part Two.

In reality you may have to settle for the only space you have. If you find that any of the above are lacking, for example if the only possible site for your plot is exposed and cold, the soil is waterlogged, or if your garden is in deep shade for much of the time, then it may be best to look for an allotment to rent instead (see page 18).

No place like home?

There are advantages in having a patch in your own garden: there is likely to be a ready source of water; security will be

better, so less worrying about your tools disappearing in the night, which in turn means you won't have to carry them backwards and forwards; and if your veggies are literally at the bottom of the garden, it is easier to get out there and pull a few weeds or harvest a few tomatoes when you have some spare minutes than if you have to make a special trip. Lastly, with allotments being in short supply, you may be forced to look further afield than you would like for a plot to rent.

The perfect plot

The picture shows the perfect site for a patch on which to grow most popular types of vegetables. Of course, this also applies if you are looking for an allotment to rent. Given the choice of two or three sites, opt for the one that best fulfils the criteria for good light, shelter and soil.

The plot shown has a south-facing aspect, which provides maximum light in spring and summer when it is needed most. It is sheltered from cold winds by a windbreak, but this will not cast shade. Also there are no tall buildings, trees or fences on the borders of the plot to cast shade on the soil. The land slopes slightly towards the south to make the most of the available sunlight and this helps to warm the soil in the spring.

On the perfect plot there will also be a source of water nearby and a small greenhouse, complete with power supply, in which to propagate seedlings in the spring and to grow tomatoes, peppers and cucumbers in the summer. There might also be an unheated polytunnel and a secure shed for tools.

Remember that this is the ideal – if your site ticks at least half of these boxes, go for it!

Chilled out

The start and end of the UK season is dictated by the time of the first and last frost. This varies greatly from place to place: in the south mid-May is usually a 'safe' time to plant out tender crops such as tomatoes and courgettes; in the Midlands the end of May is the benchmark; whereas in the far north the end of June may be more usual. There are always exceptions to the rule and it is best to check with a neighbour to see when they consider it safe to plant out.

Many traditional vegetables are reasonably hardy, indeed some, such as the brassica (cabbage) family, are capable of withstanding very low temperatures and yet still maintain leafy growth.

The growing season for most of us runs from March to the end of October, unless we have a greenhouse or polytunnel to offer some protection in winter, although global warming is slowly pushing the boundaries at each end of the season.

Beware frost pockets

While frosts dictate when we can plant or sow tender crops outside, there are ways to minimise its effect. One of these is to avoid siting your plot in a frost pocket.

A frost pocket is simply an area at the base of a slope where dense, cold air collects. If a solid object such as a wall, fence or undergrowth prevents this cold air from escaping it will build up and can make the temperature close to the ground several degrees colder than the air above, causing much more damage. It may be easy to remedy this problem – by raising the crown of the offending trees to allow cold air to seep away, for example – but your control over this factor may be limited, so bear it in mind when planning.

This is a beautiful site for an allotment, but the slope may encourage cold air to collect in the gully at the bottom

Designing Your Plot

Straight rows

The traditional method adopted by most vegetable growers is to grow crops in long, straight rows. This has the advantage of making reasonably good use of space and with the crops in uniform rows it is easy to tell them apart from the weeds in the early stages, making hoeing more straightforward. Crops which need plenty of space, including brassicas, are usually planted out in staggered rows after having been started off in straight 'nursery' rows or a 'nursery' bed. Many gardeners seem to like the orderly nature of this system, but the drawback is that the necessary paths giving access to the crops have to be dug each year to break up any compaction, since they are not 'fixed'.

Other systems (see below) are gaining in popularity and prove that vegetables can be grown in an efficient yet attractive way and need not be consigned to the bottom of the garden.

Choose this method if:
- ■ You do not want to go to the expense of buying edging for raised beds or parterres and material to cover permanent paths.
- ■ You prefer the idea of growing your crops in simple straight rows.
- ■ A lack of time means that regularly running the hoe down straight rows is a better option for you than hand weeding.

Raised beds

Raised beds are now almost as popular as traditional rows. They are a great option if your existing site is waterlogged or consists of very heavy clay or a thin soil over chalk since they allow you to grow over the problem area. Being raised, they also warm more quickly in the spring.

Raised beds can be very efficient in terms of space; leafy crops such as brassicas are grown closely in staggered rows so that when mature the leaves touch to form a weed-suppressing cover over the soil. If the crops are harvested as baby veg the planting density can be increased even further.

Growing in raised beds can also make planning easier, especially if you are following a four-year crop rotation (see page 48), and have four or eight beds.

Beds which are raised more than the standard 15cm (6in) or so can help less able gardeners by making the crops more accessible by reducing the need to bend.

Raised beds fit in perfectly with the no-dig method of growing advocated by some gardeners (see page 44). If you build them so that you can easily reach the middle of the bed from the path, you need never walk on the soil, so avoiding compaction and maintaining aeration. Around 1.2m (4ft) is the recommended width for raised beds, but you should experiment to find the perfect size for you (see 'Building a Raised Bed', page 14).

Choose this method if:
- Your site is often waterlogged or has some other soil problem.
- You want to follow the no-dig method of growing your crops (although this can be done on an open plot).
- Organising your crops in fixed units would be easier for you.
- You want to make an attractive feature out of your plot (boarding can be painted with coloured preservatives).
- You want to bring the crops closer to you to reduce strain.

TOP TIP

WHICH PLANTING METHOD?

If you are unsure as to which of the methods described here is for you, try the traditional method of planting in straight rows— you can always convert your plot to another system later.

Parterres

Parterres offer an attractive alternative to straight rows and were popular in many great gardens of the past. They were developed by the French in the 1500s and the technique reached its pinnacle in the gardens of Versailles. The formal planting consists of a series of symmetrical boxes surrounded by clipped box or similar hedging, or sometimes stones or low walls. The idea was soon adopted in Britain and examples can be seen in many of the country's wonderful stately homes such as Kensington Palace.

Modern parterres are less elaborate and more modest in size, but can offer an attractive way to grow edibles, often in combination with colourful ornamental plants. Remember that traditional edgings such as box require regular maintenance and come at a high initial cost.

Choose this method if:
- You want to make a real feature out of your vegetable patch.
- The formal look of the parterre appeals to you and fits in with the design of your garden.
- You wish to combine flowers and vegetables (although this can be done with the other planting systems).

TOP TIP

SAVE YOUR ENERGY

Consider the length as well as the width of the beds. If you are not going to walk on the soil – one of the advantages of raised beds – you will have to walk around the outside. Aim to make a path every 5m (16ft) or so to save your legs.

Growing on a grid

This option is particularly suitable if you have little space in which to grow your vegetables, or if you require only small amounts of each crop. It makes use of every inch of available soil, but if you are used to growing in straight rows on a traditional plot, you may find it difficult to adapt at first as it is radically different.

The bed, which can be of any size to fit your garden, bearing in mind that the middle should be comfortably accessible from the paths, is physically divided into squares, traditionally measuring 30 x 30cm (12 x 12in) each, but they can be adapted to suit your space. Raised beds are particularly suited to this method although it can be practised on the open plot or even in large containers.

String, laths or canes can be used to mark out the squares. When they are planted up, the idea is to adapt the number of plants per square to suit the crop, but to plant as many as possible to make best use of space. So, for example, you would plant one tomato plant per square, but four lettuces or 16 radishes, 12 carrots and so on.

Once a square has been harvested, the soil is simply refreshed with a handful of well-rotted compost (not root crops) and a little general fertiliser is added before replanting or sowing.

There are a few crops that don't easily lend themselves to this method. Trailers such as squashes and cucumbers present some problems, but they can be trained up canes to prevent them from encroaching on surrounding squares. Large, leafy brassicas such as Brussels sprouts are also a challenge, but others, such as spring cabbages, kale and crops that are usually considered long-term, such as leeks, can be harvested young.

Consider this method if:
- You have limited space in which to grow your veg.
- You have time to plan and keep on top of the successional sowings required to keep the bed full and so get the most from this system.

Building a raised bed

If, having studied the options, you decide that raised beds are for you, you will need to draw up a plan, positioning

your beds to make best use of available space. The orientation of the beds (north–south, or east–west) will probably be decided by the site and is not critical, but if you have a choice it is best to have the longest side of the rectangle facing the sun to reduce shading and help warm the soil in spring.

The next stage concerns what you use to build the retaining walls. Timber is the usual choice since it is easy to cut into the required length or shape on an irregular site. It is rarely cheap, although some allotment sites may find cut-price or even free sources nearby. Scaffold boards are the

---

TOP TIP

LET THEM SEE THE LIGHT

Tall plants, such as tomatoes and sweetcorn, should be placed at the back of the bed, at the north end if it faces south, or the east end if it faces west, so as not to shade low-growing crops.

TOP TIP

TREAT IT WELL

If you are buying timber to make the retaining walls, always go for tanalised (pressure treated) wood as this will last longer. If you have bartered or begged the wood and it is not pre-treated, paint it with a plant-friendly wood preservative before use. This also includes the pegs to hold all but the heaviest timber boards firmly in place.

perfect length and thickness for this purpose and local companies have to replace them from time to time, providing allotment holders with a bargaining opportunity.

If wood is not to your liking then there are other options: bricks, breeze blocks, rock, in fact anything that is capable of holding the soil in place will do. Kits made from recycled plastics are available and these provide a good long-lasting alternative to timber and are largely maintenance free. Some are twin-walled, offering excellent insulation and helping to warm the soil in spring.

TOP TIP

ONE SIZE DOESN'T FIT ALL

Beds can be made to any shape to fit the most awkward spaces, but remember the golden rule: you should always be able to reach the middle of the bed without straining or stepping on to the soil.

Building a raised bed from wood

1 To make your raised beds you will need suitable timber. Scaffold boards are ideal, but recycled railway sleepers last for life since they are well preserved (see note below). You will also need timber to make pegs.

2 Having decided where your beds are to go the timber can be cut to length. Sleepers (or the equivalent) are easy to cut with a chainsaw, but only attempt this if you are competent to use it.

3 In order to hold the timber in place you will need some wooden pegs long enough to hold the timber in place when knocked into the soil. Cut these to length and saw one end to a point to make hammering in easier.

4 With all the beds in place take a step back and have a last look at the positioning to be sure you are happy with the arrangement. Check for a final time that the beds are square and secure with the pegs.

5 The turf can now be skimmed off of the surface and placed back in the base of the bed, grass side down. On heavy or compacted soil, fork over the base of the bed before replacing the turf. Top up with good topsoil.

NOTE: Due to treatment with tar-based preservatives, genuine sleepers are no longer permitted for sale. Use modern untreated equivalents available from some garden centres and timber merchants.

Building a raised bed using a kit

1 Mark out your beds, making best use of the available space. Build in paths to reduce the amount of walking you have to do to get around the beds and make them wide enough for a wheelbarrow. You should be able to reach the middle of the bed from one side without straining. Then get digging!

Do not dig the areas reserved for pathways – if you do they will only sink later, and the less digging you have to do the better.

2 You now need to cover the paths with ground cover fabric. First move any soil from along the edges of the beds to facilitate burying the soil covering fabric.

3 Having dug out the bed edges cut them vertically into the soil with a spade or lawn edging knife. Roll the soil covering fabric out over the paths.

4 Push the edges of the fabric into the soil with hands or spade. This prevents weeds or grass from growing along the edge.

5 Where paths cross allow plenty of overlap when cutting the fabric as weeds or grass will find any gaps and grow through very quickly.

6 Most fabrics are easy to cut with scissors. If you can select a non-woven material as this will not fray when cut to size.

7 Pull the soil back to the edge of the bed with a rake to hold the fabric firmly in place and prepare the bed for edging.

8 Lay out the materials to edge the beds. In this case we have used low maintenance recycled uPVC plastic sections which simply clip together.

9 Our raised bed kit simply slots together using the joints supplied. Fit the bed together roughly at first and straighten it up afterwards.

10 Once the bed has been put together, check that it is in the right place in relation to other beds and that it is square and the edges straight.

11 Our kit (Link-a-Bord) comes with lengths of dowelling made from the same recycled material as the beds. It is cut to size with secateurs.

12 Hammer home the lengths of dowelling. It should be driven into the soil by at least 20cm (8in) to ensure all remains secure.

Taking on an Allotment

If you haven't got space in your garden for a vegetable patch, an allotment offers a good alternative. But before taking one on, ask yourself honestly if you have the time to spare. Tending a full-sized plot takes a minimum of two days a week – many plot holders spend considerably longer – and if time is scarce then an allotment may be something to consider for the future. However, if you feel the time is right, or if the whole family is prepared to chip in and help, then go for it. It's great fun!

After a boom in the 1970s the popularity of allotments slumped and many sites disappeared. Now demand has soared and allotments can be hard to come by in many areas; you may have to put your name on the waiting list, or look further afield.

Local authorities have a responsibility to provide land if there is sufficient demand. In fact, all it takes to trigger the process is for six adults who are on the electoral register to get together and write to the local authority (town, borough, district or parish council) requesting an allotment, to oblige them to act. The exceptions to this are Scotland and inner London where the advice is usually to look outside your own borough for the nearest site to you.

Allotments offer some great advantages:
- They provide the space you need to grow significant amounts of fruit and veg.
- They are often quite cheap to rent.
- Most sites have their own social scene and old hands willing to offer advice to those who want it.
- Some of the larger sites have great facilities – these may include a shop, free hire of machinery, even toilets and a rest room.

Where to start

First find your nearest site. You should find details of the person you need to contact on the gate, but if not have a chat with a plot holder. Failing this your local library might be able to help, or get in touch with your local authority. Not all allotments are owned by the local authority – local trusts, the church or a private landowner may have responsibility.

Having found a site with plots available, book a visit and see what your prospective allotment has to offer. Here's what to look for.

BOUNDARY WAY
ALLOTMENTS

NO TRESPASS. NO RIGHT OF WAY.
Official allotment holders only

Enquiries:
LEISURE SERVICES
WOLVERHAMPTON BOROUGH COUNCIL
Telephone: 01902 555155

SITE HEALTH CHECK

- Is the site well-tended? All sites have a few overgrown areas, but check the state of the site as a whole: is it run down or thriving?

- Ask about facilities: for example, not all sites have running water. If this one has water, can you use a hosepipe in the summer?

- Are buildings permitted? Some landowners will not allow sheds, greenhouses or polytunnels on site, since they can lead to problems with theft and vandalism.

- Is the site secure, with a gate and well-maintained security fence? Plots are often situated in the middle of a residential area and this can work in your favour since if some of the residents are plot holders they will have a vested interest in keeping an eye open for problems.

- Chat to existing plot holders – ask them about any problems they may have had either with the site, or the soil. The soil can vary greatly, even in different areas on the same site.

- Is there access for deliveries of bulk items such as manure?

TOP TIP

SELF-MANAGEMENT

Many sites are self-managed by an elected committee of plot holders who are responsible for the day-to-day running. They work in conjunction with the landowners and together with the other plot holders take responsibility for much of the general maintenance. They will organise fund-raising events and police the smooth running of the site. This generally works very well and some of the best sites are self-managed.

THE STATE OF THE PLOT

The next consideration is the plot itself. Don't be put off if it is very weedy, although if you are presented with a sea of waist-high brambles you might think twice. Some landowners will clear the area and turn the soil for a new allotment holder. If that isn't the case, you need to consider whether you are up to the task of restoring the plot, although you can usually clear enough space to get started quite quickly.

TOP TIP

SIZE MATTERS

Allotments are often measured in rods (one rod equals about 5m or 5½yd) and 8 to 10 rods is common, but size varies greatly. Many sites now offer half plots and these are great for beginners. You can always apply for a full plot later.

Some landowners will clear and rotovate the plot for you before you take over, saving you much backache.

Taming a New Plot

The overgrown allotment

The chances are that unless you have a kind landowner who is prepared to clear the ground for you, or you are lucky enough to be taking over immediately from a dedicated tenant, the plot will be seriously weedy. In reality you may well face quite a challenge to get your plot into a fit state and this can be daunting. You are about to learn one of the inescapable truths about growing your own veg – digging is hard work! Don't let this put you off. Here are some simple rules to follow, which will make the whole process far easier and highly enjoyable:

1. Don't bite off more than you can chew. Faced with a weedy plot, in your mind divide it into three or four sections and concentrate on clearing and digging one of them. The others will need to have the

major growth taken off the top to prevent things getting worse while you get on with the good bit – growing some veg.

2. Cover the partially cleared areas with thick ground covering fabric. This is available from most garden centres or via mail order and simply smothers the weeds. Hold it down securely with anything you can lay your hands on (not old car tyres as you will be charged when you eventually try to get rid of them).
3. Sow your seeds on the cleared land and while they grow uncover the next section and get digging to clear the roots of perennial weeds such as brambles, docks and creeping thistles, leaving the rest of the plot temporarily in darkness.

CLEARING THE WAY

Assuming that your new site is not already run along organic lines (i.e. the use of chemicals is forbidden), you have to decide whether you wish to grow your veg organically or not. If the answer is not, then the first job, if taking over the land during the growing season (April to September), is to spray with a glyphosate-based weedkiller, being careful not to allow any to drift on to neighbouring plots. This will be absorbed into the leaves and will travel to the roots, killing all but the deepest and most persistent (which may need another treatment later). Glyphosate will not affect the soil or subsequent crops.

Once dead (this takes about three weeks), the top growth can be removed and the area covered to prevent regrowth until you have time to dig it.

If you are taking over between October and March it is better to cut back the dormant growth to ground level and to leave further work until the spring when soft, new shoots will emerge; these will absorb the weedkiller much more effectively.

Chosen to be an organic gardener? Then cut back the top growth as soon as you get the keys to the gate and cover the ground as above.

The new plot at home

If you have just moved in and are clearing ground for a new plot in your garden, you may be faced with a similar situation to that of the overgrown allotment, in which case you can follow the technique outlined above.

On the other hand, you may be converting part of an established lawn to the cause. If so, mark out the perimeter of your new plot and, if you are happy to use weedkillers, the grass and any weeds can be killed with glyphosate. Alternatively, you can mow the grass for the last time to ensure that there is as little top growth as possible, then dig the area and turn the turf into the soil where it will gradually rot (see tip above).

KNOW YOUR SOIL

Discovering Your Soil Type

The secret is in the soil

Once you know what type of soil you have and armed with the information in Part Six of this book, you can avoid crops that are likely to fail. You will also know how to treat your soil to get the best from it year after year.

The diagram shows the range of different common soil types. There are three main types: clay (the most common),

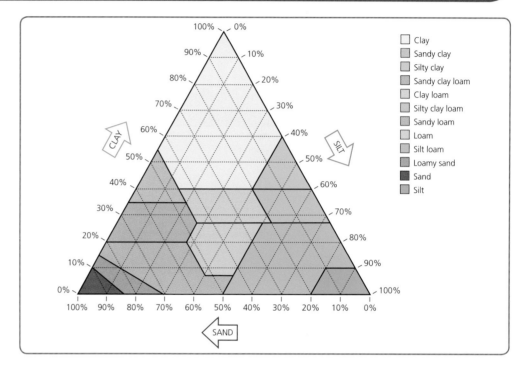

sand and silt. A mixture of all three of these in the perfect proportions is called loam.

The type of soil you have also depends on the underlying rock; most overly clay, but chalk is also common. Chalk soils tend to be quite thin and alkaline in nature.

One last soil type, which is less common, but presents its own challenges is peaty soil. Peaty soils are unique in that they are formed by many layers of organic matter that has broken down over many millennia. They are often very acidic and so on their own will only support plants that are adapted to grow in such conditions (see chart, page 27). They often remain very wet in the winter, but can be quite dry in the summer, so need careful management. In these circumstances it is often easier to grow your veg in raised beds using imported loam.

Soil size matters

The relative sizes of the various soil particles can be seen in the diagram and these have a great influence on the properties of the soil; for example, how well it drains, holds on to nutrients and how much air it contains. The mixture of particles of differing sizes is described as the soil's texture.

You can gain some idea of the

mixture of particles that make up your soil by half filling a jam jar with soil and then topping up almost to the top with water. Shake the jar for a few seconds and then leave to settle. Large particles such as stones and sand will sink immediately while tiny particles such as clay may remain in suspension for many days. Organic matter such as little bits of plant waste will float. After a week, look at the layers in the jar to gain some insight into the make-up of your soil. To get a better idea of the type of soil you have, however, follow the steps outlined on the next page.

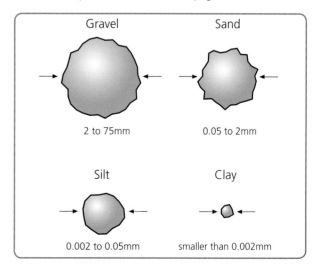

Gravel	Sand
2 to 75mm	0.05 to 2mm

Silt	Clay
0.002 to 0.05mm	smaller than 0.002mm

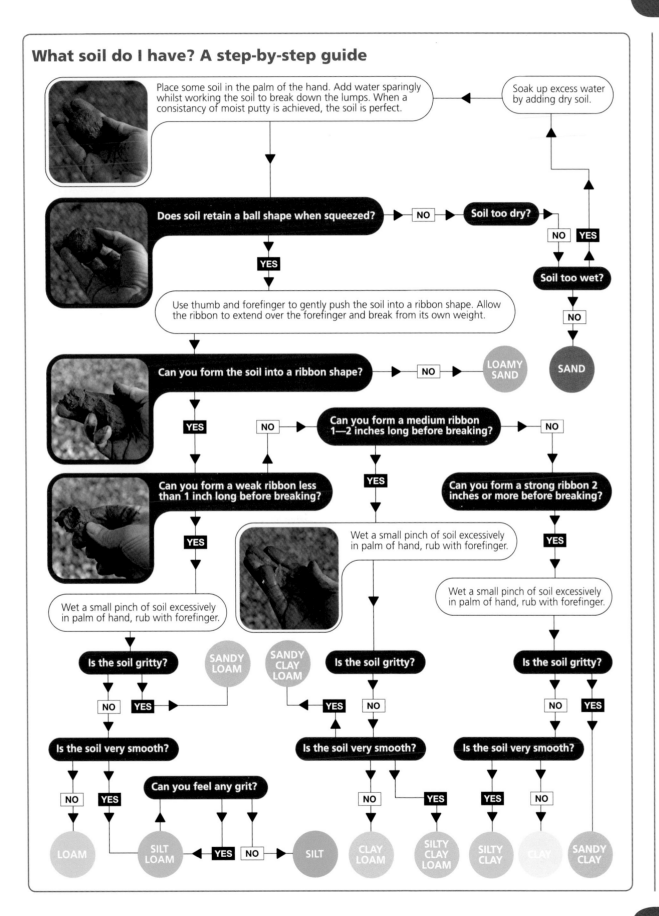

What soil do I have? A step-by-step guide

Place some soil in the palm of the hand. Add water sparingly whilst working the soil to break down the lumps. When a consistancy of moist putty is achieved, the soil is perfect.

Soak up excess water by adding dry soil.

Does soil retain a ball shape when squeezed? — NO → **Soil too dry?**

NO / YES

YES

Soil too wet?

NO

Use thumb and forefinger to gently push the soil into a ribbon shape. Allow the ribbon to extend over the forefinger and break from its own weight.

Can you form the soil into a ribbon shape? — NO → **LOAMY SAND**

SAND

YES

Can you form a medium ribbon 1—2 inches long before breaking? — NO

NO

YES

Can you form a weak ribbon less than 1 inch long before breaking?

Can you form a strong ribbon 2 inches or more before breaking?

YES

Wet a small pinch of soil excessively in palm of hand, rub with forefinger.

YES

Wet a small pinch of soil excessively in palm of hand, rub with forefinger.

Wet a small pinch of soil excessively in palm of hand, rub with forefinger.

Is the soil gritty?   **SANDY LOAM**   **SANDY CLAY LOAM**   **Is the soil gritty?**   **Is the soil gritty?**

NO / YES   YES / NO   NO / YES

Is the soil very smooth?   **Is the soil very smooth?**   **Is the soil very smooth?**

NO / YES   **Can you feel any grit?**   NO / YES   YES / NO

LOAM   **SILT LOAM**   YES / NO   **SILT**   **CLAY LOAM**   **SILTY CLAY LOAM**   **SILTY CLAY**   **CLAY**   **SANDY CLAY**

Well drained soils such as this sand are ideal for certain crops, such as asparagus.

I know my soil type, what next?

Different soil textures need different management to give their best. They also have advantages and disadvantages, which are handy to know. But before taking spade to plot you need to discover your soil's structure.

What is soil structure?

The structure of a soil simply describes the network of channels, pores and spaces within it, created as the particles clump together (rather than the percentage of particles themselves). Different soils have different structures depending on the percentage of clay, silt or sand they contain. This percentage also determines how easily the structure can be damaged when cultivated.

The soil structure determines how many air spaces there are in the soil and also how well it drains. Soils with lots of little spaces, i.e. clays, tend to hold on to water much more strongly and are less free draining than sands which have lots of large spaces. Plant roots grow into these spaces and obtain their air and water from them

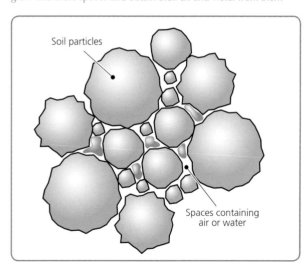

Soil particles

Spaces containing air or water

How does your soil measure up?

SANDY SOIL
Structure Coarse with large air spaces.
Pros Free draining, good aeration, warms quickly and can be worked earlier in the spring.
Cons Poor water and nutrient-holding properties so plants may starve. The structure is easily damaged when cultivating.

CLAY SOIL
Structure Tiny particles with tiny air spaces.
Pros Very fertile since the particles hold on to water and nutrients well.
Cons Remains wet and cold in spring, cracks during dry weather and becomes very hard. It is heavy to work and easily damaged if compacted, and it smears and forms hard pans (impermeable barriers) below the surface if cultivated with a rotary cultivator.

SILTY SOIL
Structure Fine with small air spaces and poor natural aeration. The fragile crumbs break down easily.
Pros Fertile and holds water and nutrients well. Faster than clay to warm in spring.
Cons Forms a crust on the surface during dry weather and puddles in wet weather. Easily damaged by over-cultivating.

LOAMY SOIL
Structure Lots of crumbs which stay together and drain freely, with plenty of air spaces.
Pros Fertile, good water and nutrient holding properties, good aeration. Slower to warm in the spring than sand, but better than clay.
Cons None

Soil Improving and pH

The essential ingredient

Vegetables are not fussy and will grow well in most soils, but it is important to build and maintain a good crumb structure, as in a loam, since this allows plenty of air to get to the roots while encouraging drainage.

A 'magic' ingredient called humus is what you need to improve poor soils and maintain good ones. It is present in all well-rotted organic matter, including animal manure and plant waste, or compost. Put very simply, humus is a jelly-like substance that is released when anything of organic origin rots. It feeds the soil flora and fauna, helps to hold water and nutrients and in combination with soil microbes which release sticky gums, binds the soil particles of all soil types together, encouraging them to form crumbs. It also darkens the soil, helping it to absorb the sun's rays so warming up faster in spring.

By adding humus in the form of well-rotted compost or manure every autumn and again when planting or as a mulch, it will gradually improve and maintain the structure and fertility of your soil and constitutes the most important job you will do each year in your vegetable garden.

Well rotted organic matter such as garden compost contains humus – nature's own soil improver

Soil pH

All soils have a natural acidity or alkalinity depending on the parent materials from which they are made, the amount of organic matter they contain (organic matter tends to be acidic), mineral content and, above all, the amount of lime present in the soil. When you measure soil pH, you are really measuring the pH of the water it contains, complete with these dissolved materials.

The acidity or alkalinity of a soil is expressed as its pH on a scale from 0–14 with 0 being very acid (the level of hydrochloric acid) and 14 very alkaline (household bleach is 12.5). A pH of 7 is neutral.

In practice, few soils fall lower than 3 or higher than 9. Plants grow best when they are in a soil that offers their preferred level of acidity or alkalinity and most are happy in a slightly acid soil, pH 6.5. This is less critical than is often suggested since most plants – vegetables included – can grow in a wide range of soil pH, certainly from 6–7.5 (see below). Much above or below this and the pH starts to affect the availablity of the nutrients in the soil and may lead to nutrient deficiencies.

pH preferences of some commonly grown vegetables	
Asparagus	6.5–7.5
Beans, climbing	6.5–7.5
Beets	6.0–7.5
Broccoli	6.0–7.0
Brussels sprouts	6.0–7.5
Cabbages	6.0–7.5
Carrots	5.5–7.0
Cauliflowers	5.5–7.5
Celery	6.5–7.5
Cucumbers	5.5–7.0
Garlic	5.5–8.0
Kale	6.0–7.5
Lettuces	6.5–7.5
Onions/garlic	5.5–8.0
Peas	5.5–7.0
Peppers	5.5–7.0
Potatoes	5.0–6.0
Pumpkins	5.5–7.5
Radishes	6.0–7.0
Spinach	6.0–7.5
Squash, crookneck	5.5–7.0
Squash, Hubbard	5.5–7.0
Tomatoes	5.5–7.5

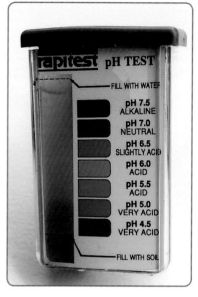

Our pH test gave a result of pH 6.5 or slightly acid – a good level for most vegetables

Testing and adjusting soil pH

Testing the soil to check its pH level is easy since all you need is a simple test kit available from your local garden centre. Place a representative sample of soil into the test tube or test pot supplied, add the reagent supplied and some distilled water and check the colour against a chart or coloured scale on the test pot.

The kit will also come with advice as to how much lime you may need to add to lift the pH to the required level. Most of us will need to raise pH rather than lower it, since rainfall and the addition of fertilisers and organic matter tend to have an acidifying effect on the soil. This is usually done by adding garden lime (ground limestone or chalk), which is the safest way of providing this nutrient. Lime can be applied once a year if a test proves it necessary, having taken account of your planned crop rotation.

Soils can be made more acidic, for example on areas overlying chalk, by adding sulphur chips. In extreme cases it is often easier to grow crops in a raised bed using imported soil rather than try to adjust the existing material.

Sulphur chips can be used to increase acidity, for example on chalky soils

TOP TIP

WHEN TO LIME

Never add lime and fertilisers together. They react when mixed, and the lime 'locks up' some of the nutrients, while making others too readily available.

Instead, plan which veg will be grown on which areas of the plot (your crop rotation plan), then lime areas where brassica crops are to be planted, since they like a more alkaline soil. Lime also deters clubroot, a damaging disease in these crops.

Do not add lime to a bed intended for potatoes, since this encourages another disease called potato scab. Give this bed a dressing of organic matter. (See Crop Rotation, page 48).

Fertilisers

Mother Nature is a great gardener. Soil left with nature in control is largely self-sustaining. If a patch of earth is left bare, it will be colonised by wild plants very quickly and depending on conditions, and whether it is grazed or not, a range of species will come to dominate. Where it is grazed animals will return the nutrients they take up in their manure; plants will live and die, also returning what they have taken from the soil.

However, on our intensively cropped plots it is all take, take, take, and we need to constantly top up the available nutrients to feed our plants. Fortunately there are several simple ways to do this.

We have already mentioned that the organic matter we add to improve the soil texture also contains some nutrients, but this is unlikely to be enough to keep your plants happy – unless you garden on the very best loam – and it will be necessary to add more.

During the Second World War the country was blockaded and people had to grow as much of their own produce as possible. In order to get the most from every scrap of land fertilisers were developed. Many of these, such as Growmore (known as National Growmore at the time), are still in use today.

Concerns about adding too much nitrogen-rich man-made fertiliser, which can leach into the water supply, have led to a backlash and many gardeners now use only fertilisers of organic origin.

Man-made feeds – the constituents of which are mainly based on natural minerals – if used carefully and in combination with organic matter, should do no harm and generally give quicker results. It is also worth remembering that too much fertiliser, whether organic or not, can cause pollution.

The choice of fertiliser comes down to personal preference. What is certain is that rising food prices and global shortages will ensure the continued use of man-made fertilisers for the foreseeable future.

Choosing a product

Having decided to use an organic or non-organic feed, or perhaps a combination of both, you will be presented with a bewildering array of products in your local garden centre and on the Internet, many designed for different plants at varying stages of growth, so which do you choose?

Fertilisers generally contain levels of the three main plant nutrients: nitrogen, represented on the packet by the letter N; phosphates (P); and potash (K, from *Kalium*, the Latin for potassium).

Most products also contain minor nutrients (those used by plants in smaller quantities, such as iron) and trace

elements (used in tiny quantities, but just as essential for plant growth, such as boron).

All this information must, by law, appear on the packet of any processed fertiliser, whether organic or non-organic, and gives you a clue as to what they are best used for.

Plant nutrients – what do they do?

The following is a simplified guide as to the uses plants have for various nutrients. There are many more minor nutrients and trace elements essential to plant growth, but in most cases these are present in the soil in large enough quantities for us not to have to worry about them.

Nitrogen (N) is mostly concerned with the green parts of the plant and is used to make green chlorophyll, which is important to the plant for the manufacture of food from sunlight.

Deficiencies show as small, pale green leaves, starting with the oldest leaves first; weak plants and poor growth. Nitrogen is easily washed from most soils and quickly used by hungry crops.

Phosphates (P) are important mainly for the internal chemistry of the plant such as in transferring energy from one part of the plant to another. They are often associated with healthy root growth.

Deficiencies are similar to those of nitrogen, but the leaves usually become a dull greeny-blue colour and fall prematurely, starting with the oldest. They are often deficient in wet areas, acid soils and some clays.

Potassium (K) This element is important for developing flowers and fruit.

Deficiencies show as scorching or browning of the leaf tips and edges, and are common on sandy soils where the potassium is easily washed away.

Magnesium (Mg) Like nitrogen, this nutrient is concerned with chlorophyll production in the leaves.

Deficiencies are often seen in fast-growing plants, such as tomatoes, and appear as a yellowing of the leaf between the leaf veins.

Calcium (Ca) is often considered by gardeners as important for adjusting the pH of the soil, but it is a vital plant nutrient in its own right. It is used to build cell walls throughout the plant and is essential for the formation of fruit. It is found in the shoot and root tips where cells are actively dividing.

Deficiencies show as a curling and browning of the shoot tips. Blossom-end rot in tomatoes (where a patch at the flower end of the fruit turns brown and extends, making the fruit inedible) is caused by a lack of calcium. However, it is rare for there to be a shortage of calcium in the soil or potting compost – a lack of water or an interaction with another mineral in the soil is usually the cause (see Soil Improving and pH, page 27).

Wash hands after use.
Storage
Store in a cool dry place.
Store away from children, pets and foodstuffs.

Analysis

NPK Fertiliser	7-7-7
Total Nitrogen (N)	7.0%
Phosphorus Pentoxide (P₂O₅) soluble in neutral ammonium citrate and water	7.0% (3.0%P)
of which soluble in water	6.5% (2.8%P)
Potassium Oxide (K₂O) soluble in water	7.0%(5.8%K)

roducts
hese

Sinclair

For further information on the use of

DOS AND DON'TS

FERTILISERS

- Never over-apply plant foods. At best it is a waste, at worst you may scorch the roots and leaves of your plants.
- Applying regular liquid feeds, for example to tomatoes, can be simplified by feeding at half strength every time you water.
- Apply top dressings, such as chicken manure pellets, to veg such as beans and onions just before or even during rain as this helps to break them up and wash them in to the soil.

- Store powdered fertilisers in a cool, dry place in a sealed container. They absorb water from the surrounding air very easily and will lose their effectiveness.

Iron is classed as one of the minor nutrients, meaning that plants use them in smaller quantities, but they are just as necessary for healthy plant growth.

Iron is important for the manufacture of chlorophyll and also has other significant roles.

Deficiency symptoms are similar to those of nitrogen. They are often caused by an excess of calcium and are prominent in lime-hating plants.

Given the information above you can see why it is essential for plants to have a balanced diet if they are to do well. Thankfully, most soils, with the exception of sandy ones, are good at holding on to naturally occurring and applied plant foods – clay is particularly good at this.

It is not too critical which fertiliser you use as long as it contains a range of nutrients. Be aware that some fertiliser products are formulated for different stages of growth. In the early stages you might choose a high nitrogen fertiliser to support healthy shoots and leaves, followed at a later stage by a high potash feed to encourage fruit production and ripening.

The other approach is to use a balanced feed, of which Growmore is the best-known example with an N:P:K content of 7:7:7 to keep matters simple.

Home-made feeds

Apart from composting your plant waste, you can make your own fertilisers at home by steeping comfrey or nettles and collecting the resulting brew. You may not be popular with the neighbours (you could assure them that something that smells that bad, must be good), but many gardeners swear by it for bumper crops. What's more, it's free!

The only drawback is that every batch will be different – no accurate measure of N:P:K here, but that should not matter too much in the case of most vegetables.

MAKING COMFREY FERTILISER
Comfrey is rich in the major plant nutrients and some minor nutrients and trace elements, especially potash. The plant has a very long taproot, which is almost impossible to dig out without breaking and allows it to access minerals from deep within the soil. The best variety to use is 'Bocking 14', available from the *Organic Gardening Catalogue* (see Useful Addresses, page 176), as it is sterile and won't seed all over the place, but ordinary comfrey will do the job. 'Bocking 14' is also happy to have its leaves cropped several times a year and it is the leaves you need for your home-made fertiliser.

Home-made comfrey fertiliser

1 Find an old plastic dustbin or bucket and make a small hole in the base. Stand it on some bricks and place a smaller container underneath to catch the liquid.

2 Cut the fresh leaves and pack them tightly into the container, weighing them down with a brick.

3 Cover and leave for three to five weeks. Use one part of the collected liquid diluted with 15 parts of water.

Comfrey leaves can also be used as mulch over the soil or as an activator in the compost heap, so it is well-worth setting aside a patch of ground to grow some.

MAKING NETTLE FERTILISER
Nettles can be used, too, as both a high nitrogen liquid feed and growth stimulant. The feed can be made in the same way as comfrey. Dilute the liquid at the rate of 10 parts water to one part nettle liquid or 20:1 as a foliar feed. Don't overdo it; undiluted it has been used as an effective weedkiller!

Green Manures

This bed contains winter tares, clover and grazing rye, three of the most useful green manures

Soil improvers consist of any bulky material of organic origin that, when added to the soil, break down to release humus. We have already mentioned animal manures and go into composting in detail, starting on page 44. Other materials are commonly available, such as mushroom compost (the recycled capping used in the production of mushrooms, often quite rich in calcium), or composted green waste available from many local council composting schemes.

There is another way to improve your soil and add nutrients at the same time and that is to grow green manures. These are seed crops which are sown direct over the soil and dug in while still young.

Different green manures provide differing benefits (see chart, page 33), but as they break down they also add humus just like ordinary manure. Some types are hardy and can be sown in late summer or autumn for over-wintering, while others are tender and are sown in the spring and

DOS AND DON'TS

GREEN MANURES

- Choose the right green manure for the time of year.
- Always dig in green manures before they become too established and woody and before they set seeds.

- Allow a few weeks between digging in over-wintered green manures, such as grazing rye, and sowing new crops in the spring. This allows the green manure to rot down, during which time lots of nitrogen is temporarily lost from the soil as the bacteria work to break down the vegetation.

- Remember that most green manures (except for grazing rye) are related to certain cultivated vegetables such as peas and beans and so must be fitted into your crop rotation plan (see page 48).

- As can be seen from the chart (right), most green manures that are related to peas and beans (*leguminosae*), such as clover, add lots of nitrogen so are good to precede brassicas.

- If a green manure becomes too woody to dig in, pull it up, run it through a shredder or put it on the lawn and chop it up with the mower before putting it on the compost heap.

summer. Green manures have several other important uses:

■ They protect the soil from the rain; the covering of foliage helps to reduce damage to the soil structure, particularly during the winter, and by soaking up unused nutrients they lock them away, preventing them from being washed out of the soil.

■ They help to stimulate biological activity in the soil as they rot down and return nutrients at the same time. Some, namely those belonging to the pea family, add nitrogen thanks to the nodules they have on their roots, which are home to beneficial bacteria called rhizobia. These bacteria fix nitrogen from the air and supply it to the plant in a usable form.

■ They help to suppress weeds on areas that are not being used to grow anything else and protect soil flora and fauna from the extremes of the weather in winter.

■ They can be grown on any area of bare soil, in between other crops, but need careful management as some are vigorous and liable to become weeds if not controlled.

Above: Phacelia is a pretty plant much loved by bees.

Right: Buckwheat provides good ground cover and can be sown from April to August.

Popular green manures

Green manure	Type	Hardy	When to sow	Group for rotations	Fixes nitrogen	Other uses
Alfalfa	HP	Yes	Apr–Jul	Peas/beans	Yes	Deep roots bring nutrients to the surface
Beans (field)	HA	Yes	Sept–Nov	Peas/beans	Yes	Very hardy
Buckwheat	HHA	No	Apr–Aug	Anywhere	No	Good ground cover
Clover	HP	Yes	Apr–Aug	Peas/beans	Yes	Good ground cover and bulk
Clover (red)	HA	No	Apr–Sept	Peas/beans	Yes	Good ground cover and bulk
Fenugreek	HHA	No	Mar–Aug	Peas/beans	No	Can also be picked for salad leaves
Lupin	HHA	No	Mar–Jun	Peas/beans	Yes	Good for acid soils, deep roots bring nutrients to the surface
Mustard	HHA	No	Mar–Sept	Brassicas	No	Can be used for wireworm control
Phacelia	HA	Yes	Mar–Sept	Anywhere	No	Attracts pollinators if allowed to bloom
Radish	HB	No	Jul–Sept	Brassicas	No	Deep roots bring nutrients to the surface
Rye (grazing)	HA	Yes	Jul–Sept	Anywhere	No	Very hardy, good ground cover
Rye (grass)	HA	Yes	Mar–May/ Sept–Nov	Anywhere	No	As above
Tares	HA	Yes	Mar–Sept	Peas/beans	Yes	Good ground cover
Trefoil	HB	yes	Mar–Aug	Peas/beans	Yes	As above

(HP hardy perennial; HA hardy annual; HHA half-hardy annual; HB hardy biennial)

ESSENTIAL TOOL KIT

Basic Tools

Before you buy tools remember that it is never a good idea to buy cheap ones – they won't do the job and will soon break. A good tool should last for many years if treated with respect and, in the case of wooden-handled tools, it will become more comfortable as time goes by.

Fork

A fork is useful for digging, emptying compost bins, weeding and picking up piles of weeds, lifting root crops, loosening and levelling the surface of the soil and mixing compost and other materials.

Buying guide
See Spades, below.

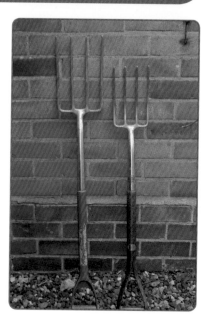

Hoe

There are many kinds of hoe and in recent years some truly wacky shapes have appeared. Modern versions, such as the Swoe (Wilkinson Sword) and the Winged Weeder (Burgon and Ball), have small blades and are ideal for weeding in among existing crops.

The traditional, tried-and-tested types remain the most popular, such as the Dutch and draw hoes. The Dutch hoe has a forward-facing blade and is perfect for killing weeds, for making a shallow furrow for sowing, or for chopping up larger clods of soil.

Spade

A spade is essential for digging, as well as for skimming off weeds and grass, chopping up green manures and cabbage stems, digging holes and chopping through unwanted tree roots.

Buying guide
Spades come in a variety of handle lengths and weights, so try a range and choose one that feels comfortable for you. Stainless steel blades are said to glide through the soil more easily, but they are expensive and can be a little heavy for long-term use.

There are many different designs of hoe. Here (left to right) we have the Push-Pull hoe, Swoe and traditional Dutch hoe

The draw or swan-necked hoe has a downward-facing blade and is ideal for pulling and levelling soil, breaking up large clods and chopping weeds, making seed drills and earthing up potatoes.

Buying guide
Look for a tool with a long, strong handle and a sharp blade. If the hoe is blunt when you buy it, put an edge on it with a file or angle grinder – it will slice through weeds much more effectively.

Rake
A flat or garden rake is essential for levelling and breaking

down the seedbed before sowing and for collecting debris from the soil surface. The edge can be used to make a furrow for seed sowing.

The wider soil or hay rake (see picture top of page 36) makes levelling soil much easier and is good for collecting stones and other debris from the soil surface.

Buying guide
The handle should be long, to give a good reach and reduce bending, strong and comfortable. Look for a model that is not too heavy, as raking puts lots of strain on the tummy muscles.

Wheelbarrow
Essential for carrying tools and moving heavy loads such as manure and compost; folding types are handy for allotment holders who need to carry their wheelbarrow in the car.

Buying guide
Pneumatic tyres are generally better than solid ones for comfort and ease when pushing over uneven ground. But they puncture easily, so if you have a holly or hawthorn hedge surrounding your plot, don't even consider them.

Our picture shows from left to right: Trowel, onion hoe, hand fork, garden line and in the front a general purpose knife and secateurs

Essential small tools

HAND TROWEL AND FORK
A hand trowel and fork are essential for planting plug plants and potatoes, lifting small weeds and many other tasks.

Buying guide
Good quality is essential, as cheap models often bend. The handle should be comfortable to reduce the risk of blisters.

ONION HOE
A smaller version of the draw hoe. The blade is handy for making short seed drills.

Buying guide
Make sure the tool is well made and that the handle is comfortable, again to avoid blisters.

SECATEURS
A good pair of secateurs is useful on the vegetable plot for slicing through the tough, woody stems of cabbages and Brussels sprouts, as well as for trimming canes and speeding up the harvesting of peas and beans without damaging the plants themselves.

Buying guide
There are two sorts of secateurs: 'anvil', where the single cutting blade cuts against a solid block of metal or plastic; and 'bypass', where two cutting blades pass each other with a scissor action, so slicing the material between.

Both are excellent, but whichever you choose it should feel comfortable, light and have an effective lock.

POCKET KNIFE

There are many types of knife available and the two most useful are a general purpose/propagation knife, with a straight blade, and a heavy-duty pruning knife, with a curved blade. The latter is tough enough to take on some of the tasks that secateurs might be used for.

The smaller, general purpose knife is ideal for taking cuttings, trimming tomatoes, harvesting and cutting string.
Buying guide
Look for a knife with a comfortable handle and good quality stainless steel blade. It should also have a reliable locking mechanism or a strong spring to prevent the blade closing on your fingers in use.

GARDENER'S LINE

Essential for marking straight lines for seed drills and plantings, a gardener's line is simple to make from a couple of canes and string, but for a more elegant long-term solution a Victorian-style line is worth investing in.

MEASURING STICK

One final tool which can be very useful as an alternative or in addition to a gardener's line is a measuring stick, the straight edge of which can be used when marking out seed drills. The markings of course are a great guide when it comes to planting out plug plants so allowing you to make the most of available space on the plot.

How to make a measuring stick

1 Find a straight, sturdy length of timber.

2 Cut the timber to the required length i.e. the width of your beds.

3 Mark at 5cm (2in) intervals along its length.

4 With a pencil and try square, go over the marks and rule straight lines across the wood.

5 With a sharp saw, make shallow cuts across the timber, following the pencil marks.

6 Take a permanent marker and draw down the saw cuts to make them stand out.

Tool Care and Storage

Looking after your tools

Even the best tools cannot be expected to last if they are abused. Here are a few simple guidelines to ensure that you get many years of service from them:

- **Keep tools dry** Always wipe moisture from blades and handles after use and store in a dry place.
- **Keep tools oiled** Have an oily rag handy to wipe the blades of cutting tools to prevent rust. Oil any moving parts and springs after each use.
- **Keep tools sharp** Hoes, secateurs and knives work more effectively if kept sharp with an angle grinder or file. Sharp knives are safer to use than blunt ones, since less pressure is needed to cut through woody material.
- **Hang tools up** Small tools can be hung by a thong or loop of string on a secure hook or nail so they are easy to find and less likely to be damaged. Large tools should be hung just off the floor on a good rack – not overhead where they could cause injury if they are accidentally knocked down.

Sheds and tool stores

Whether vegetable gardening at home or on an allotment, you will need a secure, dry place to store your tools, fertilisers and chemicals, and keep stored crops such as onions in good condition until needed. It could also double as a great place to get out of the rain, sit down and have a cup of tea. Unfortunately, not all allotment sites encourage plot holders to build sheds or store tools on site, in which case everything will have to be carried backwards and forwards.

A tool store is cheaper and easier to install than a shed and adequate for housing hand tools and small bits and pieces so that you don't have to remember to pack everything you need when travelling to the allotment. They can be handy at home, too, if you are lucky enough to have

TOP TIP

CLEANING FORKS AND SPADES

After taking off as much soil as possible, larger tools such as forks and spades can be thrust into a bucket filled with oily sand to coat them lightly and remove any light traces of dirt. Old mower or engine oil poured into gritty sand is good for this purpose.

a sizeable garden, saving your legs if the only storage space is some distance from the veg plot.

Many allotment sheds are home-made from second-hand timber or, indeed, anything else that comes to hand such as old double-glazed window frames or even garage doors.

Whatever you use for your store, it should be:

- Rainproof
- Vermin proof
- Secure
- Offer some protection from frost
- Not be an eyesore to fellow plot holders or surrounding residents
- Have a sturdy, level floor.

Security

- Fit strong locks to the door.
- When fitting door hinges and hasps for padlocks, fix them in place with blank-headed bolts and file down screw heads to prevent anyone getting a grip with a screwdriver.
- Consider doing away with windows altogether, or fitting shutters or bars over them. It may be wise to replace glass with thick, shatter-resistant polycarbonate sheeting.
- If you are building the shed yourself, consider installing anchor points set in concrete under the floor; these can be used to secure heavy-duty chains which can then be passed through the handles of all your most valuable tools and locked with a good quality padlock.
- If you intend to store valuables such as a Rotavator, mower or power tools, fit a security device such as the Shed Shackle.
- At home, install a security light over the door of your garden shed or store to deter thieves, as well to make life easier for you in the winter.

ESSENTIAL TECHNIQUES

Digging and Soil Care

Whether you have a back garden plot or an allotment, your soil is your most precious resource. On an allotment you might assume that the soil will be good, but this is not always the case since not everyone appreciates what is necessary to keep it in good heart.

In the garden the fertility of the soil may depend in part

Avoid walking on or cultivating the soil if it is wet enough to stick to shoes or spade in a sticky layer, wait until it dries a little

on whether you live in a new home as the builder may have left you with some problems that need dealing with, or you may be turning over an area of lawn or ornamental border in an established garden to growing vegetables, in which case that too will need improving.

Single or double digging

Faced with a weedy allotment or a virgin patch in the garden you will need to take a deep breath, pick up your spade and start digging. Old gardening books will tell you about double digging, a technique whereby the soil is dug to a depth of two spades (two spits), removing weed roots and incorporating organic matter. Unless there is a problem with the soil, double digging is not essential. Single digging, the turning of the top layer of soil, is enough for most sites. At the same time, be sure to remove weed roots, especially those of perennial weeds such as creeping thistles, ground elder and bindweed.

There are some commonsense rules to bear in mind when digging:

- Keep your digging sessions short.
- Mark out an area that you feel you can comfortably manage in one session and stick to it.
- Warm up before you start by doing some lighter work, or completing a few stretches; cool down slowly afterwards.
- Keep your back as straight as possible.
- Choose a spade which best suits you; shop around for one with a length and weight that feels comfortable.
- Wear stout footwear, preferably with reinforced soles.
- Wear gloves to prevent blisters and to protect your hands from sharp objects.

No-dig gardening

Having cleared the soil initially it is usual to dig every autumn as a means of clearing weeds and incorporating organic matter, but you can use the no-dig method. By not digging you will:

- Leave the soil undisturbed so that you will not bring buried weed seeds to the surface.
- Allow channels in the soil created by worms and plant roots to remain intact, improving drainage and aeration.
- Apply organic matter to the surface, allowing the worms to pull it into the soil and incorporate it.

There are drawbacks to this technique. Removing deep-rooted weeds is a conundrum and enthusiasts recommend keeping on top of weeding so that they are taken out while still small, but this is easier said than done. If you are not an organic gardener, a spot treatment with glyphosate would be an alternative.

Single digging

1 Dig in manageable chunks – use your spade to measure a rough 1.2m (4ft) width and stick to this.

2 Dig out a trench as wide as the blade of your spade and the same depth. Soil from the very first trench is placed in a wheelbarrow or piled at the other end of the plot.

3 Fork over the base of the trench to improve drainage and break up any hard layers (pans) below the surface.

4 Fill the trench with well-rotted organic matter such as garden compost, manure or mushroom compost.

5 Measure your next trench, using the blade of your spade to cut down both ends of the new trench, so keeping things neat. The soil from your second and subsequent trenches are thrown forward into the previous trench.

6 When you reach the end of the plot the stored soil can be used to fill the final trench. Your vegetables can now benefit from the new organic matter you have incorporated.

Heavy soils often become compacted and an annual digging breaks up the surface, helping you to form a fine tilth for sowing. This is not the case with a no-dig plot and at least until the regular dressings of organic matter start to improve things, some cultivation will be required.

There is a middle way and some advocates of no-dig growing turn the soil every four or five years to remove persistent perennial weeds and deeply incorporate organic matter.

When to add organic matter

Organic matter is usually added in the autumn and dug in once summer crops have been harvested. This gives it the winter to break down in the soil, giving up its humus and nutrients in time for sowing and planting in the spring (see Soil Improvement, page 27). Thirsty crops such as squashes and beans benefit from a little extra organic matter when planting and mulches can be added to the surface of the soil at any time.

Composting

Let's talk rot

There can't be many hobbies that can claim to be as environmentally friendly as vegetable growing. All the green waste generated – even the weeds – are recycled to produce more food.

The compost heap or bin is the powerhouse of the plot. With good organisation and care it should be possible for any plot not only to feed the gardener, but itself, too. Should you have a shortfall, there is always the possibility of scrounging waste from friends and neighbours.

The secrets of composting

Any pile of organic matter dropped into a compost bin will rot eventually, but to turn it in to the very best compost you need to know a few basics.

Good composting comes from keeping the bacteria and fungi happy, as they do the work of breaking down the waste. This means keeping them fed, warm and letting them breathe. Mixing various types of waste in the right proportions guarantees that the flora and fauna will receive the diet they need.

Composting experts will quote carbon:nitrogen ratios and explain how important they are to good composting. But if you make sure you add similar amounts of woody material (carbon) and green 'wet' material (nitrogen) to the heap you won't go far wrong. The woody material will serve to keep the heap open allowing air to enter and excess water to run away. The green material, such as grass clippings, adds moisture and also heats up quickly thanks to the frantic activity of the bacteria once they get working on it.

Heat is important as it encourages the bacteria to breed and also kills weed seeds, although in practice it is a confident composter who can guarantee to produce weed-free compost. A good heap can achieve temperatures of 60–70°C (140–160°F) in the middle when 'cooking' and although not essential it makes for faster composting if the cooler outer layers are mixed with the hotter core now and again. Heat can also help to kill plant pests and diseases.

What can I add to my heap?

You can add virtually any vegetable waste including:

- Trimmings from harvested veg
- Excess crops which may have run to seed before they could be harvested
- Woody prunings and debris from the end of a crop
- Vegetable waste from the kitchen
- Non-flowering weeds
- Dried roots of perennial weeds
- General organic waste from the rest of the garden
- Shredded newspaper and cardboard
- Tea bags
- Crushed egg shells
- Small quantities of leaves (see below).

What should I avoid adding?

- Meat scraps, raw or cooked (these can be safely disposed of in a Bokashi bucket, see page 46)
- Unshredded woody material
- Perennial weeds which are flowering or seeding
- Diseased plant material
- Too much garden soil (a thin layer now and again can be useful to inoculate the heap with worms, bacteria and fungi).

Composting bins

You don't need a compost bin to make good compost, heaps can be built in the open, but few of us have the space, or want to look at decomposing waste. Apart from keeping the heap neat and tidy, a bin will also help by retaining heat, keeping out excess moisture in winter and keeping it in during the summer.

A heap should not be smaller than about a cubic metre, or there will not be sufficient volume to build up heat and the heap will remain cool and composting may grind to a halt. Wooden pallets nailed together are popular since they are about the right size and can often be obtained free of charge.

Small plastic bins are best avoided in most cases; the volume of compost they contain rarely heats up sufficiently and, in summer, if sited in full sun they may dry out.

A covering of some sort will prevent the waste becoming wet and cold in winter. Slatted sides, or raising the heap off of the floor, helps to draw air into the waste, whereas building the heap on bare soil allows worms and other

COMPOSTING ESSENTIALS

- Add woody and green material at the rate of 50:50.
- Shred woody material to speed the rotting process.
- Dry the roots of perennial weeds in the sun before adding to the heap or submerge in a bucket of water for a week.
- Weeds and other plants that are seeding freely should be burned or disposed of with your green waste collection. The ashes from a bonfire are a rich source of potash.
- If possible turn a traditional heap at least once while composting to speed the rotting process. Rotary bins are turned every day.

TOP TIP

organisms to enter freely. There is rarely a need to add worms – they seem to appear from nowhere in a good heap. Earthworms don't thrive here, it is the red, striped brandlings or tiger worms – the worms favoured by anglers – that are best when it comes to working the heap.

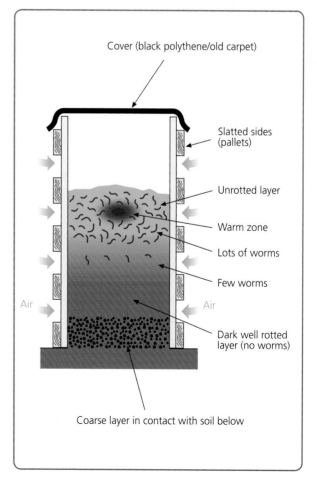

Cover (black polythene/old carpet)

Slatted sides (pallets)

Unrotted layer

Warm zone

Lots of worms

Few worms

Air   Air

Dark well rotted layer (no worms)

Coarse layer in contact with soil below

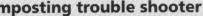

Composting trouble shooter

Despite your best efforts, things can sometimes go wrong. Here are some common problems and solutions to help you.

Tiny black flies have appeared in my heap. Are they doing any harm?

These are fungus gnats or sciarid flies and are harmless both to you and the compost, in fact their larvae help to break the waste down. Turning the heap should reduce their numbers.

I have ants in my compost heap. How do I get rid of them?

Ants in the heap are a sign that it has become too dry and the rotting process may have stopped. Turning and wetting the heap, by watering or allowing rain to enter, should send them packing and get the composting process going again.

Weeds sprout from the soil after I've added my compost. I thought the weed seeds would be killed?

It takes a high temperature to kill weed seeds and few heaps get hot enough. Do not add flowering or seeding weeds to the heap unless you are prepared to hoe them off once returned to the soil. Increase the temperature in the heap by adding more green material, but don't overdo it or the heap will become too wet.

My compost heap is wet and not heating up at all. What can I do?

It may contain too much wet, green material – try adding some shredded woody waste or paper. You may have to empty the bin and start again: place a layer of unshredded woody material in the base of the bin and raise the bin up on bricks to help air to permeate from the base. You could try kick-starting the compost by adding an activator.

Compost activators

These speed the rotting process and take the form of either a liquid or a powder. They feed the bacteria by adding nitrogen and other nutrients and lime to maintain the pH balance.

Natural activators, such as layers of comfrey leaves or nettles, can also be used, but in a well-managed heap activators are not essential.

The wormery

Wormeries offer a fun and effective way to convert kitchen waste into compost, plus liquid plant food. Ordinary garden worms are not suitable and you can buy brandlings or tiger worms, among others, from specialist suppliers (see Useful Addresses, page 177) or angling shops.

The principle is simple. The worms work on the waste from the bottom up, leaving a layer of digested waste – a pleasant, crumbly material, rich in plant nutrients, behind them. As a waste product they produce a liquid – worm wee in effect – which is collected in the base of

BOKASHI BUCKET

The Bokashi Bucket consists of an 18-litre bucket into which you place your kitchen waste, including fish, meat and other cooked scraps. This is sprinkled with a bran-based material, which also contains composting organisms and molasses. The bucket is sealed with a lid to keep in any odours and the initial stages of the rotting process take place, after which the waste can be put on the compost heap or into a wormery without attracting unwanted attention from vermin. As with a wormery, a liquid feed is also produced and this is drawn off via the built-in tap.

the wormery and drawn off as a liquid feed. Many wormeries are made in sections, allowing you to remove and empty a finished section as the worms move up into the one above.

You won't ever be able to compost all your garden waste in this way, but it is a useful addition to the composting armoury and the 'worm compost' can be used as a constituent for home-made potting composts or as a soil improver. The liquid should be diluted with water before using it as a feed for any plants around the garden, including vegetables.

There are drawbacks: fruit flies and ants may be a problem if sugar-rich waste such as fruit is added, so always fit a lid. Some gardeners find the management of a wormery to keep the worms happy takes practice. Wormeries are expensive to buy, although it is possible to make your own.

Composting leaves

Apart from the usual green waste already mentioned, many gardens benefit from an annual influx of leaves in the autumn. Once rotted down, these too can be very useful for improving the soil or adding to homemade potting composts.

Leaves are relatively woody and tend to rot very slowly; large quantities are best dealt with separately, although it is perfectly permissible to mix small amounts in with the waste in your compost bin.

There are two ways to compost leaves, both of which require about 18 months to two years to break down the leaves thoroughly. The first method is simply to fill black plastic bin bags or old compost sacks with leaves, packing them in tightly. If the leaves are dry, splash in a little water before sealing the tops and puncturing the sides in several places with a garden fork. The second method, which works well with large quantities of leaves, is to collect them in a simple bin made from a square of chicken wire supported with four stout stakes.

Making a wormery

You will need: two plastic dustbins, preferably identical (any other container which does not allow light through is also fine. Check that one stacks into the other easily. A worm starter kit (ours came from Original Organics and included worms, bedding, lime mix (for adjusting pH), a colony of worms, worm bedding, a tap with washer and nut). A saw, drill and suitable bits (the drill for our tap was 22mm), a sheet of newspaper, further bedding (we used shredded newspaper, well-rotted leafmould and a little potting compost, a small amount of kitchen waste.

1 First drill a hole in the outer bin to take the tap, taking care to select the right drill or your worm bin will leak 'worm juice'!

2 Fit the tap securely but do not over tighten or you may damage the thread.

3 Having removed the top of the second plastic bin with a wood saw, drill a small number of little holes in the base of the bin.

4 Place a brick or similar in the base of the first bin before slipping the second container inside. This creates a sump in the base of the first bin.

5 Place a single sheet of newspaper in the base of the bin and empty the worm bedding onto it so that it forms a small heap.

6 About a quarter of a bucketful of additional bedding is placed on top of the worm bedding supplied in the starter kit.

7 Gently empty the composting worms into the middle of the pile of bedding in the base of the container. The bedding also contains some worm eggs to boost your colony.

8 Cover the worms with a little kitchen waste. Place the lid on the bin to exclude light and place your new wormery in a sheltered, cool but frost-free place.

9 After a week your worms should have started work. Add three to four handfuls each week for the next two weeks. After that you can add a little each day.

Note: *Keep the lime mix aside and add a little now and again to prevent the compost becoming too acid. This may happen if too much citrus peel is added to the bin at any one time.*

Crop Rotation

Mix it up!

Crop rotation has its benefits, because growing the same crops in the same patch of soil year after year encourages a build-up of diseases, and since each crop has its own nutrient requirements the plants will deplete the patch of those ingredients. Certain crops, including legumes such as peas, add nutrients to the soil, benefiting those that follow, while others, such as potatoes and squashes, smother weeds.

There are drawbacks to this method. Crop rotation works well on a large plot, but it may not be so easy where space is limited. It also takes a fair amount of planning, recording and discipline to get a truly good rotation going, making a crop diary essential.

Dividing the plot into beds can make the job easier (see page 12), since it is easy to visualise the groupings and to remember where each vegetable was grown in the previous season. On very small plots it may not be possible to rotate the various groups effectively and you may have to make do with a 'notional rotation'. In other words, you may just have to do your best not to grow the same crop in the same patch of soil and here the grid system described on page 14 will be useful.

Organising your vegetables

What goes where depends first on whether specific crops are related and secondly, in the case of crops that are not related, on their preferred growing conditions.

The longer you can avoid growing the same crop in any one patch of soil, the better, but realistically the best that most gardeners can hope to manage is a three- or four-year rotation.

How do I start?

Divide your plot into the required number of sections: three for a three-year rotation, four for a four-year plan.

THREE-YEAR CROP ROTATION

A three-year rotation allows for simple groupings, such as brassicas (cabbage family), roots (carrots, potatoes and beetroot) and everything else (tomatoes, sweetcorn, spinach, onions).

FOUR-YEAR CROP ROTATION

With a four-year rotation you stand a better chance of keeping pests and diseases at bay. Your groupings may include:

- ■ **Bed 1** Potatoes, tomatoes, peppers and, where they can be grown successfully outside, aubergines. You can also add the cucumber family to help smother weeds. In winter, over-wintering onions.
- ■ **Bed 2** Root crops such as carrots, parsnips and beetroot, parsley, spinach, chicory, endive, chard, lettuce, sweetcorn. *Green manure*: grazing rye in winter or phacelia.
- ■ **Bed 3** All the brassicas, including summer and winter cabbage, sprouts, kale, calabrese, kohl rabi, swedes, oriental cabbage, turnips, radish. *Green manure*: mustard.
- ■ **Bed 4** All onions, including garlic and leeks, plus peas and beans. *Green manure*: winter tares.

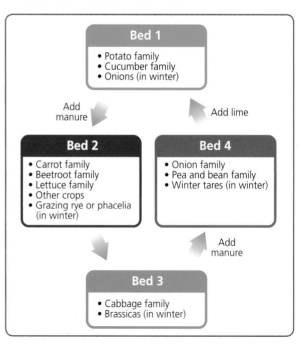

Green manures

You will notice that green manures are included in the rotation. These offer an important way to add nutrients, protect the soil and smother weeds. However, it is important to remember that some are related to the crops that you will be growing to eat and they must be considered with everything else in the rotation.

Manure and lime

When considering your rotation, remember that certain crops benefit from having lime or manure added to the soil before planting, while others do not. Hungry crops such as brassicas benefit from manure; they also benefit from lime, which can help to deter club root disease. It is not good practice to apply both manure and lime together (the lime reacts with the manure, 'locking up' many of its nutrients), so apply them in alternate years instead. Only apply lime if a soil test suggests it is necessary (kits are available from your local garden centre, see page 28). The rotation described above avoids the possibility of manuring before sowing root crops, which can give rise to forked roots.

What if I can't rotate certain crops?

It is not always practical to rotate crops such as runner beans, which require strong supports, and, having got the soil just right, some gardeners prefer to grow onions and pumpkins on the same bed every year. Many gardeners manage to get away with this, but there are risks attached (as described already) and you may eventually be forced to start again if problems arise.

Which crops are related?

Here is a detailed list of plants that are related and should therefore be planted together when possible.

Pea and bean family
Peas
Runner beans
French beans
Broad beans
Green manure: clover,
winter tares, trefoil

Carrot family
Carrots
Parsnips
Celery
Celeriac
Fennel
Parsley

Potato family
Potatoes
Tomatoes
Aubergines
Peppers

Onion family
Leeks
Onions
Shallots
Garlic

Lettuce family
Lettuce
Endive
Radicchio
Chicory
Salsify
Scorzonera
Jerusalem artichoke

Cabbage family
Cabbage
Cauliflower
Brussels sprouts
Kale
Calabrese
Swede
Kohl rabi
Turnip
Radish
Oriental cabbage
Green manures:
mustard

Cucumber family
Cucumbers
Gherkins
Marrows
Squash
Pumpkin
Melon

Beetroot family
Beetroot
Sugar beet
Spinach
Chard

Other crops
Sweetcorn
New Zealand spinach
Lamb's lettuce
Green manures:
grazing rye, phacelia,
buckwheat

Catch cropping

Catch crops offer a great way to make best use of available soil. Quite simply they are fast-growing crops such as salads, grown in the bare soil between slower-growers such as Brussels sprouts. Crops such as lettuces, salad onions and radishes make good catch crops.

Marker crops

In a similar way, fast germinating seeds such as radishes can be sown among slower germinating types such as carrots or parsnips to mark the row and make full use of available space.

Crop Protection

Many popular crops can be sown direct into the soil, but some are best started off in trays and planted out once established. In fact, the majority can be started in this way if you wish.

Crops that are best started in trays include: tender tomatoes, peppers, courgettes, squashes, aubergines and sweetcorn. Since most of these crops require a long growing season, they should be sown early in the spring (see page 56), protected from cold winds and frost, and hardened off (acclimatised to life on the open plot) before planting out.

Crop protection – whether hardening off, holding until the weather is warm enough to allow planting, or while growing in rows on the open plot – can be provided in many ways. Coverings range from a simple layer of newspaper or crop protection fleece or net, to a cloche or cold frame, or, for maximum protection, a frost-free greenhouse or polythene tunnel. The greenhouse or polytunnel can also be used right through the season to provide extra warmth for crops such as melons, peppers and sweet potatoes.

Insulating fleece

Insulating fleece is invaluable at the beginning of the season to allow earlier sowing of crops such as carrots and lettuce. It also provides good protection from birds, caterpillars and other pests.

Fleece comes in various weights or thicknesses and can be doubled for added protection. Use it to lie directly over the crop or to cover a home-made cloche (see page 52), and hold it in place with stones, ground pegs or by pushing the edges of the sheet into the soil with a spade.

Some good-quality fleeces can be washed and most will last for several years with care.

Crop protection material

Another crop protection material is fine netting. The close weave of fleece tends to restrict air movement and light, whereas fine netting allows air, light and water to reach the plants and keeps out most insects, but it does not provide protection from the cold.

Like fleece, netting can be laid directly over the crop, for example cabbages or carrots, and left there for the life of the plants.

Cloches

Cloches come in all shapes and sizes, including the traditional bell shapes, glass cloches and those using polythene or fleece in varying thicknesses.

Clestics are ideal for covering rows of plants to protect them from the worst of the winter weather. They also provide some protection from pests such as marauding birds.

Cold frames

These simple structures have been used for many years to protect crops from early cold and to grow tender crops from sowing to harvesting. Lighter versions can be lifted and moved from one crop to another as required. A good cold frame, if well built and insulated, offers better frost protection than a cloche or fleece.

As with cloches it is possible to build your own (see page 56). The simplest cold frames are made using bales of straw for the sides and some old window frames as a covering. Alternatively, timber, such as recycled scaffold boards, provides a permanent material for making the sides of the frame and both timber and window frames can often be obtained by 'skip dipping' or from a reclamation yard.

If you are not too handy at do-it-yourself, consider buying a flat-packed cold frame from your local garden centre or a mail order company. Although more expensive, hardwood is the best option, or choose a metal-framed model and insulate the sides in the coldest months with polystyrene sheets, covering the top with old carpet.

Hot beds

Hot beds are an extension of the cold frame and have been used for many years in kitchen gardens, providing heat for free. Fresh manure or compost is contained within an insulating wall of timber or straw bales and is covered with a layer of soil. As the manure decomposes and heats up, a cold frame is placed over the top to keep the heat in. After a week or so, the manure starts to cool and seeds can be sown directly into the

warm soil. Later in the season the heap makes an ideal place to grow hungry plants, such as squashes or pumpkins, and finally can be spread over the plot to enrich the soil.

Greenhouses and polytunnels

For the ultimate in crop protection many gardeners turn to a greenhouse or polytunnel. Of the two, glass-clad greenhouses generally offer the best insulation and light transmission, but are more expensive unless picked up second-hand. Polytunnels offer an affordable alternative and new developments in the plastics used to clad the framework mean that they last longer, retain heat better and let through more light than before.

These structures are great for over-wintering crops, raising young plants and providing summer-long protection for tender plants, such as tomatoes, peppers, aubergines, and for growing fruit such as peaches and grapes. Even unheated they can extend the UK season by at least a month at either end and are well-worth considering if you have the money and space.

Mini greenhouses

If you lack space in the garden or on your allotment, or perhaps only plan to grow a small number of plants, a mini greenhouse might be the answer. Mini greenhouses are widely available from garden centres and mail order companies supplying cold frames and cloches. Most are large enough to accommodate a reasonable number of seed trays and removable shelves allow the same unit to be used to house a growing-bag planted with three tomato plants or peppers.

Look for a model with a strong, ventilated cover and simple, clear instructions.

Making a cloche

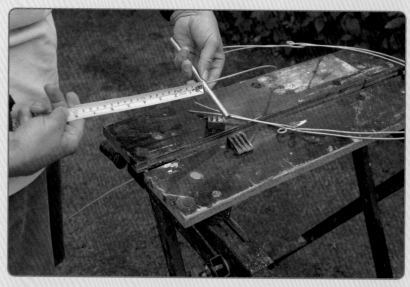

1 Cut some heavy duty galvanised garden wire into 1.2m (4ft) sections. Then, measure 20cm (8in) in from the end.

2 Bend a loop using the shaft of a large screwdriver or metal bar to turn the wire around.

3 Repeat the process in the other end of the wire section to form a second loop.

4 Bend the wire section around to form a neat hoop. Check each hoop to make sure they are all of the same size.

5 Push the hoops into the ground an equal distance apart over the row of plants you wish to protect. Cover the hoops with fleece before tying string to one loop, running it over the fleece and securing to the loop on the opposite side.

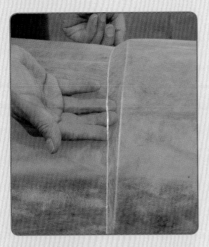

6 Sitting just behind each hoop, the string should be taut enough to prevent the fleece from blowing away as shown.

7 Trapped between the wire hoops and the string the edges of the cloche can be lifted to gain access to the crop beneath.

8 The end of the fleece tunnel can be gathered together and held closed with a brick, slate or similar to keep out cold.

Making hoops for a raised bed.

Look on any allotment site and you a re likely to see evidence of blue alkathene water pipe. It is ideal for making hoops for a raised bed and offcuts can sometimes be begged or found in skips or reclamation yards. If you are unable to obtain water pipe the same aluminium piping can be used to hold bamboo canes

1 Cut some aluminium piping into 30cm (12in) sections with a hacksaw.

2 Knock these into the ground 90cm –1.2m (3–4ft) apart in pairs down each side of the bed using a rubber mallet so that half their length protrudes above soil level.

3 Cut the alkathene pipe to the desired length with a hacksaw and slip one end over the thinner metal pipe. Gently bend the pipe, slipping it over the pipe support opposite.

4 Netting or fleece can now be draped over the top of the bed and left in place to protect against cold or pests. Weight down the edges to prevent it blowing away.

Make a lightweight cold frame

CUTTING LIST:
You will need:
2 packs x 5 x 2.4m x 93mm
    tongue and groove cladding
1 x 20mm x 40mm stripwood
3 x 10mm x 25mm stripwood
Wood glue and screws
1 sheet 1.8m x 1.2m
    polycarbonate sheeting

CUT THE CLADDING INTO:
7 x 1.2m lengths
    (4 for the back, 3 for the front)
8 x 60cm lengths (4 for each end)
Cut the 20mmx40mm stripwood
    into:
2 x 26cm lengths for the front
2 x 36cm lengths for the back
1 x 58.7cm length for the centre
    cross piece
Cut the 25mmx10mm stripwood
    into:
2 x 56.5cm lengths
2 x 61cm lengths
1 x 131cm length

1 Measure and cut the cladding to the necessary lengths.

3 Fit the sections together tapping with a rubber mallet if necessary.

5 Cut along the line with a hand saw or jigsaw.

7 Place the back of the cold frame on a firm surface and butt one of the sides flush against its edge. Draw a line.

2 Apply wood adhesive to the tongue of each piece of cladding.

4 Draw a line from the top to bottom corner of each of the two pieces of cladding intended as the topmost boards on the two ends.

6 Cut the 20mm x 40mm stripwood to the lengths specified above and the body of the cold frame is ready to assemble.

8 Use the line to gauge where the first 36cm baten should be fixed and glue and screw it into place.

9 Fix the side to the back of the coldframe.

10 Repeat this for the other side, securing it to the back.

11 Measure 2cm up from the bottom of the front section (the bottom board has the groove visible) and remove this strip with a saw. Secure the front of the frame to the other three sides.

12 Drop the polycarbonate sheeting onto the top of the frame and cut to size with a saw or knife. Allow a 2cm overhang at the front.

13 Make a shelf of stripwood to prevent the polycarbonate cover from sagging by cutting and fixing sections of 25mm x 10mm timber between the corner batens. They should be fixed so that the polycarbonate is flush with the top of the body of the cold frame (see step 14).

14 Cut two further strips of 20mm x 10mm stripwood, 61cm long and screw these to the top of the frame along the sloping edges. A gap wide enough to allow the polycarbonate to slide should now be formed between these strips and the stripwood 'shelf'.

15 Fix the centre cross piece of 2cm x 4cm timber in place by screwing through the back and front of the cold frame body.

16 Slide the polycarbonate in place. To ventilate the frame simply leave the desired gap between the polycarbonate and the back of the frame.

Propagation

Raising your own plants

Even old hands will tell you that they never fail to be fascinated by the simple act of sowing a seed or taking a cutting and watching it grow. Most vegetables are propagated from seeds, but some, notably rhubarb, can also be propagated by dividing established clumps, and herbs such as sage and lavender are propagated using cuttings.

A quick, cheap and easy method is to sow seeds direct into the open soil in a seedbed (see below), but the open plot is a hostile place for seedlings and many plants benefit from being sown in seed trays or cell trays (trays divided into little compartments of various sizes).

Although more expensive, sowing seeds in cell trays and keeping them in a greenhouse, cold frame or on a warm windowsill for as long as possible offers the following benefits:

- Allows better control over growing conditions
- Extends the growing season for tender crops
- Minimises root disturbance when planting out
- Protects the seedlings from pests such as birds and slugs
- Makes it easier to water evenly
- Shelters the young plants from the weather
- Prevents competition from weeds.

Trays are not suitable for plants with long taproots such as carrots and parsnips, but most other plants, including all brassicas, onions, leeks, beans, sweetcorn, salads and even beetroot, benefit from starting off in trays. Crops such as Florence fennel, turnips and swedes are notorious for bolting (running to seed prematurely) if they suffer root disturbance and should be sown either straight into the soil or planted out from their cells while still small.

What every seed needs

All plants have a few basic needs that must be met if they are to germinate and grow successfully. The A to Z Guide, starting on page 92, offers details of the specific requirements for each vegetable, but depending on the variety, each of the following is important:

Moisture After being sown, seeds quickly absorb water, which kick-starts germination. Once germination begins, water levels must be maintained or the seeds will die. However, they must not be allowed to become too wet or they will drown and the excess moisture will encourage diseases, which will attack the seeds. (For more advice on watering, see page 82.)

Humidity is important for tiny seedlings of tender veg when the young shoots emerge and is usually provided by covering trays or pots with a clear plastic propagator lid or polythene bag. After a few days the cover should be removed for an increasing length of time each day to allow the young

plants to acclimatise and to reduce problems with diseases.

Air Like humans, seeds need air to survive. In waterlogged soil or compost the air is driven out and the seeds will suffocate and rot. This problem is easily solved by using a good, well-drained compost in your seed trays and ensuring that the soil in your plot is well prepared and maintained.

Heat The requirement varies greatly depending on the hardiness of the vegetable. Tender plants such as melons, cucumbers and courgettes need high temperatures, while cabbages require little or no heat at all. Too much heat can prevent germination in a few crops such as lettuce, which are 'programmed' to sit out a hot dry spell until conditions improve, and may cause others to grow too quickly and to become weak.

Darkness After sowing, most seeds should be covered to their own depth with soil, compost or vermiculite to exclude light, but a few need light for germination and are best left either uncovered or beneath a light sprinkling of vermiculite. This allows enough light to reach the seed, but prevents it drying out. Advice on the correct planting depth can be found on the seed packet.

TOP TIP

SUCCESSFUL SOWING

- Always use clean trays and pots. Old containers should be washed thoroughly in a garden disinfectant before use – a good winter job.
- Always buy fresh compost at the beginning of the season and avoid using compost that may have been sitting in the garden centre over the winter.
- Ensure that your seeds are fresh. All seeds have a shelf-life during which their viability reduces.
- Sow thinly to give each seed enough space to develop properly. Overcrowding tends to encourage disease and is wasteful.
- Older seeds should be sown more thickly to compensate for losses.

More advice can be found in the A to Z Guide (page 92) and on the seed packet.

How to sow

1 Fill the cells with fresh seed compost ensuring that any lumps are broken up or removed. Sieve if necessary.

2 Tap the filled tray on the bench to settle the compost and dib a shallow depression in the top of the cells with your finger to the depth required for your chosen seeds.

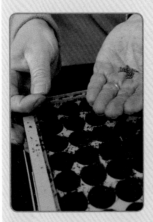

3 Drop a seed into the dibbed depression before covering with sieved compost or vermiculite. Water, label and cover with a propagator lid. Place on your heated bench or in a propagator.

4 Remove the propagator lid once the majority of seeds have germinated and when well established your young plants can be hardened off ready for planting.

Making a heated bench

Before starting this project consider the strength of your greenhouse staging and whether you feel it can take the considerable weight of the wet sand used to fill the soil warming bench. If not consider placing it on the floor (although this will be colder and absorb more heat) or strengthening your staging.

The size of your warming bench will depend on the width of your greenhouse bench and how long you wish to make it. It is a good idea to have some seed trays handy to help you decide on the measurements as obviously it makes best use of available heated space if the trays fit neatly inside. Our bench fits nine standard seed trays, or 18 half trays, perfectly and measures 102cm long front and back with 66cm long sides. Obviously if you make a much bigger frame you will need a longer warming cable.

YOU WILL NEED:
Two pieces of 2.4m x 125mmx13mm planed timber
One piece 1.2m x 606mm 6mm exterior plywood
Thick polythene to line
Wood screws
Wood adhesive
Panel pins
1 x 75 watt 6m soil warming cable
Sharp (gritty) sand

NOTE: *Electrical sockets must be rated as suitable for outdoor use and fitted by a qualified electrician. Any plugs must be properly fused and also suitable for outdoor use. If in any doubt consult a professional.*

1 Measure and cut the timber for the back, front and sides of the frame to the length required.

2 Sand rough edges with some fine sandpaper and check that the sawn ends are square.

3 With one side held square against the edge of the timber for the back of the frame, score a line.

4 Drill three holes at equal distances between your pencil mark and the edge of the back of the frame. Repeat this for the other end.

5 Apply adhesive to the sawn edge of the side of the frame and secure with wood screws.

6 Place the frame on the plywood base and mark where it needs to be cut. Cut the plywood to size with a handsaw or jigsaw.

7 Apply a bead of wood adhesive around the bottom of the frame.

8 Put the plywood base in position on the bottom of the frame making sure that the edges are flush and secure with panel pins.

9 Paint the finished case and base with several coats of plant friendly wood preservative in a colour of your choice.

10 Put the warming frame case in position on the bench. We placed ours on some timber laths to support the front of the frame which overhangs the staging.

11 Cover the base of the frame with some thick polythene to further protect the wood from the damp sand. Hold in place with staples.

12 Drill a hole in the back of the frame to take the cable and fill the base with 2.5cm of gritty sand.

13 Feed the end of the cable through the hole in the back of the frame before fitting a plug. The plug must contain a suitable fuse – in this case 3A.

14 Space the double loop of warming cable out over the sand ensuring that the two loops do not touch. Hold in place with handfuls of sand.

15 Top up the sand to cover the cable by about 2.5cm and water thoroughly. For good heat distribution the sand must be kept damp when in use.

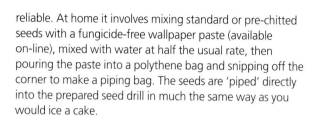

Types of seed

As well as loose seeds, companies supply seeds in different forms, all designed to make sowing and growing easier.

Seed tapes

Seeds supplied pre-spaced on strips of thin tissue paper. Sowing thinly is not easy with small seeds; tapes ensure that every seed is perfectly positioned. The paper is quickly absorbed into the soil.

Seed mats These are similar to the above, but instead of strips the seeds are sown between paper discs that fit on top of a pot and can be easily covered with compost.

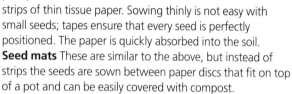

Pelleted seeds Some tiny seeds are encased in a ball of clay making them easier to handle and sow thinly (the technique was developed for commercial growers using machines to speed up the sowing process and the clay in commercial seeds often also contains insecticides or fungicides to protect the seedling as it grows). Provided the soil is kept moist, the clay will break down, otherwise the clay will set hard and the seedling will die.

Primed and pre-chitted seeds It is possible to buy seeds that have been treated to start the germination process, so improving the success rate and, as with pelleted seeds, this is a popular technique with commercial growers.

You can do something similar at home by pre-chitting (pre-germinating) your own seeds to improve the germination rate – this works well with parsnips, for example (see Parsnips, page 134).

Fluid sowing

This technique was developed in the commercial world to make sowing in the open plot faster and germination more reliable. At home it involves mixing standard or pre-chitted seeds with a fungicide-free wallpaper paste (available on-line), mixed with water at half the usual rate, then pouring the paste into a polythene bag and snipping off the corner to make a piping bag. The seeds are 'piped' directly into the prepared seed drill in much the same way as you would ice a cake.

Multi-sowing

If you intend to grow mini veg or to produce plants using the grid system or in beds, it is possible to sow up to six seeds per cell or pot, or per station in the soil, and to grow them, in effect, as one plant. When it comes to planting, the individual clumps are given a little more room than conventionally sown seedlings, but thinning out is eliminated. The plants are harvested as tasty young mini veg. Try it with onions, leeks, beetroot and carrots.

Aftercare of seedlings

Newly sown trays must be checked every day for dry patches; pay particular attention to the edges and corners. Spray with tap water to wet the compost (do not use water from a water butt as it may contain disease spores).

Once around 70 per cent of the seedlings have germinated the plastic covering should be removed or ventilated to slowly reduce humidity and within a few days can be removed completely.

The bottom heat from the propagator (where supplied) can also be reduced and once the seedlings are large enough to handle (as soon as the seed leaves open out fully) seedlings sown in standard trays can be pricked out. Pricking out involves splitting the seedlings up into individual plants, taking care not to damage the roots, and planting into cell trays or small pots to grow on.

Hardy veg can be grown on in a frost-free place such as a cold frame or cold greenhouse; tender crops such as tomatoes and aubergines need a warm greenhouse.

Even hardy veg must be gradually acclimatised (hardened off) to outside temperatures over a period of 10–14 days before planting out once conditions are suitable.

Sowing in the open plot

The alternative to sowing in pots and trays is to sow your seeds direct into the open soil and indeed this method is best for some crops, notably those with taproots such as carrots and parsnips which do not transplant well or which bolt if subjected to root disturbance.

It is also cheaper since you don't need to invest in trays and compost, but does render the seedlings more vulnerable to attack by pests and the weather.

Having made your basic soil preparations in the autumn (rough digging to remove weeds and incorporate organic matter), the soil can simply be raked down in the spring to produce a fine, crumbly seed bed suitable for sowing. When raking any large stones and pieces of debris are removed and the soil levelled. It is then simply a case of making a straight drill (groove) in the soil to a suitable depth for the seed to be sown (see A to Z guide) using the edge of a hoe or cane. The edge of your measuring stick (see page 38) or a garden line can be used to produce a straight line.

Sow the seeds thinly into the drill before covering with soil and watering well. In very dry weather it can be a good idea to use a technique called 'dry mulching' and this simply consists of watering the bottom of the drill before sowing and then covering the seeds with dry soil. Because the soil is dry, water is slower to escape through it leaving the area around the seeds wetter for longer, so improving the chances of germination.

Once your seeds have germinated, take precautions against pests such as slugs and maintain watering during dry spells. Keep the rows weed free by hoeing and hand weeding as necessary.

Sowing direct in the soil

1 Use the edge of a hoe or a cane to make a drill to the correct depth for the seeds to be sown 13mm (½in) is usual.

2 Sow seeds into the drill as thinly as you can either straight from the packet or by tapping seeds from the palm of you hand.

3 Cover the seeds with soil before watering the row thoroughly. Use your hand or a hoe to gently pull the soil back into the drill.

4 Label the row with the name of the variety and the date. This marks where the row is and gives you an idea of when to expect the seeds to emerge.

Thinning out

Despite your best efforts to sow thinly your seedlings are likely to need thinning out as they develop to give the remaining plants room to grow to maturity. This is usually done in one or two stages and many thinnings, such as those of salad leaves and onions can be eaten rather than wasted.

To thin, simply remove the weakest plants to leave a few inches between those remaining. Don't remove too many at first since pests and the weather may well take their toll yet. More plants can be removed later on if necessary as they grow. By the time the plants are well established they should have been thinned to allow sufficient room between each for them to mature – an idea as to how much space to allow between each plant is often given on the seed packet.

Success with cuttings

Cuttings offer an alternative way to propagate many plants, particularly perennials such as herbs. The conditions required are much the same as for seeds grown in containers – gentle warmth, moist compost and humidity – until their new roots have formed. Once the new roots have begun to grow the cover can be removed and the plant acclimatised to the outside world.

TOP TIP

HOW DO YOU TELL WHEN YOUR CUTTINGS HAVE ROOTED?

Give the cutting a gentle tug to check for resistance, or turn the pot upside down, remove the pot and look for signs of roots showing around the sides of the rootball.

Taking cuttings

1 Select a plant with healthy, pest-free shoots such as this sage plant. This plant is old and will be replaced by the new cuttings.

2 Remove a healthy shoot, 7–10cm (3–4in) long, with a sharp knife. Remove the bottom leaves to leave 2.5cm (1in) of clear stem.

3 Dib into a pot or tray filled with seed and cutting compost or a 50:50 mix of gritty sand and peat or peat substitute. Water well, label and place in your propagator to root. Keep the compost moist, but not wet.

Young plants

Mail order seed companies and garden centres offer young vegetable plants for sale at appropriate times and these can be a real boon. Propagating plants can be a delight, but raising seedlings can also be the most challenging stage. Ready-grown plants are available in several forms; you can buy young seedlings for pricking out, or larger plants, known as plug plants, produced in their own little plug of compost. These are offered in various sizes.

While being a more expensive option than home sowing, they offer convenience and are great if you only require a few plants of, for example, cabbages or lettuces, to satisfy your needs.

Weed Control

Perennial weeds like this field bindweed often have deep roots which will re-shoot if left in the ground

Coping with weeds

Weeds can out-pace virtually any cultivated crop and are a particular challenge to those taking on a new allotment. Once the ground is cleared, things will become easier providing you keep on top of them. The old saying that 'one year's seeding equals seven years' weeding' is true since some weeds, such as chickweed, are capable of producing thousands of seeds in a season and many of these will remain dormant in the soil for seven years or more, coming back to haunt you just when you thought you had won the battle.

WHAT IS A WEED?

The definition of a weed is 'any plant growing in the wrong place', but there is more to it than that. Weeds tend to be vigorous growers, prolific seeders and are capable of flowering at an early stage in their development.

Some weeds, such as docks, produce taproots, which are hard to remove without breaking. Others, such as creeping thistle, bindweed and mare's tail, have long, fragile creeping stems or roots. If you leave even a tiny piece of root in the soil it will sprout again.

WHY ARE THEY BAD NEWS?

Weeds deprive crops of light, water and nutrients. They also harbour pests and diseases and often carry them over-winter to infect new crops. This can be a particular problem in the case of weeds that are closely related to crop plants, such as shepherd's purse and bittercress (cabbage family) and wild garlic and leeks (onion family).

Types of weeds

As with any plant, weeds belong to one of three groups: perennials (live for three years or more), biennials (complete their lifecycle in two years) and annuals (flower and set seeds in one year). Most weeds are annuals or perennials. Annuals are prolific producers of seeds, perennials are often deep-rooted and/or produce creeping stems or roots. Knowing which group a weed belongs to can help you to select the best method to tackle it. For example, some weedkillers are better at controlling perennials than others. Hand-weeding or burning off the tops of annual weeds with a flame gun will often be enough to kill them, while perennials must be removed, roots and all.

Weeding techniques

There are several ways to eradicate weeds in the vegetable garden.

Digging The best way to remove most weeds, particularly perennials, is to dig them out by hand, but this requires time, patience and a strong back. However, as long as things have not got out of hand, a few hours' weeding can be therapeutic. It is essential to remove weeds before they become established to avoid disturbing the roots of your crops.

Hoeing can be an effective way to control annual weeds

Hoeing A sharp hoe is very effective for controlling young annual weeds where simply cutting the tops off is enough to kill them. It is less effective in the case of established perennials where this 'pruning' can actually encourage them to shoot even more prolifically.

TOP TIP

- When using a hoe, always work backwards, especially when hoeing on a traditional plot where you will be walking on the soil. This avoids treading the weeds back into the ground where they may root once more.
- Always hoe in dry, sunny weather so that the severed weeds quickly dehydrate and cannot recover.

Weedkillers can be a useful way to control weeds in certain situations, but you need to choose the right one for the job

Weedkillers

Although not for organic growers there is no doubt that weedkillers can be useful, especially on new plots, paths or areas that have laid fallow for some time.

Just as there are different types of weeds, there are different weedkillers to control them.

Contact weedkillers burn off the top growth and are useful for young weeds or annuals. The effect can often be seen within hours.

Residual weedkillers often have two active ingredients: a fast-acting contact weedkiller to remove existing growth and another persistent product to prevent regrowth. They are good for paths, but must not be used on soil intended for cropping.

Systemic weedkillers are absorbed by leaves and moved around the entire plant, including the roots. They are based on an active ingredient, glyphosate, and are neutralised on contact with the soil, which means that they can be used with care around wanted plants. They are slow-acting and the results may not be seen for up to three weeks.

Mulches

Virtually anything that smothers weeds and retains moisture can be used as mulch, including both organic and non-organic materials. Only apply after removing perennial weeds and when the ground is moist.

Organic mulches

include anything that rots down naturally in the soil, such as grass clippings, straw, paper and chipped bark. They rot slowly, and as they do so they release humus into the ground. Any remnants can be dug in at the end of the season. Sprinkle a little general fertiliser or ammonium sulphate over the soil before applying organic mulches. This helps to compensate for the nitrogen that bacteria in the soil will absorb when breaking down the mulching material.

Non-organic materials include permeable soil covering

materials and black or white polythene. They are great for reducing weeds from around long-term crops such as asparagus, strawberries and fruit trees.

> ### TOP TIP
>
> *Remember!* Mulches only work effectively if they are applied in a thick layer – 5cm (2in) is ideal – top up occasionally to maintain the cover.

Weedkiller products

A selection of products that are freely available from garden centres.

Product	Active ingredient	Weeds controlled	Where to use
Doff Fast-Acting Natural Weedkiller Spray	Acetic acid	All, but best on annuals	Hard surfaces
Doff Knockdown Systemic Weedkiller Spray	Glyphosate	Annual and perennial weeds	Anywhere with care
Bayer Glyphosate Kills Weeds & Roots	Glyphosate	Annual and perennial weeds	Anywhere with care
Bayer Glyphosate Ready To Use	Glyphosate	Annual and perennial weeds	Anywhere with care
Bayer Advanced Spot Weeder for Beds & Borders	Glyphosate	Annual and perennial weeds	Anywhere with care
Scotts Weedol 2	Diquat	Annual and perennial weeds	Anywhere with care
Scotts Weedol Max	Pelargonic acid	Annual and perennial weeds	Anywhere with care
Scotts Roundup GC	Glyphosate	Annual and perennial weeds	Anywhere with care
Scotts Tumbleweed Ready To Use	Glyphosate	Annual and perennial weeds	Anywhere with care

Pest and Disease Control

Treating your crops

Most vegetables have a few pests and diseases that regularly attack them – if you grow cabbages you will have to deal with cabbage white butterflies and if you grow leeks, they will be attacked by leek rust. Although pests and diseases are potentially damaging, most are nothing to worry about and plants often survive to produce a good harvest.

So, which pests and diseases do you need to tackle and which can you leave to their own devices, and what treatment, if any, should you give your crops?

Fewer and fewer pesticides (a blanket term that includes insecticides and fungicides) are available each year due in part to a shortage of new active ingredients, but more to regulations phased in over the last few decades. Gardeners are having to look for more chemical-free ways to control pests. That is not to say that there aren't still a number of products, both organic and non-organic, available for use on vegetables and these are detailed in the chart (see page 68).

IDENTIFYING THE PROBLEM

Before reaching for the sprays you need to know what you are dealing with. Some pests, such as greenfly and caterpillars, are familiar to many of us. Others are a little less easy to identify, or more elusive, and it is a good idea to invest in an up-to-date pests and diseases guide to help you, and to check out websites such as www.garden-care.org.uk for advice as to the correct product to choose.

THE OPTIONS

Your choice of pest control will be partly governed by whether or not you wish to use chemicals. There is a range of off-the-shelf sprays available in garden centres that are approved for organic gardeners and these are often based on fatty acids. Some organic gardeners are also happy to use pyrethrum, and there are barriers for pests such as slugs, snails, winter moth and flying pests.

Biological controls (a treatment using a natural pest predator or parasite) offer another option, but they require the correct conditions to work well and can be expensive. Slugs, aphids, whitefly, red spider mite, caterpillars and carrot fly can be dealt with using biological controls.

Being living things, biological controls cannot be purchased off the shelf and have to be ordered in advance from a specialist mail order supplier (see page 177).

Common pests and diseases

APHIDS (GREENFLY AND BLACKFLY)

Aphids are a problem not just because they suck the sap

from the tips and leaves of plants, but because they spread a number of viruses as they do so. The viruses cause distortion and poor growth, reduce yields and shorten the life of perennial crops.

Plants attacked: Most vegetable crops, but common on carrots, broad beans, lettuces, globe artichokes and cardoons, potatoes, brassicas, aubergines, peppers, parsley.

Symptoms: Clusters of insects on the shoot tips and underneath the leaves, usually at the top of the plant. Distorted growth and puckered, discoloured leaves. Sticky honeydew given off by the feeding pests attracts black, sooty mould on the leaves below. Often associated with ants which 'farm' aphids for the honeydew they produce.

Organic control: Squash small numbers of pests between finger and thumb. Cover crops with crop protection fleece. Under cover introduce a biological control.

WHITEFLY

These little, white moth-like insects suck the sap from the leaves of many plants. Like greenfly, they breed very quickly and can be present in large numbers. There is a hardy outdoor type, often to be found on brassicas in winter, and a more slender pest that thrives in the protection of the greenhouse or polytunnel. There are several distinct stages in the lifecycle from egg to a tiny, pale yellow-green scale, to

adult. Both the adult and scale are damaging, weakening the plant when present in large numbers and producing honeydew, which blocks the pores of the leaves and encourages sooty mould.

Plants attacked: Brassicas, tomatoes, aubergines, peppers.

Symptoms: Tiny white 'moths' on the underside of the leaves, together with limpet-like scales and sticky honeydew, often colonised by black mould. Leaves may become pale and droop in hot weather if attack severe.

Organic control: Under cover use sticky yellow traps to reduce numbers and introduce the parasitic wasp, encarsia, in summer.

CARROT FLY

If you grow carrots, you will experience carrot fly. Inconspicuous little flies are attracted to the crop by its scent and lay their eggs on the soil around developing roots. The eggs hatch and the tiny creamy-coloured maggots tunnel into the root, causing damage to the surface and allowing diseases to enter.

Plants attacked: Carrots, parsnips and parsley.

Symptoms: Scars and shallow burrows on the surface of larger roots (the damage on larger roots can often be removed when peeling). Small roots may be tunnelled and the maggots often found inside.

Organic control: A low barrier of fine netting 45–60cm (18–24in) around the crop helps to deter the adult flies. Sow thinly to reduce the need for thinning out as the resulting smell can attract flies from long distances. Cover the plants with crop protection netting, providing you are confident that the pest is not pupating in the soil from a previous crop. Select a resistant variety (see page 110).

SLUGS AND SNAILS

Often voted the most troublesome pests by gardeners, slugs and snails cause damage to many crops. Seedlings and young plants are most vulnerable, but even mature plants and fruits can be attacked, especially in damp weather. They are much less of a problem during hot, dry summers.

There are many species of slugs and the most damaging are the small ones, such as the black keeled slug, which live underground for much of their lives. Garden snails are found in large numbers in many areas of the country and often congregate in nooks and crannies where they survive the winter and prolonged dry spells. Snails require calcium to make their shells and so are less troublesome on acid soils. Slugs and snails breed in the autumn or spring depending on species.

Plants attacked: Most seedlings and soft, young growth. Beans, tubers and roots such as potatoes and carrots, lettuces, radishes, brassicas.

Symptoms: Irregular holes in leaves, holes and craters in tubers and roots. Slime trail sometimes visible, although pests are often elusive during the day.

Organic control: Slug pellets based on ferric phosphate and parasitic nematodes (slugs only) are popular with organic gardeners. Slug and snail hunts at night often reveal pests, which can be picked off plants and disposed of.

There are a number of products available designed to form a barrier around the crop to prevent attack, including copper strips and mats, crushed rock or shells, powder-filled barriers.

Slug traps can be effective, either purchased or home-made and filled with beer or sugar water. Half an empty grapefruit or orange skin placed on the soil to form a shelter attracts slugs and they can be collected each morning.

Clear away rubbish and fallen leaves regularly to deprive molluscs of places to hide.

CATERPILLARS

The caterpillars and larvae of many butterflies, moths and beetles will attack the leaves, fruits and roots of various vegetables. Pest species include cabbage whites, pea moth, turnip moth (cutworms), tomato moth and chafer grubs.

Plants attacked: Brassicas, peas, root crops such as turnips and carrots, tomatoes and aubergines.

Symptoms: Holes eaten in leaves, sometimes leaving only a skeleton of leaf veins. Peas and tomatoes tunnelled, seedlings and young plants eaten off at soil level. On cabbages, severe attacks from cabbage white caterpillars is obvious as the leaves are laced and a strong cabbage smell can be detected from the droppings.

Organic control: Pick off pests and squash eggs where seen. Cover crop with crop protection fleece. Spray with a biological control based on parasitic nematodes.

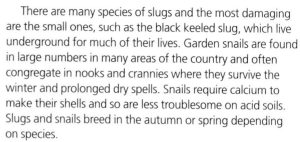

RED SPIDER MITE

This tiny pest causes problems under cover during the summer. Females over-winter in the structure and in cracks and crevices in staging, etc, emerging as light levels improve in the spring to lay their eggs. In summer they migrate to the open garden where they may cause problems on crops outside.

Plants attacked: Peppers, aubergines and cucumbers.

Symptoms: The surface of the leaf appears to have been sprinkled with white pepper, and each tiny dot being a feeding mark. Leaves often turn yellow and then white as the pests feed. The pests themselves can be seen with a magnifying glass on the underside of the leaf and in severe attacks very fine webbing is produced, which the pests use to move around the plant.

Organic control: Spraying host plants with water helps by preventing the pests from moving about on the leaves and increases humidity. A biological control using a predatory mite, *Phytoseiulus persimilis*, is effective under cover.

ONION WHITE ROT

White rot is a fungal disease that lives in the soil and attacks the roots and base of the bulb. The spores survive in the soil for many years and once the ground is infected there is nothing that gardeners can use to eradicate it. Some gardeners use the same onion bed year after year and never see it. Others are not so lucky and the usual advice is to rotate crops regularly to avoid growing onions on the same site each year (see page 48).

Plants attacked: Onions, leeks and, to a lesser extent, shallots and garlic.

Symptoms: Yellowing of the leaves and general poor health. When the plants are lifted they come away easily from the soil and a dirty white mould, sometimes with large black over-wintering spores, can be seen around the roots and base of the plant.

Organic control: Crop rotation. Gardeners with infected land do not always have the luxury of being able to move onions around significantly. Some manage to continue growing on the land, removing any obviously infected plants as soon as they are seen and taking care not to transfer

infected soil from one part of the site to another. This will, however, inevitably lead to a build up of the disease.

If all else fails, it is possible to plant onions and leeks in pots or beds isolated from the infected ground and indeed many exhibitors growing large onions for showing do it this way.

CLUBROOT

This is another long-term soil-borne disease that attacks cabbages and other members of the same family except radishes, which have some resistance.

Plants attacked: Brussels sprouts and cauliflowers, turnips, swedes, Chinese cabbage and wallflowers, which are all members of the same family.

Symptoms: Wilting, initially during warm weather, but then permanently. The leaves may become discoloured, often with a pinkish tint, and when lifted the plants have swollen roots or what appears to be one large root.

Organic control: Some resistant varieties are available (see brassicas, page 104). Always buy plants from reputable sources and do not accept young plants from others unless you are confident that their land is free of disease.

If land should become infected do not use it for brassicas and take care not to spread contaminated soil to clean areas. Grow plants in pots for as long as possible before planting out. They should then be able to produce a crop before the disease takes hold.

Finally, the soil-borne spores of the disease prefer acid soils and so some gardeners find that dusting the planting hole liberally with garden lime can help to reduce problems.

POTATO AND TOMATO BLIGHT

These diseases are one and the same. The spores first infect potato crops, usually in August when the day and night temperatures are a constant 10°C (50°F) and the air humidity is at 75% or above for a period of 48 hours or more. Having established on potatoes blight will often attack outdoor tomatoes. Indoor crops are usually protected and often remain unscathed.

Plants attacked: Potatoes and tomatoes.

Symptoms: Brown spots on leaf tips spread to cover the entire leaf. Plants collapse soon afterwards. The spores are washed into the soil where they infect tubers.

Tubers which are apparently healthy when lifted often become inedible soon afterwards. Brown spots appear on tomato fruit and these quickly become inedible.

Organic control: Some maincrop varieties of potato, known as the Sarpo strain, are currently resistant to blight, including 'Mira' (red) and 'Axona' (white) with more on the way. Tomatoes 'Ferline', 'Legend' and 'Fantasio' are said to have good resistance, too.

Early varieties are usually harvested before the disease strikes and if maincrops are attacked the haulms (top growth) should be removed to prevent the spores from infecting the tubers.

MILDEWS

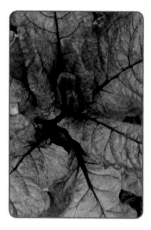

Powdery mildew tends to attack during dry weather

Downy mildew is often worse during wet conditions

There are two types of mildew that attack vegetables. The most common and widespread is powdery mildew, but the unrelated downy mildew can also cause problems in damp seasons and on certain crops.

Plants attacked: Powdery mildew affects squashes, cucumbers, courgettes, brassicas, peas, spinach, radishes, turnips, swedes. Downy mildew is a problem on lettuces, onions, peas and spinach.

Symptoms: Powdery mildew gives rise to a distinctive white coating over the upper surface of the leaves and stems. The affected parts of the plant turn yellow and the leaves wilt. Downy mildew leads to pale green or yellow spots on the upper surface of the leaf, often followed by a corresponding dirty white or purplish mould over the underside of the leaves of lettuce and on the foliage of onions during wet weather. The spots then turn brown and the plant becomes stunted. In onions the leaves turn yellow from the tip down, but the mould growth appears in much the same way.

Organic control: Powdery mildew is a disease of dry conditions and plants suffering from drought are much more susceptible. Regular watering can keep it at bay. Avoid feeding with too much nitrogen, which gives rise to soft, disease-prone growth. Allow space between plants for air to circulate.

As mentioned, downy mildew is much more common in wet conditions and allowing space between plants to reduce humidity around the leaves may help.

Different strains of downy mildew, of which there are many, generally only infect a narrow range of plants and there is good resistance to many strains in some crops, notably lettuce (see page 124).

STEM AND ROOT ROTS

These diseases are caused by different fungi and tend to appear as a result of wet conditions or poorly drained soils.

Plants attacked: Many, but most commonly squashes, cucumbers, lettuces, carrots, parsnips, seedlings (damping off).

Symptoms: General ill-health of the plant followed by yellowing and collapse. When examined, the stem at soil level may be obviously soft and infected or brown underneath when the bark is scraped away with a thumbnail. Roots may show similar symptoms and plants may simply come away from the soil when tugged gently.

Organic control: Improve drainage and on heavy soils consider planting squashes and cucumbers on ridges. Sow thinly and when sowing in trays indoors avoid over-watering. Sowing in cell trays can restrict the spread of damping off disease.

Products for pest control

Pest	Product	Active ingredient	Organic (O)/ Chemical (C)	Comments	When to use
Whitefly	Agralan Yellow 'Sticky' Traps	Non-toxic glue	O	Can be used in conjunction with biological controls	All season
Aphids, caterpillars, red spider mite, whitefly	Doff All-In-One Garden Pest Killer	Bifenthrin	C		All season. Cabbage white caterpillars from June onwards
Aphids, caterpillars, whitefly	Doff All In One Insecticide Spray	Pyrethrins	O		As above

Pest	Product	Active ingredient	Organic (O)/ Chemical (C)	Comments	When to use
Aphids, caterpillars, whitefly	Doff All In One Bug Spray	Pyrethrins	O		As above
Aphids, caterpillars, red spider mite, whitefly	Bayer Garden Sprayday Greenfly Killer Plus	Bifenthrin	C		As above
Aphids, red spider mite, whitefly	Provado Ultimate Bugkiller Concentrate	Imidacloprid	C		All season
Aphids, caterpillars, whitefly	Provado Ultimate Bugkiller Ready-To-Use	Thiacloprid	C		All season. Caterpillars from June onwards
Aphids, caterpillars, red spider mite, whitefly	Bugclear For Fruit and Veg	Rape seed oil	O		All season. Cabbage white caterpillars from June onwards
Aphids, red spider mite, whitefly	Bugclear Gun For Fruit and Veg	Natural pyrethrins	O		All season
Aphids, caterpillars	Vitax Py Insect Killer Powder	Pyrethrum	O		All season. Cabbage white caterpillars from June onwards
Aphids, caterpillars, whitefly	Vitax Py Spray Garden Insect Killer	Pyrethrins	O		As above
Aphids, red spider mite	Vitax Organic 2 in1 Pest & Disease Control	Natural Plant and fish oils	O		All season
Aphids	Vitax Py Spray Garden Insect Killer	Pyrethrum	O		As above
Aphids, red spider mite, whitefly	Ready-To-Use Organic 2 in 1 Pest & Disease Control	Natural plant and fish oils	O		As above
Aphids, caterpillars, whitefly	Westland Bug Killer		C		All season. Caterpillars from June onwards
Aphids, whitefly, red spider mite and other pests	Growing Success Fruit & Veg Bugkiller Concentrate	Natural plant extracts	O	Claims to control eggs and adults	As above
Aphids, whitefly, red spider mite and other pests	Growing Success Ready To Use Fruit & Veg Bugkiller	Natural plant extracts	O	Claims to control eggs and adults	As above
Slugs	Growing Success Advanced Slug Killer	Ferric phosphate	O	Pet and wildlife friendly	All season, paying particular attention to new sowings and plantings
	Doff Slug Attack	Metaldehyde	C		As above
	Doff Slugoids Slug Killer	Metaldehyde	C		As above
	Bio Slug and Snail Killer	Metaldehyde	C		As above
	Vitax Slug Off	Absorbent granules	O	Absorbent granules form a barrier around plants	As above
	Growing Success Slug Barrier	Copper	O	Adhesive copper tape	As above
	Growing Success Slug and Snail Trap		O	Use beer or yeast tablets to trap pests	As above
	Growing Success Slug Stop	Absorbent granules	O	Absorbent granules form a barrier around plants	As above
	Slug Rings	Copper	O	Copper rings for surrounding individual plants	As above
	SnailAway Slug and Snail Barrier		O	Mini electric 'fence' deters pests	As above

Harvesting and Storing

Gathering in the harvest

There is little point in growing lots of fresh produce if you don't pay attention to harvesting. This may sound obvious, but when you are busy growing and tending to your plants, it is easy to forget this end of the operation and to start wasting good veg. This is especially true of fast-growing crops that mature during a relatively narrow window, such as courgettes, tomatoes, peppers and salads.

Before you sow seeds in the spring, consider which vegetables your family eats the most of and whether they are easy to grow. Growing the veg that you buy regularly in the shops ensures that you will cut your food bills and you will be more likely to use up the harvest that you reap.

Having decided on the staple items that you want to grow – such as carrots, onions and potatoes – look at the list of veg that you might see as being of secondary importance, such as peas, beans and cabbages.

How much space you devote to the secondary vegetables will depend on how much you use and whether they can be stored effectively. Peas and beans freeze brilliantly so are

always worth growing. Cabbages can be left in the soil for some time and also store well in nets hung in a cool place. They can be shredded and frozen or pickled, but you might decide that it is better to grow small batches from regular sowings to produce a succession.

Courgettes come thick and fast during the summer, but can be frozen in slices or made into delicious pickles. The list

TOP TIP

HARVEST REGULARLY

Some vegetables, such as beans, peas, courgettes and aubergines, tend to crop for longer if they are harvested regularly and this may mean every day in the summer. Get into the habit of checking daily and cutting produce as necessary. Use it immediately, while it is at its freshest, or store as described in the A to Z Guide, starting on page 90).

TOP TIP

THE TASTIEST TIME

It is often a good idea to harvest your crops while they are as young as possible. You do lose total weight of crop if you do this, but the veg will be tender and flavoursome. This also allows you to get them out of the soil as quickly as possible so that new sowings can be made, so making best use of available space. Crops such as turnips, carrots and beetroots are nice harvested young, although left in the ground for longer they will gain more bulk.

The exception to this are the later crops, for example swedes and carrots, which are destined for winter storage where a greater bulk is desirable for over-wintering.

goes on and more advice can be found in the A to Z guide, starting on page 90.

Next look at the perishables, such as lettuce, spinach, radishes and cucumbers. You may eat lots of these and as they are often expensive to buy in the shops, they are always worth some space, but you need to be realistic about how many you can eat. Sowing little and often is the best policy here. If space is limited, consider growing them in patio pots and tubs, trays, or even in the ornamental garden (see page 80).

Finally take a look at the vegetables you eat the least of and decide whether you have space and time to devote to them. If you eat very little, or they are very cheap to buy, then you might decide that it is better to devote more resources to the vegetables in your lists above. Here, though, you can choose to grow a few novelties, such as salsify and scorzonera, just for the fun of it. If your then decide you like them, you can grow more next year. It is best to try just one or two novelties each year.

Preserving your crop

Vegetables can be preserved in a number of ways and there are few that can't be frozen or made into a delicious pickle, dried or stored in other simple ways.

FREEZING

Vegetables for freezing should be of good quality, without too many blemishes. Any less than perfect bits should be removed, along with all soil and other impurities.

Larger vegetables, such as carrots, parsnips, courgettes and runner beans, are best sliced before freezing (carrots and parsnips should also be peeled). Most vegetables also need to be blanched: place them in boiling water for just a few minutes to maintain colour, flavour and nutrient content, and then allow them to cool before freezing in batches of one serving. Freezer bags offer a good way to store the frozen produce and allow you clearly to label what is in the bag and when it was frozen.

Freezing should be done quickly – use the fast-freeze facility of your freezer if it has one, and don't open the door until the process is complete. Most vegetables will remain in perfect condition for approximately six months.

DRYING

Drying offers a simple way to store crops such as tomatoes, peppers, mushrooms and beans. Beans and peas for drying should be allowed to mature on the plant fully before

PERFECT PARSNIPS

Parsnips are best left in the ground and lifted as required, or stored in a sheltered spot (see Storing in the ground), as they tend to dry out and become unpalatable once out of the ground.

harvesting and picked on a dry, sunny day. Store in airtight plastic or glass containers.

For fleshier crops, sun-drying is the best option, but since we rarely receive enough sun in the UK to make this feasible, the alternative is to slice peppers and tomatoes and put them on a metal tray with a little space between each slice. Place over a gentle heat near a radiator, in an airing cupboard or, better still, in an oven set to the lowest heat possible (70°–80°C) and allow the slices to dry very slowly, turning occasionally. For large quantities you could invest in a food dryer

STORING IN THE GROUND

Hardy vegetables can be stored in the ground providing that the soil does not remain too wet or waterlogged during the winter – this includes carrots, parsnips and swedes. The only drawback is that they can be impossible to lift when the soil is frozen and may need to be lifted and 'heeled in' (loosely replanted) in a sheltered spot to guarantee a supply during cold snaps.

In mild areas a layer of straw held in place with some netting may be enough to insulate the roots from the worst of the cold.

VEGETABLES IN CLAMPS

Clamps offer the same protection as leaving roots in the ground, but the veg will be easier to get to in very poor conditions. Vegetables such as carrots are placed on a bed of straw in layers separated by more straw, before being covered with a final layer of straw and buried under a mound of soil to insulate them. The drawback is that the mound, or clamp, is easily attacked by rodents and is liable to become soaked through, although it can be covered with polythene during wet spells.

STORAGE IN SACKS AND BOXES

Before the days of refrigerators, storing vegetables in boxes of sand or straw, in pits or clamps, was very common.

Hessian or paper sacks remain the best way to store potatoes. Carrots can also be stored in this way, although they, along with other root crops such as beetroot, celeriac, salsify and scorzonera, are more commonly stored in boxes in layers of sand, peat or peat substitute, each root placed in the sand so that it has a little space between it and its neighbour and covered with an inch or so of the substrate.

Nets offer the ideal way to store onions, garlic bulbs and heads of cabbages.

RIPEN ON THE VINE

At the end of the season, when you are anxious to clear old plants from the greenhouse, the summer's tomatoes and peppers can sometimes get in the way yet may still be holding a good crop of semi-ripe fruit.

Simply lifting the plants and hanging them upside down on the back of a shed or garage door gets them out of the

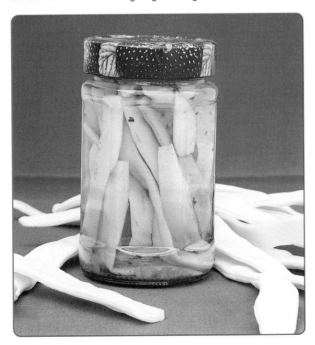

TOP TIP

TOMATO TRICK

If your tomatoes are slow to ripen, try hanging a banana skin in the branches near a truss of fruit. The ethylene gas given off (the sweet smell that rises from the fruit bowl indoors) helps to ripen the tomato fruit. The same trick can be used indoors to ripen picked fruit in a dark drawer or similar.

way and encourages natural ripening, but do use the fruit as quickly as possible.

PICKLING

Lots of vegetables can be pickled and this is a simple and delicious way to ensure not only that waste is kept to a minimum, but that you have pickles, chutneys, relishes and whole pickled veg throughout the winter months.

Of course onions and beetroot are the crops that most will think of when considering pickled veg, but there are plenty of other things to try – even beans can be preserved in this way (see picture).

Storing crops – the rules

- ■ Only store top-quality, sound produce; blemished or damaged vegetables should be used straight away.
- ■ Check stored produce regularly and remove any items that are rotting.
- ■ Store produce in a cool, frost-free, airy, dry, dark place, out of the reach of vermin. A cool shed or garage is fine as long as the temperatures remain above freezing during the winter.

For more information about individual vegetables, see the A to Z guide, starting on page 90.

TOP TIP

IN THE DARK

It is especially important to keep potatoes in the dark to prevent them from turning green and bitter. The bitter taste results from the production of solanine, a naturally occurring chemical that is common to members of the potato family, *solanaceae*. It is toxic and green tubers should be discarded.

Seed Saving

Compared with the cost of buying vegetables from the supermarket, seeds are relatively cheap. However, with the seed bill to keep a family of four in vegetables for most of the year likely to be around £60 per year (including seed potatoes), it is worth saving seeds from your own crops. But there are more than financial reasons for doing this. Saving seeds:

- allows you to select seeds from your best plants, so developing your own strain of veg, which suits your conditions
- allows you to continue growing varieties that you prefer for taste, even if they are no longer available from the catalogues
- allows you to share seeds with friends and family or to join local seed swapping schemes and events
- helps to maintain rare or heritage varieties which are no longer available commercially
- it's fun!

How to save seeds

If during the growing season you notice a particularly good plant of any vegetable, mark it with some coloured wool or a stake and remember not to lift it at harvesting time, but allow it to flower, fruit and set seeds. In the case of some plants such as carrots or leeks, this may not happen until their second year since they are naturally biennial (grow in their first year and flower and set seeds in their second). If they are in the way they can be lifted and moved carefully, or potted using fresh potting compost.

As the seed pod or head ripens, and just before it opens to scatter the seeds, choose a dry day and cover it with a paper bag (not polythene), tying it securely around the stem.

TOP TIP

SEEDS TO AVOID

Do not try to save seeds from F1 hybrids, since these will not come true to type (they won't have the same characteristics as the parent plants due to intensive cross breeding). Only open-pollinated varieties – those which do not have the prefix F1 after their name – are usually worth saving.

TOP TIP

DISEASE-FREE SEEDS

Do not save seeds from plants that show any signs of virus or other diseases. Beans in particular may carry certain diseases over from one crop to another on their seeds.

Snip the pod or head from the parent plant. Note that it is essential not to remove the seed head too soon or the seeds may not be ripe and germination may be poor.

Hang the seed head upside down and shake the bag occasionally to encourage the seeds to fall out into the bag. Once the seeds are in the bag, the remains of the head or pod can be discarded, along with any unwanted bits and pieces, and the seeds stored in the bag or transferred to an envelope. Write the name and date on the package and seal it.

Envelopes of seeds can be stored in a cool drawer or, if they are completely dry, in an airtight container. Rather than envelopes, it is possible to use any other secure container, such as plastic film canisters or matchboxes.

Keep the seeds away from mice if storing in the shed and make sure that they do not become damp or exposed to light, especially strong sunlight.

As soon as seeds are harvested or fall from the plant in the wild, they begin to deteriorate, but some deteriorate much faster than others. The carrot family, which also includes parsnips, rapidly lose their viability and should be sown the following year. Brassicas may last for many years in storage, however the longer they are kept, the fewer are likely to germinate when sown, so it is always best to use seeds as quickly as possible.

This also applies to commercially produced seeds; when you purchase a packet of seeds it will have been tested to show that it is viable before it can be sold. It will usually then be packed in a hermetically sealed foil packet (the exception are large seeds such as peas and beans). Inside the foil, the reduced humidity and oxygen levels ensure that the seeds stay fresh for at least two years and each pack will have a 'sow by date' printed on it.

Once opened, the seeds deteriorate and should be used as quickly as possible.

Saving seeds

1 It is essential to allow the seeds to ripen fully on the plant and seeds must be dry. During wet spells whole plants like these drying beans can be lifted and hung upside down in a dry place to 'cure'.

2 In the case of beans simply remove the seeds from their pods at the point where they are about to open naturally and scatter their cargo.

Saving seeds from fruit

Seeds from fruit such as tomatoes will often be surrounded by a pulp which has to be removed before the seeds can be dried and stored. To do this squeeze the seeds from the ripe fruit into a jar and allow to stand for three or four days.

Then, fill the jar with water and stir or shake gently to mix and remove the pulp from the seeds. Viable seeds should sink to the bottom while non-viable seeds will tend to float. Pour these off the top before pouring the rest of the seeds into a fine sieve and washing thoroughly under running water.

The clean seeds can then be dried in a dish in the airing cupboard or on a warm windowsill before storing in paper envelopes in a cool, dry place.

3 If you have plants with lots of tiny seeds such as amaranth, beet, lettuce etc, plants can be brought inside and the heads covered with a paper bag or sack or hung over a piece of polythene.

4 When dry and any chaff removed, store your seeds in paper envelopes making sure that you label and date them clearly. Larger seeds can be stored in clean, dry jars or plastic containers. Keep your seeds in a cool, dark place until needed.

TOP TIP

JOIN THE HERITAGE SEED LIBRARY

The vegetable varieties featured in seed catalogues tend to reflect what is popular among commercial growers. As better varieties in terms of disease resistance or yield come along, old varieties disappear since it is no longer profitable for the breeders and suppliers to maintain them on the approved varieties register. The Heritage Seed Library, a part of Garden Organic, Britain's largest organic gardening charity, maintains many of these old varieties and keeps them available to members. To join, tel: 024 7630 8210 or visit www. gardenorganic.org.uk

Companion Planting

Companion planting is a simple technique for protecting crops without using pesticides. It also helps to attract pest predators and in some cases is beneficial for improving growth. It simply involves inter-planting two crops, one often with a pungent smell or nectar-rich flowers – such as garlic or calendula (pot marigolds) – with your main crop.

and fungi, which may benefit both themselves and a partner. Advocates also believe that certain crops should never be grown together, such as onions with beans or peas, tomatoes or cucumbers with potatoes.

Scientific proof for this is scanty, but some gardeners are convinced that it works for them.

Scenting lunch

Many pests, such as carrot fly, rely on scent to find food. Interplanting with garlic, for example, can help to mask the scent of the carrots, so reducing damage. Another technique is to select a plant that often suffers from attack by a pest, such as nasturtiums which invariably attract blackfly and caterpillars, and to use it as a decoy or sacrificial crop to draw pests away.

Natural stimulants

There is a school of thought that suggests that certain crops when planted together provide mutual benefits. How this may work is unclear, but some plants are known to produce chemicals through their roots or to form partnerships with beneficial bacteria

Getting physical

Some relationships are easier to understand, such as the technique of using tall plants to shelter smaller crops from the elements and from pests. This can be taken a stage further – growing crops in small groups or patches rather than the usual straight lines and mixing them with prickly raspberries and blackberries (polyculture), protects crops by forming a physical barrier and makes them harder to home in on. Leaving small, controlled areas of wild plants, such as nettles, provides a home for beneficial insects.

Mixing crops together in small patches rather than rows can help to confuse pests

Good companions

The following are just a few examples of crop plants and their suitability for growing together.

Crop plant	Companion plant	Incompatible	Comments
Asparagus	Dill, coriander, tomatoes, parsley, basil, comfrey, marigolds	Onions, potatoes, garlic	Marigolds and tomatoes are said to deter asparagus beetle
Beans	Summer savory, aubergines	Tomatoes, peppers, onions, brassicas, beetroot	Beans add nitrogen to the soil
Beetroot, leaf beet	Lettuces, onions, brassicas, kohl rabi	Beans	
Brassicas (Cabbage, kale, broccoli etc)	Dill, onions, coriander, rosemary, nasturtiums	Tomatoes, peppers, mustard	Nasturtium is a sacrificial plant for blackfly and caterpillars. Rosemary deters cabbage root fly
Carrots	Peas, lettuces, onions, sage, tomatoes, wormwood	Radishes, dill, parsnip	Onions and wormwood deter carrot fly
Leeks	Celery, carrots	Beans, peas	Leeks deter carrot fly
Lettuce	Radishes, kohl rabi, carrots, beans, mint, sage	Celery, brassicas, parsley	Mint, sage and other aromatic herbs are said to deter slugs
Onions	Carrots, tomatoes, peppers, aubergines, potatoes, brassicas	Beans, peas, parsley	Onions are said to deter slugs and snails, also aphids, carrot fly and cabbage root fly
Peppers	Tomatoes	Beans, brassicas	Tomatoes shade the smaller peppers
Potato	Horseradish	Tomato	
Spinach	Peas, beans		Peas and beans provide nitrogen and shade
Sweetcorn	Beans, squashes, potatoes, cucumbers, parsley	Tomatoes, celery	
Tomatoes	Marigolds, peppers, asparagus, carrots, onions, nasturtiums	Sweetcorn, peas, dill, potatoes, beetroot, brassicas	Marigolds deter whitefly
Cabbages	Aromatic herbs, celery, beets, onion family, chamomile, spinach, chard	Strawberries, tomato, dill	
Celery	Nasturtiums, onion, cabbages, tomatoes	Sweetcorn	
Cucumbers	Beans, peas, sunflowers, radishes	Aromatic herbs such as sage and mint, potatoes	Flowering herbs attract bees and other pollinators
Lettuces	Carrots, radishes, strawberries, cucumbers, onions		Onions deter aphids
Onions	Beets, carrots, lettuces, cabbages	Beans, peas	
Parsley	Tomatoes, asparagus		
Peas	Carrots, radishes, turnips, cucumbers, beans	Onions, potatoes	
Potatoes	Beans, cabbages, horseradish, marigolds	Sunflowers, cucumbers, tomatoes	
Radishes	Peas, nasturtiums, lettuces, cucumbers	Hyssop	
Spinach	Strawberries, beans		
Tomatoes	Onions, marigolds, asparagus, carrots, parsley, cucumbers	Cabbages, fennel, potatoes	
Turnips	Peas	Potatoes	
Flowers (including nasturtiums, flowering herbs, limnanthes, marigolds, sunflowers)			Attract predatory and pollinating insects

VEGETABLES IN THE FLOWER GARDEN

Vegetables in the Border

Many vegetables are highly decorative and lend themselves to growing in the ornamental garden. Climbing and runner beans, for example, are particularly attractive and can be mixed with other climbers such as sweet peas. The beans then reap the benefit that the sweet peas provide in attracting pollinating insects and the sweet peas add even more colour, scent and flowers for the home.

Coloured lettuces, such as those mentioned for use in containers in the chart on page 85, or larger-growing types, such as red and green salad bowl, make a super edging for the border, as do many hardy radicchios, varieties of which turn red in the autumn.

Dwarf French beans make an attractive dot plant towards the front of a display, too, while leaf beet, beetroot and chard varieties

often have coloured leaves or stems. Jerusalem artichokes produce bright yellow sunflower-like blooms in summer and being tall and strong can be used as a windbreak at the back of a border or veg plot, but they spread rapidly, so beware. Globe artichokes and the related cardoons are highly

Soil and planting

Like any vegetable growing in the open plot, vegetables in the flower border need a well-drained soil and reasonable fertility. They should also receive plenty of sunlight.

Remove any weeds before planting or sowing and dig in a little well-rotted organic matter or general fertiliser. If planting early in the year, bear in mind that the rapid growth of herbaceous plants might swamp small crops such as lettuces and allow enough room for this, though salads also grow quickly and should be large enough to harvest before long.

Remember to sow new batches of seeds every three to four weeks so that there are always new plants to fill in any holes as short-term crops are harvested.

Cut-and-come-again crops, such as salad leaves, are useful for sowing along the front of a mixed border since they do not leave gaps in the planting as they are harvested.

Remember, the vegetables in question do not have to be planted in the beds – containers can be dotted among the flowers and moved around or replaced as required (see page 82). The growing and care of any veg in the flower garden is the same as that in the vegetable plot. See the A-Z guide starting on page 90 for further details.

Flowers in the vegetable garden

There has always been a place in the vegetable garden for flowers. Traditionally gardeners have grown flowers such as chrysanthemums, roses, gladioli, dahlias and sweet peas for cutting for the home or for the local horticultural show, and this also has the advantage of brightening up the veg plot and attracting pollinators.

Some allotment sites have a policy of asking plot holders to keep the first few yards of their plots as an ornamental garden and this can be a wonderful way of adding colour to an allotment site and encouraging local people to visit and maybe even to rent a plot.

architectural plants and make a bold statement when dotted through a border. A few flowers, if allowed to open, are a spectacular sight, forming a pin-cushion of purple blue, like a giant thistle.

Peppers and aubergines can be grown outside in the open garden and look attractive, but will not do well in a cool summer. They may be best grown in containers where they can be moved indoors or out as conditions dictate.

Many squashes can be grown as climbers up a strong wigwam of canes, an arch or pergola. Some of the most decorative are not edible; the gourds come in all manner of shapes and sizes and fascinate children and adults alike. Cured and varnished, they make interesting indoor winter decorations that will last for months.

Sweetcorn can be decorative, and there are several varieties with coloured cobs, such as 'Red Strawberry', 'Double Standard' and 'Indian Summer'.

Vegetables in Containers

You don't need an allotment or even a garden patch to grow vegetables. A patio tub, hanging basket or window box is quite enough to provide a tasty harvest of tomatoes, sweet finger carrots, salad leaves, peppers, cucumbers, fresh herbs, potatoes and much more.

What's more, vegetables and herbs can make an attractive as well as a productive addition to the ornamental garden, whether in a container or planted among ornamental plants in the flower borders.

Choosing a container

Virtually any container is suitable for growing vegetables, but it must be well-drained, deep enough to accommodate the roots and should not be so small as to constantly dry out. The best bet is to grow several types of veg in a large patio tub or pot, as the greater volume of compost will make it easier to manage your plants' water needs and will keep the roots cooler during the summer.

TOP TIP

POT DRAINAGE

Always ensure that your containers are well-drained; drill additional holes in the base of plastic pots if required. Raising your containers up on some pot feet, bricks or short pieces of timber will assist drainage.

Watering

When growing in containers, vegetables are dependent on you for water and food. Most also need sunshine and the compost

can quickly dry out on a hot, sunny day. Shading the pot in some way – perhaps by standing pots together in groups – can help, but if you can't be around to water regularly, you may have to consider installing a simple watering system, available from most garden centres and irrigation specialists.

DID YOU KNOW?

Plastic pots tend to be hotter than terracotta, which are cooled by the water as it evaporates from the porous surface of the pot. Black plastic pots absorb the most heat.

For a cheaper alternative, stand your pots in saucers or trays of water during hot spells, but remember to remove them during persistent wet weather if plants are growing outside.

Composts

Vegetables are not too fussy when it comes to composts, but those rich in nutrients are probably best avoided since they can encourage soft, lush growth at the expense of fruit or roots. Multi-purpose composts are suitable and manufacturers produce a variety of composts especially for containers – some even make a vegetable compost.

Thirsty plants, such as tomatoes, might benefit from a small amount of water-retaining gel added to the compost before planting, but use this with care as it is easy to over-wet the compost during cooler, rainy spells. Do not use the gel for cucumbers and squashes, as they are prone to root and stem rots.

Growing-bags

Growing-bags offer a great way to cultivate all sorts of vegetables from tomatoes to salad leaves. The shallow root run that a bag offers larger plants, such as peppers and tomatoes, means that the soil dries out quickly and is difficult to rewet. To overcome this, when planting such crops it is advisable either to use the compost to fill a deep pot (15cm/6in or larger) or small bucket with drainage holes drilled into the base, or to use the bags as part of a ring culture system (see Step-by-Step guide on page 86).

Grow three plants to a bag in the case of tomatoes, or two per bag in the case of cucumbers. One growing-bag should be able to support four peppers or three aubergines.

Feeding

Liquid fertilisers are ideal for containers since there is less chance of over-feeding and scorching the roots. A general fertiliser containing more potash than nitrogen is best in order to avoid leafy growth at the expense of a good crop. If you are growing a 'green' crop where leafy growth is more desirable, as in the case of salad leaves, a high nitrogen feed could be used instead.

If you are using a watering system, feeding can be given via a dilutor fitted between the tap and the pots. (Dilutors are available from garden centres.)

The liquid fertiliser usually recommended for feeding vegetables is a tomato feed, which will not only be rich in potash, but minor and trace elements, such as magnesium, too.

How much fertiliser you need to give your plants and how often will depend on what is being grown. In the case of salad leaves a few feeds towards the end of their useful lives is often enough to produce a last flush of tender leaves, whereas heavily cropping tomatoes require feeding every 7–10 days during the summer once the first truss has set. As a rule it is better to under- than over-feed, because an excess of nutrients can build up quickly in the confines of a container.

Controlled-release fertilisers offer an alternative to liquid feeds and can be incorporated into the compost in the form of granules, pellets or sticks, before planting. They release nutrients in response to the temperature and water content of the compost and so prevent over-feeding. One dose of controlled-release fertiliser should be enough to see the plants through from planting to harvest and means that you don't have to worry about feeding for the life of the crop.

Siting containers

Most vegetables require a sunny, warm, sheltered spot. Avoid a windy, exposed area as this will cause rapid drying due to water loss through the leaves and perhaps snapped branches. Pollinating insects might be deterred from visiting your plants if they are constantly being battered by the wind.

Supporting the plants

It is not as easy to support plants in containers as it is in the border. Beans and other climbers can be provided with a wigwam of canes, home-grown hazel or willow stakes, or a ready-made decorative obelisk.

Growing-bags are an easier proposition since there are proprietary supports on the market that incorporate a tray for the bag and canes or a frame for the plants, or you can

make your own. You could also consider siting pots holding taller plants near a trellis against a sunny, warm wall.

Hanging baskets

Hanging baskets and other hanging containers offer a great chance for anyone to grow some tasty fresh veg. Bush tomatoes are the classic variety to try, but bushy peppers, mini cucumbers, salad leaves and herbs are also well-suited. Hanging the container close to the kitchen door is a good idea, providing growing conditions are suitable, as the produce will be close at hand no matter what the weather.

Baskets are even more prone to drying out than other containers, so a dose of water-holding granules or 'planting' a mat incorporating similar material in the base is a good idea. Alternatively, place a small pot saucer in the base of the basket before planting up. Lining with moss or moss substitute and then with a layer of polythene cut from an old compost sack is another way of helping to prevent evaporation during hot weather.

Controlled-release fertilisers and water-retaining gels (see above) are perfect for use in hanging baskets.

See Step-by-Step guide on page 87.

Vegetables for containers

Most vegetables can be grown in containers, and the chart below offers some suggestions for those which are especially suited for this purpose. For more information see the A to Z guide starting on page 90.

Vegetable	Type	Variety	Comments
Aubergines		Any	
Beans	Runner	'White Lady' (climbing), 'Hestia' (dwarf), 'Painted Lady', 'Sun Bright', 'Celebration', 'Snow White'	'Sun Bright' with yellow leaves also looks great in the flower garden. 'Celebration' has pink flowers, 'Painted Lady' bears red and white blooms
	Dwarf/ climbing French	Any	Those with coloured pods can be highly attractive. Green, yellow and purple-podded types are available
	Broad	'The Sutton'	
	Borlotti	'Firetongue'	Green pods splashed with red
	Lablab		Pretty purple flowers
Beetroot		Any when harvested as baby beet. 'Moulin Rouge'	Eaten young, beetroot leaves are delicious and nutritious. Bull's Blood' is grown for its deeply coloured red leaves
Chard		'Rainbow Chard'	Great in containers or the flower border. Single colours are also available
Brassicas	Cabbage	'Primero F1', 'Guardian F1', 'Excel F1', 'Minicole F1'	'Primero' is an attractive red variety
	Calabrese	'Lucky F1'	Compact grower
	Cauliflower	'Candid Charm F1', 'Igloo'	Eat when tennis-ball size
	Kale	'Dwarf Green Curled', 'Redbor'	
Carrots		'Amsterdam Forcing – Sprint', 'Parmex', 'Sugarsnax', 'Paris Market Baron', 'Mignon'	
Courgettes		'One Ball', 'Eight Ball', 'Black Forest', 'Crystal Lemon', 'Paris White'	'Black Forest' can be grown as a climbing plant
Cucumbers		'Sunsweet F1', 'Miniature White', 'Cucino F1', 'Green Fingers F1'	'Cucino F1' is a greenhouse type
Kohl rabi		Any	Harvest when young and tender
Leeks		'Armor', 'Jolant'	
Lettuces		'Freckles', 'Little Leprechaun', 'Little Gem', 'Roxy', 'Marshall', 'Dazzle'	Many decorative varieties available in seed catalogues. Sow in succession.
Peppers		'Redskin', 'Hungarian Hot Wax', 'Apache', 'Etna', 'Prairie Fire', 'Pyramid', 'Mohawk F1'	Small bushy types are ideal
Potato		'Swift', 'Moulin Rouge', 'Carlingford', 'Orla, 'Vivaldi'	Early and salad varieties are best for containers and Christmas cropping
Radish		All summer varieties	
Salad leaves		All types suitable	Sow every few weeks, avoiding July and August
Salad onions		All. 'Crimson Forest', 'North Holland Blood Red – Bloodmate', 'Purplette'	Red varieties add colour to salads
Spinach		All. 'Bordeaux'	'Bordeaux' has attractive red stems
Squash		'Straightneck Yellow', Gemstore F1', 'Little Gem Rolet'	Butternuts and smaller squashes can be grown as climbers up a strong obelisk
Sweet potatoes			Provide shelter in a greenhouse or polytunnel in all but hottest summers
Tomatoes (containers)		'Maskotka', 'Vilma', 'Totem', 'Incas F1', 'Red Robin'	Numerous varieties; some bush types have been bred for use in pots and containers
Tomatoes (baskets)		'Tumbling Tom',	Choose a trailing type
Turnips		'Aramis'	Harvest at golf-ball size

Planting growing-bags

1 First roll the bag on the ground to break up the compost inside.

2 Take three large pots and remove the bases with a hacksaw.

3 Sit the pots on top of the bag and cut around the base with a knife.

4 Remove the polythene from beneath the pots, push the bases into the compost and put some extra compost in the bottom of the pots.

5 Remove the plants from their original pots – the roots should be well established.

6 Put the rootball into the new pot and fill around with compost.

7 Tie the plants to supports where required and water well.

Planting a hanging basket

1 Stand the basket on a large pot for stability. Fill the base with compost.

2 Place a taller-growing plant such as a bush tomato in the middle.

3 Lower-growing plants are planted around the outside.

4 These nasturtiums were sown five to a pot and can be divided carefully.

5 The trailing nasturtiums are planted around the edge and angled over it. Fill in carefully around each rootball with compost so as not to leave gaps.

6 Hang the basket in a sunny, sheltered spot and water well.

Growing Without Soil

For many years commercial growers experimented with raising crops without soil, particularly tomatoes and cucumbers, and in the Second World War soil-free systems were used to produce food to feed the troops. Since the 1970s commercial crops of cucumbers and tomatoes have been grown in Rockwool blocks 'planted' into channels of constantly moving nutrient solution. This may seem strange at first, but the method has many benefits; it eliminates the problem of soil-borne diseases and the need for crop rotation, and overcomes the fact that soil in a greenhouse or polytunnel can quickly become depleted of nutrients and home to pathogens if used year-after-year for the same crop.

Growing without soil, or hydroponics, used to be something that could only be attempted by professionals because it required very careful management to ensure that the plants received the correct levels of nutrients. Today's small, modern systems offer anyone the chance to grow crops in self-contained, soil-less units that are very easy to take care of. What's more, since the water they contain is constantly recycled, they are very efficient and only need topping up occasionally, so they are ideal for people who are out at work all day, even in the hottest summers.

How does it work?

Plants destined to be grown in a hydroponic system can be raised in compost in the early stages in the same way as any other, or they can be sown directly onto Rockwool blocks or similar. The blocks are made from an inert material that holds lots of water, but drains very freely. The base of the block sits in a shallow tray of water, allowing the roots of the plant to take up the moisture and nutrients they need, yet still have access to the air that the roots must have to stay healthy.

If germinated in compost, some systems demand that the roots are washed before being introduced into the nutrient system, while with others the pot in which the plant has been grown is removed and the rootball simply stands on a layer of capillary matting (a highly absorbent synthetic material) in a covered tray above a water reservoir. As the roots grow they move out of the rootball and into the matting where they are free to take up water. A pump constantly moves water through the matting, and back into the reservoir (see below).

There are other systems such as 'ebb and flow', which periodically floods the root zone with nutrient solution and then slowly drains it away again.

Nutrient solution

Below the 'growing tray' is a reservoir that needs to be topped up with a water/nutrient mixture as the plants take it up – perhaps twice a week in the heat of summer. The solution is circulated by a tiny pump, using no more power than a small light bulb, and heated very gently by an aquarium heater in the early stages when ambient temperatures in the greenhouse are likely to be low.

The nutrient solution must circulate continuously around the roots to ensure that there is always a constant and adequate supply and that the water is always well aerated. It also acts to wash away any impurities. The plants simply take up what they need, but because most of the roots – and the stem – are out of the water, they have access to plenty of oxygen and should never become waterlogged.

The pH balance of the solution must also be maintained and each week it is important, especially in hard water areas, to take a sample of the water and test it with the simple kit provided, adding a few drops of special solution as directed to keep the pH at the right level.

Suitable plants

Virtually any plants can be grown in a hydroponic system and it is ideal for tender greenhouse types such as tomatoes, cucumbers, peppers and aubergines. Apart from the different planting technique, plants are grown in exactly the same way as those in a standard compost mixture.

It is possible to grow different kinds of plants in the same unit and because plants never suffer from a lack of water (provided the reservoir is topped up and the pump kept running), yields can be up to three times heavier than from conventional methods. Water-related problems such as blossom end rot should be much reduced, too.

A TO Z OF VEGETABLES

Artichokes and Cardoons

It is the scales or chokes of the flower heads of globe artichokes (*Cynara scolymus*) that are considered such a delicacy when squeezed from their tough outer coat.

Cardoons (*Cynara cardunculus*) are a close relative, but it is the fleshy midrib of the leaf and tip of the stem that is eaten after blanching rather than the choke.

Chinese artichokes (*Stachys affinis*) are grown for their little potassium-rich tubers, which have a pleasant nutty taste. Jerusalem artichokes (*Helianthus tuberosus*) are related to sunflowers. They produce tasty tubers and pretty, yellow daisy-like blooms in late summer.

Cardoons

Preparing the ground

Artichokes will thrive on well-drained, reasonably fertile soil. Globe artichokes and cardoons prefer a sheltered spot, but being large and decorative they make good dot plants for the flower border.

Jerusalem artichokes are tough, invasive plants that are better grown in isolation. Growing up to 1.8m (6ft) tall, they make great windbreaks and are also ideal for suppressing weeds and breaking up the soil. Low-growing Chinese artichokes are also invasive and should be grown in a separate bed.

Lime very acid soils before planting and dig in plenty of well-rotted manure or garden compost to improve fertility on poor sites.

Propagation

Globe artichokes can be grown from seed, but the plants are often poor. It is generally better to buy in plants of named varieties, which are often supplied as rooted suckers and should be planted in May.

Cardoons Sow seeds into small pots or deep-celled modules. They can also be sown direct outside in April once the soil has warmed; thin to remove the weak plants as seedlings develop.

Jerusalem artichokes Plant tubers during March or April, 10–15cm (4–6in) deep in rows 30cm (12in) apart.

Chinese artichokes Plant tubers vertically 5–7.5cm (2–3in) deep and 15cm (6in) apart in well-prepared soil in March or April. If the season is very cold, start tubers off in pots or trays in the greenhouse.

Growing on

Globe artichokes and cardoons can be moved to their permanent positions in well-prepared soil once plants are well established. Plant 60cm (2ft) apart, allowing up to 90cm (3ft) between rows. Water well and keep the soil moist until the plants have established. Mulch with a thick layer of organic matter around the roots to retain moisture and keep the roots cool in the early stages.

Grow on globes and cardoons during the first summer and remove flowers as they appear. In cold winters, or exposed areas, protect the crowns of globe artichokes with fleece or straw; remove this before growth begins again in the spring.

Globe artichokes and cardoons are harvested during the second and third years, but are best replaced after that to keep them young and vigorous. To increase stocks lift plants in May and remove healthy suckers with plenty of roots and at least two good shoots. Replant immediately.

Jerusalem and Chinese artichokes are simply allowed to grow and develop. Beds should be weeded regularly before the crops have established a good weed suppressing leaf cover. Water well during dry spells and, as with globe artichokes, cover the beds with insulating material if the ground is likely to freeze over before the crop is harvested.

Harvesting

Cut the flower buds of globe artichokes before the scales (chokes) begin to open, generally from August onwards.

Stems will produce one main 'terminal' flower head and will then go on to grow several more on shoots that emerge from the leaf joints.

Globe artichoke

Cardoons should be blanched to produce the tender hearts and midribs. This is done in the autumn: first tie the leaves against the stem with soft string before covering with cardboard, newspaper or black polythene – anything that will exclude light from the stems. Blanching takes three or four weeks after which the wrapping can be removed and the plant lifted. Leave blanching plants in situ until required for harvest.

Jerusalem and Chinese artichokes are also left in the soil until needed.

Pests and diseases

Slugs Few pests attack these plants, although slugs will nibble the leaves, especially in spring, and may set up home in the wrapping around cardoons when blanching. Use your favoured form of slug control or pick them off.

Powdery mildew can cause problems on cardoons in dry seasons. Regular watering and mulching will help to keep it at bay, or treat with a fungicide.

Varieties

Globe artichokes: 'Green Globe' is widely grown. 'Purple Globe – Romanesco' is an attractive alternative, producing red heads.
Cardoons and Chinese artichokes: Only the species are available.
Jerusalem artichokes: 'Fuseau' is the main variety, although you will also find the species on offer as 'common'.

Chinese artichoke

Jerusalem artichoke 'Fuseau'

Globe artichoke												X = ok XX = ideal
Month	J	F	M	A	M	J	J	A	S	O	N	D
Plant				XX	XX							
Harvest								X	XX	XX	X	

Jerusalem/Chinese artichoke												X = ok XX = ideal
Month	J	F	M	A	M	J	J	A	S	O	N	D
Sow		X	XX	XX								
Harvest	XX	X	X							X	XX	XX

Cardoon												X = ok XX = ideal
Month	J	F	M	A	M	J	J	A	S	O	N	D
Sow				XX	XX							
Harvest										XX	XX	

NUTRITIONAL INFORMATION

Globe and Jerusalem artichokes contain iron, potassium, magnesium, phosphorus and trace elements. Cardoons and Chinese artichokes are also rich in potassium.

Asparagus

Asparagus is well-worth growing as it is always expensive to buy in the shops. Being a long-lived perennial – it can crop for up to 20 years – it requires quite a commitment in terms of space.

DID YOU KNOW?

Asparagus (*Asparagus officinalis*) is a member of the lily family. Plants are either male or female and breeders have worked to develop better all-male varieties to reduce problems caused by prolific seeding.

Propagation

Asparagus plants can be raised from seed, but the seedlings are usually inferior and it is better to invest in good crowns of a named variety.

Growing on

Planting is carried out in spring (March) or autumn. The latter allows the roots to establish over winter for an early start the following spring. Check suppliers for availability of varieties at various times.

As soon as plants arrive soak the roots in a bucket of

Asparagus needs very well-drained, rich, deep soil and since this is a long-term crop it is well worth paying attention to soil preparation before planting.

Commercially, plants are often grown on ridges, but providing your soil does not remain waterlogged during the winter you should be able to produce a good crop on your plot. Before planting dig in plenty of garden compost or well-rotted manure. If the soil is acidic add lime to adjust the pH to 6.5–7.5. Make sure that all perennial weeds are removed; on weedy soil, dig over before covering with a thick mulch or apply a glyphosate-based weedkiller.

Commercially asparagus is often grown on ridges

water and then 'heel in' (plant temporarily) while you make final preparations.

Dig a trench 30cm (1ft) deep with a 10cm (4in) mound of soil or sharp sand on the base to ensure good drainage from the crown, which is prone to rotting. The soil that is dug from the trench is temporarily placed down the centre of the bed. Trenches should be spaced 90cm (3ft) apart.

Space plants at 30–45cm (12–18in) intervals with their roots fanned out either side of the mound. Cover the crown with about 5cm (2in) of soil using that placed down the centre of the bed. As the shoots develop add a little more soil to cover them, in effect 'earthing them up'. All the excess soil should be used up by the autumn.

Remove weeds by hand, as hoeing may damage the delicate and shallow roots. Mulching with a layer of weed-free organic matter in late winter or early spring can help to suppress early weed growth and prevent water loss during the summer. If your site is exposed plants may need some support.

In the autumn cut back the yellowing ferns, leaving a few inches of stem protruding to show the location of the plants during the winter.

Harvesting

Resist harvesting in the first two years after planting to allow the plants to establish. In the third year take a small crop and by the fourth year plants should be in full production.

The main harvest takes place from April to June and a few spears can be taken until midsummer. Crowns then need the remaining foliage to build up their strength for next season or you will have thin, weak spears the following year. Harvest by slicing through the spears with a sharp knife 2.5–5cm (1–2in) below the surface of the soil.

Spears are best eaten immediately after harvesting, but will remain fresh in the fridge for a few days, or stand them in a glass of water for a day or two to keep them turgid. Spears can also be frozen: wash well and blanch for a few minutes; allow to cool before placing in labelled and dated freezer bags.

Pests and diseases

Crown rot and grey mould (botrytis) are common on heavy soils. Improve drainage and plant on a mound.

Asparagus beetle will attack plants even in their first year,

so keep watch for the yellow and black adult beetles and grey larvae and pick them off.

Slugs cause losses to young spears before they emerge, especially in the early stages after planting. The little black soil-dwelling keeled slugs can be controlled by watering the soil with a biological control. Scatter organic or non-organic pellets over the surface to kill snails and surface-living slugs.

Varieties

'Connover's Colossal': a tried and trusted old variety.
'Backlim F1': a modern, heavy-cropping variety said to have good disease resistance. Mid- to late-season.
'Gijnlim F1': an all male variety producing green shoots with purple tips. Early cropping.
'Crimson Pacific': purple spears sweet enough to eat raw. Steaming helps to retain the colour when cooking. Mid-season cropping.
'Pacific Purple': attractive purple spears with a sweet flavour and good yields. Mid-season cropping.
'Ariane F1': green, tight-tipped spears. Good yields and very early cropping. Can be planted in the autumn.
'Pacific 2000 F1': the stringless spears can be eaten raw or cooked. Plant autumn or spring.
'Guelph Millennium': a Canadian variety that is said to suit UK conditions. A few female plants may occur. Mid- to late-season cropping. Plant autumn or spring.

Artichokes												X = ok XX = ideal
Month	J	F	M	A	M	J	J	A	S	O	N	D
Sow/plant			XX	XX						XX	X	
Harvest				X	XX	X						

NUTRITIONAL INFORMATION:
Rich in potassium, folic acid and vitamin C.

Aubergines

Aubergines (eggplants) are tender plants producing large, attractive purple-pink flowers and shiny purple or white fruits. These have a distinctive texture and a mild flavour, although they are very good at absorbing flavours from other ingredients and are an essential ingredient in ratatouille and moussaka, or as a vegetable in their own right when fried or baked.

DID YOU KNOW?

In the past the chopped fruit was soaked in salty water for up to an hour before cooking to remove bitterness, but modern varieties can be used straight from the plant.

Preparing the ground

Aubergines are related to tomatoes and peppers and need similar growing conditions, although of the three they are the most prone to cold and for this reason they are usually grown in pots and containers under cover. They can be planted outdoors in the soil in mild areas, in which case preparation is the same as for tomatoes (see page 164).

Propagation

Aubergines need a long growing season to crop well in the UK's relatively short summers. Sow from February to the end of April (the earlier the better) in a heated propagator on a sunny windowsill or greenhouse bench, maintaining 15–21°C (60–70°F). Sowing into modules (cell trays), or small pots, prevents the need for pricking out later on. Check each day and water any dry patches.

Germination takes approximately 7–10 days and once most of the seedlings have emerged remove the lid of the propagator to prevent stretching. Take plants out of the propagator, but maintain an air temperature of 15°C (60°F) in the early stages, reducing to 10°C (50°F) as plants establish.

Growing on

Once the plants are well-established pot on into progressively larger containers until you reach a maximum of 15cm (6in), which is adequate for most varieties. Multi-purpose, vegetable or potting compost is ideal for this;

alternatively you can grow three plants in a standard growing-bag or four to a vegetable planter (a larger version of the growing-bag). It is also possible to plant out into the open plot or garden border once the last frosts are over, covering with a cloche initially. However, plants will only thrive if the early summer period is warm and unless you live in a mild area of the country it is better to grow on in pots until the weather warms up thoroughly.

Pinching out the growing tips is not essential to make plants bush out, but can be done once they reach 30cm (12in). Take care when handling, as many varieties bear very sharp spines.

Once plants have been in their final pots for a few weeks it will be essential to feed with a high potash tomato feed once a week, or at half strength every watering.

Weather permitting, as plants flower they can be moved outside to encourage pollination by bees and other insects, as this is often erratic during a cool, wet summer in the greenhouse. Tapping stems or pollinating using a soft-haired brush is also an option. Both methods help to distribute the pollen. When using a brush, gently brush the flower parts moving methodically from one flower to another to transfer the pollen from the anthers (male part) to the stigma (female part) of the same flower and neighbouring blooms.

Harvesting

Harvest from July until the first frost. Once the fruit has reached full size, but is still glossy, snip off the fruit with scissors or secateurs. Use as soon as possible, although they will store well for a few days in the fridge.

Pests and diseases

Aphids (greenfly) cause mottling and puckering of the leaves. Spray with a suitable insecticide or rub off with the fingers.

Whitefly attack plants in the greenhouse early in the year, but by summer they move outdoors on to plot-grown plants. They are difficult to control because they are resistant to most of the available insecticides. In the greenhouse or polytunnel you can hang sticky yellow traps among the crop or, alternatively, introduce the parasitic wasp, encarsia. This is effective if used as soon as the pests are first seen.

Red spider mite over-winter in the structure of the greenhouse during the winter and emerge to infest plants in the spring. Clean and fumigate the structure and staging in the autumn. Spray over the foliage with water to deter the pest and restrict its movement through the crop, otherwise use a suitable insecticide at the first sign of attack. Biological control is effective using phytoseiulus, again providing that the predator, a mite, is introduced as soon as pests are seen.

'Moneymaker'

Varieties

'Moneymaker': widely available and reliable, producing large purple fruits in good numbers.
'Ophelia': small purple fruits, ideal for growing in pots on the patio.
'Black Beauty': medium-sized, rounded fruits.
'Bambino': tiny purple 'cocktail' aubergines.
'Long Purple': an old variety producing long purple fruits, ideal for slicing.
'Clara F1': attractive round, white-skinned non-bitter fruit.
'Fairy Tale F1': a compact variety. Highly decorative on the patio, producing small to medium purple fruit, each with white stripes.
'Rosa Bianca': rose pink, rounded fruits have a mild flavour.

Aubergines												X = ok XX = ideal
Month	J	F	M	A	M	J	J	A	S	O	N	D
Sow		XX	XX	X								
Harvest								X	XX	XX	X	

NUTRITIONAL INFORMATION:
Useful levels of vitamins E and K, magnesium, folate and potassium.

Beans

beans can be grown over a trench that has been filled with kitchen and soft garden waste during the winter or has had plenty of well-rotted compost dug in.

Flowers often fail to set in acid conditions, so test the soil and if necessary lime to increase the pH to 6.5–7.5 in the autumn.

Propagation

Sow French dwarf and climbing beans directly into the ground from May when fear of frost is fading, or into deep cell trays in the greenhouse in April/May to be ready for planting when the weather allows. The latter is the best option for

Beans are part of the pea (legume) family and there are many types grown as important crops worldwide. In the UK the most popular are runner beans, broad beans, dwarf and climbing French beans. Drying beans, much used in Europe, are also becoming popular in the UK as a winter standby and an ingredient of soups and stews.

Most popular beans are grown in the same way, the main exception being broad beans, which are hardy and can be sown direct into the ground in spring or autumn. French and climbing beans, including drying and runner beans, are tender and outdoor sowing should not attempted until the soil has warmed up. Give all beans a good start in cell trays.

Preparing the soil

Beans love a deep, rich, moist soil, which improves growth and flower setting, so they benefit from the addition of lots of organic matter in the autumn before sowing. Runner

early crops as it protects the young seedlings from pests and ensures that the roots are kept warm until the soil heats up. A week before sowing or planting dwarf French beans or broad beans, rake in some general fertiliser.

When sowing direct into the soil, sow runner and drying beans 5cm (2in) deep and dwarf and climbing French beans 4cm (1½in) deep in the soil. Allow 23cm (9in) between runners and 10cm (4in) between the smaller types. Rows should be spaced 45cm (18in) apart. (For broad beans, see below.)

When sowing the larger climbing beans in pots, sow four seeds per 10cm (4in) pot and grow as one plant. Alternatively, like the smaller French types, they can be sown individually in deep cell trays, sweet pea tubes or home-made paper pots.

Bottom heat from a propagator is not generally necessary by the time beans are sown in April/May, but the greenhouse should be frost-free and preferably maintained at around

10°C (50°F) for best results. It is important not to sow too soon, since climbing types start to twine around their neighbours and quickly become tangled and difficult to separate without damage. Sowing to planting takes about four weeks in the spring.

BROAD BEANS
Broad beans are hardier and can be sown in November as well as in the spring. This, together with successional sowings from February to the end of May, gives a potential

harvest period from the end of May into October. Since they freeze well it is possible to have broad beans all year round.

Sow 5cm (2in) deep and 20cm (8in) apart in rows about 20cm (8in) apart. Alternatively, stretch some bean netting between stout stakes over the soil and sow seeds or pot-raised plants into alternate squares in the netting. As the plants grow

the netting is raised up. 'The Sutton', which at only 30cm (12in) tall needs little or no support, is suitable for windy sites.

Growing on
Strong supports for climbing beans should be put in place before the beans are sown or ready to plant out. When placing pot-grown plants around a wigwam of canes, plant one pot of three or four seedlings at the base of each cane. The plants may need to be tied to the canes initially until

TOP TIP
When direct sowing any beans into the soil, place a few at the end or in between the rows to make up for any losses caused by poor germination or pests.

they begin to twine. Maintain watering during the growing season and once climbers reach the top of their supports remove the growing tips to encourage branching.

Dwarf French beans sown direct into the soil are allowed to grow on without support or pinching. Cloches or fleece will be necessary if sowing in April to protect seedlings from the cold; remove once the frosts are over. Sow every three weeks until the end of June to ensure cropping until the autumn and mix the varieties to provide a range of colours and flavours for the kitchen.

Adjust the support netting or strings for broad beans as required. Once beans start to form on the top of the plants the growing tips can be removed to discourage blackfly, which tend to congregate there.

RUNNER BEANS – IMPROVING FLOWER SET
Early in the season, runner bean flowers may fail to set. Low temperatures are one factor and this is usually rectified once the temperatures rise as conditions improve. Hot, dry weather can have the same effect; spraying over regularly with water and good soil preparation as above will help to minimise problems.

A lack of lime also leads to flower drop and this can be cured by liming in the autumn or applying 28–56g (1–2oz) of garden lime diluted in 4.5 litres (1gall) of water.

Bumblebees can cause problems with flower setting when they often discover that it is easier to reach the nectar in the flowers by biting into the back of the blossom, rather than entering through the front. Sparrows sometimes pick off the blooms for no apparent reason. Growing white-flowered varieties can help, since they don't seem to attract the attention of birds and bumblebees quite so much.

If all else fails, grow French beans – they tend to set much more readily than runners. Planting or sowing sweet peas alongside climbing beans can help to improve pollination and offers the bonus of scented flowers for cutting.

Harvesting
Harvest regularly to encourage more beans to form; this may mean checking them over every day because they grow very quickly. Never pull the beans from the plants when you pick

as you risk breaking the thin stems, instead snip or pinch the pods off.

In all cases the younger pods are the most tender. Broad bean pods, if picked very young, can be eaten whole. Young broad beans harvested and removed from the pods while still tender are far superior to anything you can buy in the shops. Leave them too long and you will have to peel away the tough outer skins before eating.

Drying beans can be eaten in the same way as runner beans, but for drying and storing pods are only harvested once they have dried and just before they split to spill their seeds on to the soil.

Pests and diseases

Beans suffer from a number of pests and diseases. Some pests – such as slugs, snails and birds, which love to eat the young growth – can be avoided by growing in pots in the early stages. Mice will dig up seeds and nip off bean shoots as they emerge – covering rows with wire netting can help and setting traps will keep damage to a minimum.

Bean seeds are often saved from one year to the next, but this may come at a price. If the seeds have any telltale small round holes in them they should not be saved since they will have been attacked by seed beetles and may not germinate.

Bean seed fly The maggots of bean seed fly may tunnel the emerging shoots of the beans, causing them to become distorted. Growing in pots avoids this problem.

Pea and bean weevils eat distinctive notches in the edges of the leaves – not a serious problem on established plants, but damaging on young seedlings. Spraying with an insecticide against other pests such as aphids should eradicate them or alternatively grow in pots.

Halo blight is a bacterial disease affecting runner and French beans

Chocolate spot (large chocolate-coloured spots) on broad beans is rarely fatal to the plants. This picture also shows some of the tiny raised orange spots of bean rust

and, like seed beetle, can be carried over on the seeds. Water-soaked spots on the leaves and pods change to dry, dark spots surrounded by a halo-like yellow ring. There is no cure and seeds from infected crops should not be saved.

Chocolate spot attacks broad beans and is common. It causes small chocolate brown spots to form on the leaves and these often coalesce to cover the leaf. It can cause the death of the plant, but is usually less serious with plants managing to produce a good crop. There is no chemical cure.

Greenfly and blackfly are common pests on beans. Blackfly attack the soft tips of the plants in large numbers. Removing the tips once the flowers have set solves the problem. Runner and French beans suffer from greenfly from time to time and these can either be rubbed off with finger and thumb or in all cases reliable sprays are available (see page 68).

Varieties
RUNNER BEANS

'Scarlet Emperor': an old variety that has stood the test of time.

'Lady Di': a stringless type with good flavour, producing pods up to 30cm (12in) long.

'Painted Lady': a popular variety for its two-tone red and white flowers and tasty medium-length pods.

'White Lady': an old white-flowered variety producing good yields.

'Celebration': pretty pink flowers make this one ideal for growing in the flower border.

'Pickwick': a dwarf plant bearing medium-sized pods of stringless beans. Needs no support.

'Hestia': as above, but with attractive bi-coloured flowers.

'Butler': a stringless type producing heavy crops of medium-length beans.

'Red Rum': an early variety producing good yields of medium-length stringless beans. Halo blight resistant.

'Sun Bright': a late-cropping variety with golden yellow leaves and red flowers. Ideal for the flower garden.

DWARF FRENCH BEANS

'The Prince': a heavy-cropping green podded type.

'Safari': a fast-maturing Kenyan type. Slender pods up to 13cm (5in) long on disease-resistant plants.

'Supremo': a borlotti type producing creamy coloured pods and seeds flecked with red. Eat the beans fresh or dried.

'Delinel': a green-podded stringless type bearing heavy yields of slender pods.

'Golddukat': attractive, tender yellow stringless pods.

'Golden Teepee': pencil-thin, tender yellow pods held well above the soil.

'Purple Queen': round, purple stringless pods.

CLIMBING FRENCH BEANS

'Blauhilde': purple, round pods up to 27cm (11in) long. Virus resistant.

'Goldfield': early cropping with flat yellow pods up to 27cm (11in) long.

'Cobra': popular, heavy-yielding variety producing green, stringless pods.

'Eva': dark green pods. Resistant to bean, cucumber and yellow mosaic virus.

ORIENTAL CLIMBING BEANS

'Yard Long': an oriental climbing bean producing pods up to 45cm (18in) long. Tender, best suited for growing in a polytunnel or greenhouse.

DRYING BEANS

'Barlotta Lingua Di Fuoco' *('Firetongue'):* the classic barlotti (or barlotto) bean with cream-coloured pods and seeds, splashed with red. Eat young as fresh pods or allow to mature and dry.

'Cannellino': dwarf bush

bean producing round pods which can be eaten as green beans when young or allowed to mature and used dry.

'Czar': a white-seeded runner bean that when left to mature can be used as butter beans.

Pea bean: attractive white round beans with a splash of chocolate brown. Eat pods whole when young and tender or use as a drying bean.

BROAD BEANS

'The Sutton': the dwarf broad bean. Short pods are less productive than some, but needs no support even on exposed sites.

'Bunyard's Exhibition': an old variety, but still very popular. Tall plants producing long pods of tasty beans.

'Aquadulce Claudia': ideal for autumn or spring sowing. Medium pods up to 25cm (10in) long.

'Stereo': often produces short twin pods from each leaf joint. Pods can be eaten as mangetout if picked very young.

'Violetta': green pods, each with four or five purple seeds. Good for freezing. Steam to retain colour.

'Witkiem Manita': matures very early from a spring sowing and produces short pods of beans with good flavour.

'Express': fast-maturing from a spring sowing and very heavy cropping. Good for freezing.

Broad beans												X = ok XX = ideal
Month	J	F	M	A	M	J	J	A	S	O	N	D
Sow		X	XX	XX	X						X	XX
Harvest					X	X	XX	XX	X			

French/climbing beans												X = ok XX = ideal
Month	J	F	M	A	M	J	J	A	S	O	N	D
Sow				X	XX	XX						
Harvest							XX	XX	XX	X	X	

NUTRITIONAL INFORMATION

Good source of vitamins A, C and E, protein and fibre.

Beetroot

Beetroot is delicious hot or cold, when grated raw into salads or pickled. Usually grown for the root, more and more gardeners are growing the tasty, sweet foliage as a colourful salad leaf.

If sown in succession, stored and pickled, beetroot can be available all year round. Seed catalogues offer a range of roots in red, yellow, pink and white, some with internal white rings, making this one of our most colourful ingredients – you can even use it as a food dye.

Growing

The best beets grow on well-drained, sandy soils, but it is not too fussy and will grow in most areas if given a sunny spot. Plants bolt if they become short of water and those that do form become woody, so dig in plenty of well-rotted garden compost or manure in the autumn and dress the soil with a general fertiliser 7–10 days before sowing. On acid soils, lime in the autumn to increase the pH to between 6.5 and 7.5.

Propagation

Wait until the soil warms in March to sow and cover early crops with a cloche. A good way to improve early germination is to grow in cell trays in March and transplant outside in April/ May when conditions are better. Later direct sowings should be fine. For early sowings choose a bolt-resistant variety such as 'Boltardy'.

Normal beetroot 'seeds' consist of a little cluster of seeds, usually two or three, and so

TOP TIP

The corky seed coat covering beetroot contains a growth inhibitor designed to prevent germination until conditions are favourable. This can be removed before sowing by soaking the seeds in water for an hour. Stir gently to assist the process.

you may need to thin to the strongest once the seedlings are large enough to handle. The alternative is to sow a monogerm variety, bred to give just one seedling per seed.

Sow one seed per station, approximately 2.5cm (1in) deep and 10cm (4in) apart in rows 30cm (12in) apart. Sowing single short rows every three to four weeks will ensure a succession.

Plants grown for salad leaves can be scattered over compost in trays or pots and covered lightly, or can be sown in drills in the greenhouse or polytunnel border.

Growing on

Germination takes about 14 days. Thin as soon as the seedlings become large enough to handle. Remove cloches from early outdoor sowings by the middle of April. Protect seedlings outdoors from birds with some netting or crop protection fleece and take precautions against slugs.

Maintain watering during dry spells to avoid growth checks and root splitting and keep weeds down by hoeing or hand pulling.

Harvesting

Lift every other plant from the row once roots reach golf ball size; they should never be allowed to grow larger than a cricket ball or they will become woody. For pickling, lift when small, young and tender.

Remove the leaves from the roots by grasping them just above the bulb and twisting so that a few inches of the leaf stalks remain attached. This prevents the colour from leaching out of the roots when cooking. Once cooked the roots and remnants of the leaf stalks can be trimmed and the roots peeled. Eat hot as a main course veg, allow to cool for salads and sandwiches.

Harvest the foliage of plants grown as salad leaves by

'Chioggia Pink': roots have alternate red and white rings when sliced through. This becomes a uniform pink when cooked.
'Burpee's Golden': attractive golden yellow roots. Germination can be poor.

either pulling up whole plants or pinching a leaf or two from each. The mature tops can be steamed and eaten as a spinach substitute.

To maintain good condition, the roots are best lifted in the autumn and stored in boxes of dry peat or sand where they should keep well until the end of March. Twist off the leaves as described above before storing. Small roots can also be frozen after first cooking, peeling and cubing.

Pests and diseases

Birds and slugs attack seedlings and roots so take precautions against both.

Boron deficiency Boron levels may be low on naturally chalky soils. Deficiency shows as corky sunken patches around the top of the root and blackened areas within. Feed with a liquid feed containing this trace element to correct problems initially. Lower the pH on problem soils using sulphur chips, or grow in containers.

Manganese deficiency is most common on poorly drained or acid soils and causes yellow blotches between the leaf veins and poor growth. Improving drainage and adding lime may help. Feed with a fertiliser rich in manganese.

Varieties

'Boltardy': bolt-resistant red roots with good flavour and colour.
'Moneta': recommended for early sowing. Monogerm.
'Cylindra': cylindrical dark red roots. Good disease resistance.
'Alto F1': sweet cylindrical roots. Earth-up as roots develop.

'Bull's Blood': grown as a salad leaf. Deep red foliage, attractive in the flower border.
'Albino': a white-rooted variety. Does not store well.
'Pablo F1': uniform, tender roots which keep well in the ground. Good disease resistance.
'Action F1': bred for baby beet. Harvest when 2.5cm (1in) in diameter.

Beetroots												X = ok	XX = ideal
Month	J	F	M	A	M	J	J	A	S	O	N	D
Sow/plant			XX	XX	XX	XX	XX	X				
Harvest							XX	XX	XX	XX	X	

NUTRITIONAL INFORMATION
Said to aid the immune system. Contains potassium, folate and vitamin C.

Brassicas

The cabbage family (*Cruciferae*) is enormous and encompasses all of our popular 'greens', such as cabbages, cauliflowers, kale, Brussels sprouts and broccoli. These crops have been staples in the UK for many years and being hardy are an important mainstay during the winter months.

With planning it is possible to harvest delicious fresh greens of one sort or another all year round. There are a few points to bear in mind: the first is that these are slow-growing long-term crops that can tie up large amounts of space if you intend to be self-sufficient in them; the second is that summer types suffer from more than their fair share of pests and diseases. Having said that, they are relatively easy to grow and highly nutritious.

Preparing the ground

All brassicas enjoy the same soil conditions: well-drained, reasonably fertile, neutral to alkaline soil (pH6.0–7.5) in a spot that receives plenty of sunshine. Being the taller of the clan, Brussels sprouts and, to some extent, kale, are best grown in a sheltered spot where they will not be battered by the wind, as the roots are shallow and easily damaged by winter gales. Staking may be necessary to prevent losses.

Check lime levels and adjust if necessary in the autumn before planting. Lots of well-rotted organic matter should be added, especially to poor soils. Perennial weeds should be removed. The soil should then be raked level and allowed to settle for as long as possible before planting, since all brassicas prefer to have their roots in a firm soil; planting in recently disturbed spots can lead to problems with 'blown' (loose) sprouts and cabbages. The same is also likely to occur if too much nitrogen is applied to the soil immediately before planting.

Propagation

Brassicas can be sown direct into the ground or into cell trays or pots for planting out later. Traditionally they are sown in nursery rows and transplanted into their final growing positions when 7.5–10cm (3–4in) tall. This is ideal if you don't have a greenhouse or polytunnel, but time-consuming. Sowing into cell trays not only saves time, but because there is less root disturbance when planting, helps the plants to establish more quickly.

If you prefer, it is possible to buy brassicas as ready-grown young plug plants. They offer a convenient way to start your crop and are very useful if you forget or don't have time to sow, or experience poor germination for any reason.

In cell trays, all brassicas are sown in the same way: drop a single seed on to the top of the compost in each cell and cover with 6mm (¼in) of fresh compost or vermiculite.

In open ground sow thinly, 13mm (½in) deep in nursery rows 15cm (6in) apart. Be sure to protect the plants with your favoured form of slug and snail control and net against attack by pigeons.

Maintain watering during dry spells and remove weeds as they occur. Once the seedlings are large enough to handle, thin to leave 7.5cm (3in) between plants. When the plants have developed four to five true leaves they can be planted out.

Growing on

Cabbages will produce a head to match the space available. Mini vegetables are gaining in popularity and if you have limited space or prefer to harvest the heads while still small and sweet, allow 35cm (14in) each way between plants. If you prefer full-sized heads allow up to 50cm (20in) between plants. The variety chosen also has an influence, so check the seed packet for further advice.

Brussels sprouts need plenty of space and lots of time to mature – up to 36 weeks from sowing to harvesting for winter types. The planting distance will depend on the variety chosen, as older varieties tend to be taller and need more room than the compact, modern F1 types. The usual advice is to allow 75–90cm (2½–3ft) between plants. It is possible to grow good sprouts using a modern variety and planting just 45cm (18in) apart, but, the closer the plants the greater the risk of diseases as air and sunlight are restricted.

Kale is easy to grow and some varieties, such as 'Dwarf Green Curled' and 'Redbor', are highly decorative. These compact varieties can be planted 45cm (18in) apart either way. Taller types need a little more room: plant 60–75cm (24–30in) apart.

Cauliflowers need much the same treatment as the other brassicas although they are a little fussier about soil conditions – too much nitrogen and they will produce leafy growth at the expense of the curd. Plant winter types 65cm (26in) apart and those for summer and autumn harvest 60cm (2ft) apart.

Broccoli should be planted 60–75cm (24–30in) apart either way in the rows and calabrese 30cm (12in) each way.

Plant all brassicas with as little soil disturbance as possible to maintain a firm tilth. Use a dibber or trowel and if plants have become leggy they can be buried up to 5cm (2in) deeper than they were in the nursery bed or cell tray. Firm around the base of each plant with the ball of your palm and water in.

Place a cabbage collar around the stem of each to deter cabbage root fly and protect plants from birds, snails and slugs immediately after planting. From June onwards you will have to take precautions against cabbage white caterpillars and the best way to do this is to cover crops completely with crop protection netting, such as Micromesh or Enviromesh, preferably suspended over a frame of canes.

Provide taller plants

DID YOU KNOW?

What is the difference between broccoli and calabrese? Generally, broccoli varieties produce lots of smaller florets from the sideshoots that run towards the tip of the main stem, although there is usually one slightly larger main head at the top. Broccoli is very hardy and crops from April onwards.

Calabrese produces one very big head in the growing point of the plant and this is the type that is often found in supermarkets, sometimes confusingly labelled as broccoli. Modern varieties of calabrese usually produce a good number of smaller sideshoots and crop from August until the first frosts.

such as Brussels sprouts, kale and larger varieties of broccoli with canes to prevent wind damage as they become top heavy.

Feeding encourages a better yield from most brassicas, but needs to be carried out with care to prevent leafy growth and loose cabbage heads and sprouts. After the first harvest from broccoli and calabrese, apply a feed of liquid Growmore or similar, or scatter Growmore granules thinly around the base of the plants.

Sprouts can be given one or two feeds using a high potash liquid fertiliser, such as a tomato feed, in late summer. Cabbages are fed with a general granular fertiliser a few weeks after planting. Follow this with a liquid feed when the heads start to firm up.

Harvesting

Cabbages are usually harvested once the hearts are firm although young plants or thinnings can be used as tender greens. Either pull up the entire plant or sever just below the head leaving the stalk in the ground. As with most brassicas if the stalk is left and two cuts are made in the top of the stump to form a cross shape, new shoots may form and these can be harvested as greens.

Sprouts are best harvested after a frost when the buttons will be sweeter. Start from the bottom of the plant up allowing those at the top more time to mature. Either twist or cut off.

In the case of kale, the whole plant can be harvested or leaves picked off as required, just taking a few from each lant at each harvesting.

The heads of calabrese and broccoli are cut before the flowers open, taking the stem back to the leaf joint below. New shoots should emerge from the leaf joints below the main head to produce further cuts of smaller heads later on.

Pests and diseases

Clubroot is devastating as it not only kills the crop, it remains in the soil for up to 20 years to infect future plantings. The symptoms are not always obvious at first, but then plants may appear poor and stunted and will often wilt, especially on a warm day, often recovering at night in the early stages. If lifted, the roots will be swollen and distorted and may show signs of rotting.

Infected plants should be removed carefully, together with all the roots and the soil around them. Avoid moving the disease from one patch to another on boots or tools. Never accept plants from friends or other sources unless you are sure they are clean. Lime discourages the disease and gardeners have had some success from liming soil to pH7 or above, or from dusting lime into the planting hole.

Growing plants in containers, such as 10–13cm (4–5in) pots, for as long as possible before planting out, enables them to survive the disease for long enough to produce a crop before the disease strikes.

There are some clubroot-resistant varieties of brassicas available and these should be chosen if the disease is suspected.

White blister is a common disease that causes puckering of the leaves, mainly of cabbages and Brussels sprouts, but it will infect any brassica crop. Yellow spots turn white and powdery as spores are produced. It is rarely fatal although disfiguring. There is no control other than to remove infected leaves and badly infected plants.

Powdery and downy mildews both affect brassicas. Powdery mildew causes a powdery white coating to appear over the upper surface of the leaf, while downy mildew causes angular brown spots between the leaf veins. During moist weather a dirty grey mould appears. Sprays are available to control both diseases and some varieties are more resistant than others.

Water well during dry spells to avoid powdery mildew. Increasing the spacing between plants and avoiding the use of high nitrogen feeds can help to reduce downy mildew.

Cabbage root fly lay their eggs around the stems of plants. These hatch and the little creamy white maggots eat into the roots and lower stem. The first sign of trouble is often when the plant wilts, the roots being too badly damaged to take up sufficient water. Plants then turn yellow and die. It is common to see occasional plants dying in a row, while others are perfectly healthy. The larvae then pupate in the soil to emerge again the following spring.

Cultivating the soil over winter should kill the pupating pests or expose them to the frost and to predators. Collars made from old matting, carpet tiles or similar, or ready-made collars from the garden centre placed around the stems at planting prevent the adults from laying their eggs on the soil.

Cabbage whitefly are little white insects seen fluttering around the leaves as you brush by. They do not cause a great deal of damage other than by encouraging black, sooty mould to form on the leaves below where the pests are feeding. This blocks the pores of the plants, reducing their vigour, and soils edible sprouts, kale and cabbage leaves.

There are plenty of sprays available, but few are very effective and it is usually easier to ignore them. They can be blasted off with a hose, but this will only have a limited effect. Covering with fine crop protection netting soon after the crop is planted is probably the best answer.

Caterpillars of many species of moths and butterflies will attack brassicas and those of large and small cabbage white butterflies are the most troublesome. Fine netting is the best way to keep them at bay, but if they do manage to reach your plants, from about the beginning of June onwards,

with powdered dry soil can deter them, otherwise run a sticky yellow whitefly trap over the leaves, just brushing the tops. This will catch many beetles as they jump. Alternatively, spray with a general insecticide.

Nutrient deficiencies are very common on brassicas. Good soil preparation and the use of lots of organic matter is the best way to prevent problems. A liquid feed using a product containing a good range of trace elements can be given if problems are suspected. Testing the soil once a year in the spring with a simple soil testing kit (see page 28) and acting on its recommendations before planting or sowing should avoid deficiencies of the major nutrients.

Most soils contain plenty of nutrients, only very sandy soils or those which have been over-limed cause problems.

start to check for the yellow eggs – clusters in the case of large whites, individual eggs in the case of small whites. These can be squashed and if any have hatched, the caterpillars picked off. Sprays are also available and are very effective.

Cabbage aphids are grey-green insects that infest the tips of the plants and form clusters on the underside of the leaves causing yellowing and severe distortion. They breed very quickly in the summer and can render the foliage inedible.

Sprays can be effective, but the waxy coating covering the pest makes it difficult to reach and several applications are usually required. Since a few plants in a row are usually badly infested, while others escape relatively unscathed, those plants should be removed and destroyed. Once again, covering the crop, while difficult, is the only way to ensure they remain unaffected.

Slugs, snails and birds just love brassicas and it will be necessary to take precautions against them from the time of planting. Birds generally lose interest once the plants have established and even quite badly damaged specimens are often capable of recovery if protected from further attack.

Flea beetles are a nuisance on young plants, eating little holes in the seed leaves (cotyledons). Infestations can cause the death of plants before they ever get going. A dusting

Pigeons cause much damage to brassicas

Varieties
CABBAGE
Spring harvest
'April': attractive pointed heads. Ideal for close spacing.
'Offenham 2 – Flower of Spring': pointed heads, matures April/ May.
'Spring Hero': spring-maturing ballhead cabbage that can also be grown for summer use.

Summer/autumn harvest
'Hispi F1': pointed heads, good for successional sowing, so can be harvested right through to the autumn.
'Minicole F1': compact round heads of white cabbage. Sow in April for a September harvest.
'Derby day': heavy, tight heads mature from mid-June to October from a February to mid-June sowing.

'Kilaton F1': a new clubroot-resistant variety, producing dense, round heads from September to December.

'Picador': compact plants ideal for those with smaller plots. Crops from August to October.

'Golden Acre': compact plants which can be grown at close spacings (down to 30cm/1ft). Crops from July onwards.

'Red Rookie F1': very early red cabbage and resistant to splitting. Harvest from mid-August.

'Red Drumhead': great fresh or pickled. Crops from September onwards.

Winter harvest

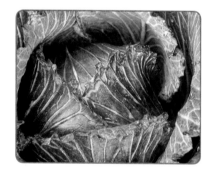

'Tundra F1': crisp, tasty, dense heads from this Savoy type cabbage.

'January King 3': reliable cropper that keeps well in the ground until needed.

'Robin F1': a January King type that has an attractive red flush to its green leaves. Keeps well in the soil until required.

BROCCOLI

'Purple Sprouting Early': very heavy crops of purple spears from March onwards.

'Purple Sprouting Late': as above, but harvest from April onwards.

'Claret': large heads mature from April onwards and plants crop for up to four weeks.

'Extra Early Rudolph': this one bucks the trend by cropping from November to February. Purple spears produced on sturdy plants.

'Wok-Brocc': purple sprouting, cropping from June to winter when sown in succession.

'Nine Star Perennial': a perennial variety. Needs lots of space, but produces a good crop of green heads year after year.

CALABRESE

'Belstar F1': produces lots of sideheads once the main head has been harvested. Small beads (flower buds) make for delicious eating.

'Kabuki': compact plants allow close spacing for smaller plots.

'Romanesco': attractive lime green heads maturing in September and October.

'Fiesta': bright green heads for cutting through the summer and autumn.

CAULIFLOWERS
Summer/ autumn harvest

'Mayflower F1': very early variety can be harvested from May to June if sown in the greenhouse in January.

'Snowball': long leaves self-wrap the curd in to protect against scorching in summer. Good raw or cooked.

'Violet Queen': attractive purple heads mature August to October.

'Clapton F1': sow March/April for a July to October harvest. Clubroot-resistant.

Winter harvest

'Jerome F1': stands well through the winter for an April harvest.

'Maystar': as above, but ready for cutting in May and June.

'Haddin F1': vigorous variety for harvesting from November to February from May to July sowings.

BRUSSELS SPROUTS
Early varieties (harvest August-November)

'Brilliant F1': high yields of tight buttons. Resistant to powdery mildew.

'Rubine': red buttons that retain their colour on cooking. Harvest in December.

'Brigitte F1': good alternative to the old favourite 'Peer Gynt', which is no longer available.

'Franklin F1': another good alternative to 'Peer Gynt' and producing early crops from the end of August.

Late varieties (harvest November to February)

'Bedford Winter Harvest': heavy yields of tight sprouts from November to February

'Trafalgar F1': uniform, sweet sprouts produced from November to January.

'Exodus F1': late variety with good disease resistance, including white blister and powdery mildew. Harvest November to March.

KALE

'Dwarf Green Curled': compact plants needing no staking. Deeply curled leaf edges. Great flavour.

'Redbor': as above, but with attractive red leaves.

'Nero Di Toscana': Italian thin-leaved variety with a distinctive strong flavour.

Cabbages												X = ok XX = ideal
Month	J	F	M	A	M	J	J	A	S	O	N	D
Spring												
Sow						XX	XX					
Harvest			X	XX	XX	X						
Summer/Autumn												
Sow		X	X	XX								
Harvest								X	XX	XX	X	
Winter												
Sow					XX	XX						
Harvest	XX	XX	X							X	XX	XX

Broccoli												X = ok XX = ideal
Month	J	F	M	A	M	J	J	A	S	O	N	D
Sow				XX	XX							
Harvest	X	XX	XX	XX	X		X	XX	XX	XX	X	

Sprouts												X = ok XX = ideal
Month	J	F	M	A	M	J	J	A	S	O	N	D
Sow/plant		XX	XX									
Harvest	XX	X							X	XX	XX	XX	XX

Kale												X = ok XX = ideal
Month	J	F	M	A	M	J	J	A	S	O	N	D
Sow/plant			X	XX	XX	XX	XX					
Harvest	XX	XX	XX	XX					X	X	XX	XX	XX

NUTRITIONAL INFORMATION

Vitamins A, C and fibre, plus iron and antioxidants.

Carrots

Carrots are delicious raw or cooked, they store well and with care it is possible to have delicious home-grown roots for much of the year. Packed with health-promoting nutrients, finger roots are a great, sweet snack food, much-loved by children. Short or stump-rooted types are ideal for growing in shallow or stony soils or in pots and tubs.

Preparing the ground

Carrots, especially early crops, like an open, sunny spot. The soil should be deep and free draining. Heavy soils are more likely to harbour slugs and these cause much damage to the roots, often allowing in diseases and other pests. Improving

DID YOU KNOW?

Carrots are biennial plants (grow one year, flower and set seeds the next). In order to survive the winter, the plant stores lots of sugars and other nutrients in its fleshy tap root, making them sweet to eat.

heavy soils with lots of organic matter will help the situation, but remember that using fresh manure on the ground in the winter before sowing will cause the roots to fork, so should be avoided.

On heavy soil delay sowing until March and then only go ahead if conditions are right and the soil temperature has reached at least 7°C (45°F).

Large stones will also encourage the roots to fork, so rake out when preparing the seedbed. About a week before sowing, rake in 28–56g (1–2oz) of general fertiliser.

Propagation

Carrots are sown direct into the soil in which they are to grow. Drills should be about 13mm (½in) deep and 15cm

(6in) apart. Water the base of the drill before sowing thinly, then cover with dry soil, so trapping the moisture beneath.

Carrot fly is a constant threat and sowing a couple of rows of onions each side of the carrots is said to be a good deterrent. Sow thinly or use seed tapes, as the smell of the thinnings will attract the pests to your plot.

The pests first emerge from the soil in May or June, so delaying sowings until then ensures that there is nothing for the pests to feed on. The alternative is to sow a row of resistant carrots in between two rows of non-resistant ones so that the non-resistant crop will act as a decoy.

Early crops should be covered with cloches to keep them and the soil as warm as possible to maximise germination.

TOP TIP

IMPROVING GERMINATION

Germination can be improved by sowing as described on this page and covering with seed compost.

On stony or heavy soils a cone-shaped hole can be made with a bar. Fill the hole with compost and sow two seeds on top, covering each with lightly with sieved compost. Water well and remove the weakest seedling if both germinate.

Growing on

To protect further against carrot fly, place low barriers of fine netting (60cm/2ft) around the crop, or cover with crop protection netting. This only works if the soil is free of over-wintering pests.

Watering must be maintained to ensure that previously dry roots do not split.

If thinning is necessary do this in stages until the roots are 5–7.5cm (2–3in) apart to allow the remainder to grow. Dispose of the thinnings well away from the row. Subsequent thinnings can be eaten as finger carrots. Keep the crop weed-free at all times and watch for pests such as greenfly.

Earth up occasionally, as the top of the root will turn green and bitter if exposed to the sunlight.

Harvesting

Simply harvest when the roots have reached the desired size either as small finger carrots or full sized roots. Roots can be left in the ground until needed in most areas, but in cold regions or soils which are home to lots of slugs they are best lifted and stored in boxes of sand, sacks or clamps.

Pests and diseases

Carrot fly has already been mentioned and barriers, crop covers and resistant varieties offer a combined solution. A biological control is available which can be useful on land infested from previous crops.

Willow-carrot aphid infests the crop in late spring and is often to be found around the growing point at the crown of the plant. Pests carry a virus that causes the leaves to become stunted and mottled with yellow and red. Spray as soon as the greenfly are spotted.

Slugs are a problem, especially on heavy soils and in wet seasons. Use pellets, traps or barriers to control them on the surface. Biological controls offer a good way to reach those living below ground.

Varieties

'Rocket F1': an early carrot. Harvest young as finger roots, or allow to mature as a maincrop.

'Maestro F1': a carrot fly and disease-resistant variety producing good quality medium-length roots.

'Nelson': an early variety, ideal for sowing in February if conditions allow. Resistant to greentop and cracking.

'Chantenay Red Cored 2': main-crop carrot producing tasty, tapering roots over a long period.

'Atlas': round, disease-resistant roots, ideal for growing in containers.

'Parmex': As above – full flavoured globe-shaped roots.

'Yellowstone': distinctive yellow roots high in vitamins A and C.

'Rainbow Mixed F1': a mixture of coloured types to provide a colourful plate and also the widest range of anitioxidants.

'Purple Haze F1': dark purple roots with an orange core.

'Sugarsnax F1': deep orange roots and very sweet. Good as finger carrots.

Carrots												X = ok XX = ideal
Month	J	F	M	A	M	J	J	A	S	O	N	D
Sow/plant		X	XX	XX	XX	XX		X				
Harvest							X	XX	XX	XX	XX	X	X

NUTRITIONAL INFORMATION
Rich in vitamin A (beta-carotene) and antioxidants.

Celery and Celeriac

Propagation

Sow seeds of celery in March or April, starting them off in cell trays or pots in a heated propagator set to 13–15°C (55–60°F). Celeriac is best sown in February to give it a longer growing season as it is slow to mature.

Once the seedlings are through, remove the lid of the propagator and grow the plants on at a temperature of 10–13°C (50–55°F), hardening off before planting out in May or June. A cold frame is useful here.

Growing on

There is no need to plant self-blanching celery in trenches to blanch (whiten) the stems as there is with traditional varieties – close planting in a block does the same trick. Plant 20–23cm (8–9in) apart in both directions. Celeriac is planted 25–30cm (10–12in) apart in rows 18in (45cm) apart.

Regular watering is essential, although celeriac is a little more tolerant of the occasional dry spell than celery, which will grow poorly and be tough and stringy if allowed to dry out. Celery also benefits from a liquid feed with a balanced fertiliser once a month during the summer months.

Once the plants are well developed from mid- to late-summer, blanching can be further encouraged by shading the plants around the edge of the block with anything that will reduce light levels, such as several layers of shade netting, boards or straw.

These closely related vegetables are invaluable for their distinctive flavour. Although celery is traditionally used in salads, the hearts are even more delicious cooked, but it is not an easy crop to grow well. Thankfully celeriac is easy and offers a low-maintenance way to enjoy the unique taste in soups or winter salads.

Preparing the ground

Celery is a marsh plant, needing plenty of water to thrive, and this is partly what makes it difficult to grow. The other difficulty is the need to blanch the stems, although modern self-blanching varieties help to overcome this and these are the types described here.

Both celery and celeriac prefer a rich, fertile, moisture-retentive yet well-drained soil. The site should also be sunny and open with a pH of between 6.5 and 7.5.

Dig in plenty of well-rotted organic matter in the autumn before sowing and, in the case of celery, add a layer of the same material in the holes when it comes to planting out. About a week before planting add 28–56g (1–2oz) of general fertiliser to the soil and rake in.

Harvesting

Lift self-blanching celery as required from late summer onwards. It is less hardy than trenching celery and so should be lifted and used before the first frost.

Celeriac is very hardy and can be left in the ground until needed, but slugs may take their toll over winter on heavy soils and you may decide to lift them to minimise damage. If plants are left in situ, cover the bed with straw or some other insulating material to keep the roots in good condition.

If lifting, cut or twist off the leaves, leaving a few inches of leaf stem intact, and store in damp sand or peat in boxes in a dark, frost-free shed.

The leaves of celeriac have a strong celery scent and taste and can be used chopped as a garnish or in soups or stews.

Pests and diseases

Celery fly (celery leaf miner) commonly attacks both crops by tunnelling into the leaves, causing a blister-like 'mine' and reduced yield.

The occasional affected leaf can be picked off or the larvae squashed, but it is probably best to cover crops with crop protection netting. If attacks are very severe plants should be burned.

Celery heart rot is a serious problem on celery plants grown under cover, such as those for exhibition, but can cause losses on garden crops, also. Bacteria attack the heart of the plant, entering though any damage, such as slug holes or where stems have been nicked with a hoe. There is no cure and plants should be destroyed.

Bolting is most common in dry seasons where celery has been allowed to dry out, or where it has been planted out too early and has suffered a growth check due to a cold snap. Instead of forming a head, plants send up a single flower spike and are useless except for soup. Maintain regular watering.

Celery leaf spot gives rise to small black or brown spots over the leaves, which reduce vigour and can kill in severe cases. It is most common in wet seasons. Lift and destroy badly infected plants. Grow resistant varieties where possible.

Varieties

CELERY

'Tango': long, smooth stalks that are resistant to bolting.
'Loretta F1': a British-bred variety, producing thick, fleshy stalks which are said to be sweet and stringless.
'Victoria F1': thick, tasty, upright stems.

CELERIAC

'Alabaster': smooth roots. Excellent raw, steamed or mashed.
'Prinz': crisp flesh, ideal for grating in salads. Disease resistant.
'Giant Prague': roots store well and have a good flavour.

Celery												X = ok XX = ideal
Month	J	F	M	A	M	J	J	A	S	O	N	D
Sow			XX	XX								
Harvest	XX	X							X	XX	XX	XX	XX

Celeriac												X = ok XX = ideal
Month	J	F	M	A	M	J	J	A	S	O	N	D
Sow			XX									
Harvest	XX	X	X							X	XX	XX	XX

NUTRITIONAL INFORMATION
Rich in potassium and vitamin C.

Chicory, Radicchio and Endive

These leafy crops are widely used in summer and winter salads. Each one is easy to grow and reasonably hardy (radicchio less so), offering a long season of cropping.

Many varieties are highly attractive and perfect for the front of the flower border. They are also ideal for the border of a cold greenhouse or polytunnel where the leaves are protected from the weather, although cloches can do the same job outside in autumn and winter.

There are two types of green chicory: forcing chicory, which is lifted in November (see below), and sugar-loaf types, which are eaten rather like lettuce.

Radicchio is a variation on the green chicories and is sometimes called red chicory. It is lettuce-like in appearance with a bitter taste. Many varieties, while green through the summer, take on lovely deep red tints in the autumn at the same time as they form hearts, making them highly attractive in the plot or in the ornamental garden.

Endives also look like lettuces; some varieties are deeply frilled and best for summer cropping. The hardier Batavian types with broad leaves are grown mainly for winter crops. Both are usually very bitter if eaten without blanching (covering to exclude light), although modern varieties of Batavian tend to have closely-packed upright leaves which are to a certain extent self-blanching.

Preparing the soil

In all cases soil should be reasonably well drained and fertile, so dig in plenty of well-rotted organic matter in the autumn before sowing or planting. The site should receive a reasonable amount of sunshine, especially if you are growing crops to over-winter.

Rake in some general fertiliser 7–10 days before sowing or planting.

Propagation

Chicory, radicchio and endive can be direct sown into well-prepared soil or into cell trays in the greenhouse. If sowing outside, seeds should be sown thinly, about 13mm (½in) deep in rows 30cm (12in) apart.

Chicory is best sown in June or July for harvesting from October onwards. Curly-leaved endives can be sown over a long period during the summer (see chart); the Batavian types for autumn and winter use are sown from July to September.

If sowing endives indoors, place trays in a heated propagator set at 20–22°C (68–72°F). Chicory and radicchio should not need any additional heat.

Growing on

Plant out once well established and hardened off, allowing 23–30cm (9–12in) between plants and rows. Ensure that plants are well watered during dry spells and that any weeds are removed.

CHICORY

Except in very mild areas, forcing chicory is lifted in October or November and the leaves cut back to about 2.5cm (1in). The long taproot is cut back to 15cm (6in) and the plants stored dry in boxes in a cool, but frost-free place until needed for forcing. They are then potted into large pots using moist peat, peat substitute or sand, six roots to each pot, leaving the crown exposed. Tape up the drainage holes in a second pot to exclude light and place this over the plants.

Place the roots in a warm place heated to 10–15°C (50–60°F), such as an airing cupboard, until the chicons (the chicory shoots) have formed and can be removed.

If forcing in the soil, cut back the leaves of plants left in the ground as needed and cover with 15cm (6in) of soil, then insulate with straw. Within 8–12 weeks the shoots should appear through the soil and can be uncovered.

Forcing chicory step-by-step

1 Lift the plants in October/November.

2 Trim the roots and topgrowth.

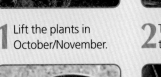

3 Pot up the roots into a large pot.

4 Cover with a pot of the same size. Cover the drainage holes.

5 Chicons (shoots) should, be ready about a month later.

ENDIVES

Endives should also be blanched for the best-tasting leaves and this is started about three months after sowing. In the case of the Batavian types, wait until the leaves are dry and then cover plants with buckets to exclude the light for about 10 days. Plants will rot if left for too long, so blanch a few at a time.

Low-growing frilly types can be blanched by covering the middle of the plant with a pot saucer held in place with a stone, or use a pot with the drainage holes covered to prevent light reaching the leaves.

Harvesting

Cut forcing chicory as soon as the chicons are large enough and before they open. They may rot if left

Non-forcing endives are lifted as needed in the same way as lettuce

covered for too long. Once harvested, old roots may sprout again and can be forced for a second time if watered well.

Forced Batavian endives should be cut after two to three weeks, while the frilly types are eaten after 10 days.

Radicchio need no special treatment and are cut as required once the heads are large enough. Alternatively, pick a few leaves from each plant over a period of weeks – only a few are needed in salads to add just enough bitterness.

Pests and diseases

Slugs and snails can cause problems with all these leafy crops, especially as they are being forced, so take precautions against them.

Endives may be attacked by aphids (greenfly) from time to time and these should be sprayed as seen.

Varieties

'Sugar Loaf'

CHICORY

Non-forcing

'Sugar Loaf' (Pain de Sucre): firm hearts that stand well in the soil until needed.

Forcing

'Witloof Zoom F1': tight-packed, dense heads
'Dura Witloof': produces fat, dense chicons when forced.

RADICCHIO

'Palla Rossa Bella': firm, red hearts and white-veined leaves.
'Augusto': deep red round heads. Strong-growing and bolt resistant.

ENDIVE (CURLY):

'Frisee Glory': finely divided leaves producing a dense heart. Alternatively, use as salad leaves.
'Blonde Full Heart': large heads of tasty white leaves when forced.

Endive												X = ok XX = ideal
Month	J	F	M	A	M	J	J	A	S	O	N	D
Sow			X	XX	XX	XX	XX	XX	X			
Harvest	XX	XX	X	X						X	XX	XX	XX

Chicory & Radicchio												X = ok XX = ideal
Month	J	F	M	A	M	J	J	A	S	O	N	D
Forcing												
Sow					XX	X						
Harvest	XX	X									X	XX
Non-forcing												
Sow					X	XX	X					XX
Harvest	X	X						X	XX	XX	XX	XX

NUTRITIONAL INFORMATION

Chicory: Good source of Vitamin A and potassium.
Endive: High in Vitamin A and iron.

Courgettes, Marrows and Squashes

True crops of summer, these prolific plants are very popular with UK gardeners. Marrows have been grown for years and are the staple of the local gardening show where enthusiasts vie to grow the heaviest fruit.

Courgettes are a newer introduction, but now possibly more popular than their larger cousin. In fact, one (the marrow) is simply a mature version of the other. Specific varieties have been bred for both and if you want to grow the best marrows, or courgettes, it is best to select a variety bred for the purpose.

Squashes come in many shapes and sizes; the summer squashes (of which marrows and courgettes are examples) are best used soon after harvesting, while winter squashes (including pumpkins) will store well for many months.

Preparing the soil

These fast-growing, heavy-cropping plants need lots of food and water, so plenty of well-rotted manure or garden compost is essential for success. Gardeners often have great results when growing squashes on top of their compost heap, or even over of a pile of very well-rotted manure into which they have made planting pockets filled with garden soil.

Choose the sunniest spot you can find and dig in the organic matter during the autumn. Check the pH of the soil, which should be between 5.5 and 6.8, and adjust if necessary – the acidifying effect of all that compost or manure should ensure that the pH is about right on all but the most alkaline of soils.

If supplies of organic matter are scarce, or you only have room for a few plants, prepare an area for each plant by concentrating the material at one spot and digging in. Before planting, open up a hole, fork over the base and refill with a 50:50 mix of the same material and garden soil. If your soil is poorly drained, overfill the hole to make a mound at the top 15cm (6in) high to drain water away from the stem which is prone to rotting. At the same time you could 'plant' a plastic drinks bottle into the top of the mound: remove the base of the bottle to make a funnel and angle the buried end of the container towards the roots. Use the funnel to channel water to the root zone in the summer.

As an alternative to the bottle, you could plant through a mulch of black polythene. Although fast-growing, in a cool spring these plants may take some weeks to get going and a polythene mulch, laid over the soil and held in place by pushing the edges into the soil with a spade, will suppress weeds. It will also help to retain moisture and warm the soil by absorbing heat. Make sure that the soil is thoroughly moist before putting it in place.

Propagation

Sow seeds individually in 7.5cm (3in) pots or large modules (cells). The usual advice to sow the flat seeds on their sides to encourage water to run off is said to reduce losses from rotting. However, the advantages are likely to be minimal. Seed size varies according to type, so as a guide bury each

seed in a pot to a depth which is twice the width of the seed. Large pumpkin seeds, for example, will need to be buried about 2.5cm (1in) deep.

Place the pots or trays in a heated propagator set to 20–25°C (68–77°F) and cover with a lid. Check watering every day, soaking any dry patches. Once most of the seedlings have emerged the cover can be removed and the plants 'weaned off' from the heat.

It is also possible to sow seeds outside from the end of May to the end of June directly into the top of the mound. Sow two seeds 2.5cm (1in) deep and cover with a bell cloche or similar to protect the emerging seedlings. A scattering of slug pellets will keep these pests at bay. Remove the cover once the seedlings are well established and thin to leave the strongest plant.

Growing on

Under cover maintain a temperature of 13–15°C (55–60°F) at first, gradually reducing this until the plants are hardened off and ready for planting out once the last frost has passed.

Planting distances depend on the type of squash being grown and whether they are trailing or bushy. In the case of courgettes and smaller bushy squashes or plants that are to be trained directly up a pergola or wigwam, allow 60cm (2ft) between plants in both directions. Large trailing varieties such as pumpkins, which will be sprawling over the ground, should be allowed 1.2m (4ft) between plants.

If you intend to grow smaller squashes up supports, the frames should be put in place before planting and the plants tied to them as the stems develop. Supports need to be strong, since the crop will be heavy.

Squashes produce separate male and female flowers on the same plant and it is common at first to find only male flowers and little or no fruit as a result, but the balance is usually restored later in the season as conditions improve. Female flowers have a tiny embryo fruit behind the bloom, but males lack this swelling and simply have a thin stalk.

If female flowers are scarce or if the weather is cool and there is a lack of pollinating insects, pick off a ripe male bloom (the pollen is visible on the male part of the flower in the centre) and peel back the petals before placing the male pollen-bearing parts in the female flower directly against the stigma in the middle; simply leave it there to wither. Later flowers should need no help to pollinate.

The stems of trailing types should be pinched (the

Right: Female flowers have a little embryo fruit behind the bloom

Planting squashes

1 Prepare the ground by adding lots of manure and rake level.

2 Dig a planting hole in the manured ground. If your soil is poorly drained, consider planting on a mound.

3 Ensure that the level of the compost is level with the soil in the bed to prevent rotting.

4 To aid watering make a watering funnel with a cut down drinks bottle and 'plant' this next to the rootball.

5 Water your plant through the funnel to ensure that it gets right down to the roots.

growing tip removed) once they are 60cm (2ft) long or have developed 4–5 leaves. This encourages more shoots to form on which fruit can be produced.

Maintain watering as the fruit forms, tying climbing plants to their supports regularly to prevent damage to the stems. Large fruits, such as pumpkins, should be placed on a bed of straw as they develop to cushion them from sharp stones and help prevent rotting. Feed with a high potash liquid feed every 7–10 days.

If plants start to outgrow their allotted space, cut back the offending shoots and in the case of large-fruited types, such as large pumpkins, remove the growing point from the parent stem two leaves after the fruit once you are sure it has set properly. Small-fruited varieties can be allowed to develop two fruits per stem. In a poor year you may have to limit the number of fruit per plant to ensure that those left grow to a reasonable size and ripen before the frosts. If you are after a very large fruit from your pumpkin, only allow your plants to develop one fruit to maturity.

Harvesting

Courgettes are harvested as soon as they are large enough to eat and grow so quickly that they need checking every few days. If necessary they can be stored in the fridge for several days before use. The flowers are a delicacy when fried in batter.

Marrows are allowed to mature on the plant. Give them a tap and if they sound hollow they should be ready. Then pierce the skin at the stalk end with the thumbnail – if ripe your nail should easily puncture the skin.

Larger squashes and pumpkins are also allowed to ripen on the plant; the plants themselves will begin to turn yellow and the fruit

take on a colour typical of the variety. The stalk may also crack and can be severed. Except in cold weather or very exposed areas, allow the fruit of winter squashes intended for storage to ripen in situ for a couple of weeks after cutting to cure. This hardens the skin and allows the stalk to dry, so extending the shelf-life of the fruit. If a frost is forecast before the fruit is ripe, move it to a frost-free place.

Once cured the fruit should be stored at a temperature of 7–10°C (45–50°F) until needed and can be kept for up to six months. Summer squashes can be harvested and eaten as required.

Pests and diseases

Aphids (greenfly) These attack plants from spring onwards causing damage and distortion, however the biggest danger they pose is the spreading of cucumber mosaic virus, which can ruin the crop. Spray as soon as pests are seen, but check the product label carefully as squashes can be sensitive to chemical sprays.

Root and stem rots Although these plants love lots of moisture, they are prone to stem and root rots. Planting on a mound as described should help.

Powdery mildew A very common and damaging disease, especially in dry seasons. Lots of organic matter and plenty of water are key to keeping powdery mildew at bay.

Slugs and snails These pests may damage the stems, especially in the early stages, and in wet weather they tunnel the developing fruit as well as nibbling the leaves. Control them with pellets, traps, barriers or a biological control.

Mice and rats may nibble the developing fruit and can be kept in check with traps or bait.

Varieties

Scores of varieties are available and in the case of squashes many produce fruit in fascinating shapes and colours.

SQUASHES
Winter squashes/pumpkins

'Bonbon F1': a compact-growing variety producing 1.5kg dark green fruits with a pale green stripe.

'Festival F1': attractive fruit, ideal for baking or stuffing.

'Blue Hubbard': distinctive large blue-grey fruit with a great flavour.

'Atlantic Giant': enormous fruit that can reach 320kg (700lb) in weight.

Butternut *'Harrier F1':* an early ripening butternut producing sweet, pear-shaped fruit.

'Crown Prince'

Butternut Squash

'Crown Prince': large, grey-green fruit with delicious deep orange flesh. Stores well.

'Turk's Turban': distinctive, colourful fruit, ideal for stuffing or cooking whole. Stores well.

'Turk's Turban'

Summer squash

Vegetable spaghetti: small to medium-sized orange or yellow fruit on bushy plants. On cooking, flesh takes on the appearance of spaghetti. Ideal for stir-fries or salads.

'Yellow Crookneck': pale yellow fruit with a distinctive shape and good flavour.

'Scallopini Mix': a mixture of green and yellow patty pan squash with a distinctive 'flying saucer' shape. Eat whole when young or slice like courgettes.

'Custard White'

'Sunburst'

'Custard White': as above, but with white fruit.

'Sunburst F1': as above, but with deep yellow fruit.

'Green Buttons F1: another patty pan with a shape much like a UFO, but this time in lime green. Highly decorative in a patio tub.

COURGETTES AND MARROWS

'Goldrush F1': compact plants bearing masses of attractive yellow fruit.

'Romanesco': lightly ridged green courgettes with a nutty taste.

'Tuscany F1': suited to the UK climate. Uniform, green glossy fruit. Good resistance to powdery mildew.

'Clarion F1': mottled, light green, tapered fruit. Plants have an open habit for easy picking.

'Eight Ball F1': round, green fruit, best picked when 5cm (2in) in diameter. Recommended for stuffing or steaming.

'Tiger Cross F1': a reliable variety, can also be picked young as courgettes. Resistant to cucumber mosaic virus.

'Long Green Bush 2': compact plants ideal for smaller gardens. Produces long, dark fruits.

Courgettes, marrows and squashes											X = ok XX = ideal	
Month	J	F	M	A	M	J	J	A	S	O	N	D
Sow/plant					XX	XX						
Harvest							X	XX	XX	XX		

NUTRITIONAL INFORMATION
Rich in vitamins B1 and E, potassium, beta carotene, folates and antioxidants.

Cucumbers

Ever popular as an ingredient of summer salads, cucumbers come in two types: greenhouse and outdoor varieties, including gherkins for pickling. You will also find some oddities in specialist seed catalogues that are well-worth searching out.

In the greenhouse, grow an all-female variety since pollinated fruit is very bitter. If growing one of the old open-pollinated types (without the prefix F1 in its name), you will have to remove the male flowers as they form.

Growing

Outdoor types are often called 'ridge cucumbers', since they are traditionally grown on ridges to aid drainage. Prepare the soil as for pumpkins, digging in lots of organic matter, but if this is in short supply, simply prepare planting pockets.

Cucumbers are tender plants and require protection. Having been started indoors, outdoor varieties can be given a better start if grown in, or covered with, a cold frame. If your frame is mobile you can pop it over the plants after planting, but, if not, the soil in the frame can be cultivated and the plants planted inside. Cloches can also be used temporarily to protect the plants should the spring and early summer turn out to be cold and wet.

If growing trailing varieties up supports, such as a low wigwam of canes, netting or a trellis, put them in place before planting out.

Propagation

This is the same for both indoor and outdoor types. Heated indoor crops can be sown in February for planting in March; outdoor crops are sown in April for planting out in May/June.

Sow seeds individually in cell trays or 7.5cm (3in) pots. Sow the flat seeds 13mm (½in) deep. Water well and place the pots in a heated and covered propagator set at 21–25°C (70–75°F). Germination should be rapid (within seven days) and once most of the seedlings are through the cover should be removed to prevent stretching.

Outdoor cucumbers can be sown direct into the soil, but because they are tender sowing is usually delayed until the end of May in the south, the middle of June in the north. To increase the chances of success with direct sown cucumbers, the seeds can be pre-germinated (Top Tip).

TOP TIP

PRE-GERMINATION

Pre-germinating seeds speeds up the germination process and can increase the rate of success in the case of expensive seeds such as cucumbers. Simply 'sow' seeds evenly and thinly on to damp kitchen towel placed in the bottom of a lidded plastic container. Pop on the lid and place the container in a warm, dark place. Check the seeds each day, re-wet the paper towel if necessary, but drain off excess water before replacing the lid.

Once the little root of the seedling is a few millimetres long, the seeds are ready for sowing outdoors or in pots and any that haven't germinated can be given a little longer or discarded.

Growing on

Once seedlings have established remove from the propagator and grow on at a temperature of 15–20°C (60–68°F). As the stems begin to grow insert a split cane into each pot and secure the plant to it with a soft wire ring. Give plants enough room so that they all get sufficient light and do not intertwine.

OUTDOOR CUCUMBERS

Outdoor cucumbers can be planted once the threat of frost has passed, but must be thoroughly hardened off first. Give them a sheltered spot or be prepared to cover with cloches or a cold frame as described above.

Prepare planting pockets as for squashes 90cm (3ft) apart and the same distance between rows. Also, as with squashes, consider covering the soil with a soil covering material before planting to keep down weeds and retain water.

Once plants have produced five true leaves pinch out the tip to encourage branching. As plants grow, trail the stems along the row or spread them out around the mound, or tie them to their supports. Do not pick off the male flowers of outdoor types. Water copiously during dry spells and feed every week with a high potash liquid fertiliser.

GREENHOUSE CUCUMBERS

Greenhouse cucumbers can be planted into the border soil of the greenhouse or polytunnel (prepare the soil in the same way as for outdoor types), but are more usually planted in pots or growing-bags to reduce the possibility of soil-borne diseases.

Once plants have developed a good root system they can be planted into 25cm (10in) pots, or two plants to a growing-bag. As with tomatoes, cucumbers can be grown using a ring-culture system (see page 86), in which case they are planted into 13cm (5in) bottomless pots placed on a growing-bag to increase the root run.

Maintain a temperature of 15°C (60°F) for open-pollinated (non-F1) varieties and 18–21°C (65–70°F) for all female varieties.

As the plants grow twist the stems around a string secured to the pot or 'planted' under the rootball, with the other end tied to the eves of the structure. Pinch out the growing tip of the plant once it has reached the eaves. Side shoots will be produced and these should be pinched at two leaves. Remove any male flowers.

Water to keep the compost moist, but not waterlogged, and only ventilate the greenhouse on warm days as cucumbers love warm, humid conditions.

Harvesting

Harvest the fruit as soon as it is large enough to encourage more to form. Do not worry if some small fruit turn yellow or black and fall off as plants produce far more fruit than they can ripen.

Pests and diseases

Powdery mildew (see squashes, page 116).
Red spider mites Often attack greenhouse varieties. Spray with a suitable insecticide, checking the label first to make sure that it will not damage cucumbers. Alternatively, use the biological control phytoseiulus as soon as pests are seen.
Whitefly Spray as above or use the parasitic wasp encarsia.

Varieties

Indoor

'Birgit F1': highly productive all-female variety.
'Femspot F1': as above.
'Baribal F1': short fruit produced on mildew-resistant plants.
'Carmen F1': all-female variety producing long fruit. Resistant to mildew, leaf spot and virus.

'Carmen F1'

Outdoor

'Boothby's Blonde': small yellow-white fruit. Can be grown indoors or out.
'Burpless Tasty Green F1': crunchy cues, resistant to mildew.
'Crystal Lemon': unusual round, yellow fruit.

'Boothby's Blonde'

GHERKIN

'Diamant F1': ideal for pickling or salads. Mildew-resistant.
'Bimbostar': all-female, disease-resistant variety.

Cucumbers												X = ok	XX = ideal
Month	J	F	M	A	M	J	J	A	S	O	N	D
Sow/plant		X	XX	XX	XX	X						
Harvest						X	X	XX	XX	XX	X	

NUTRITIONAL INFORMATION

Rich in potassium and carotenoids.

Florence Fennel

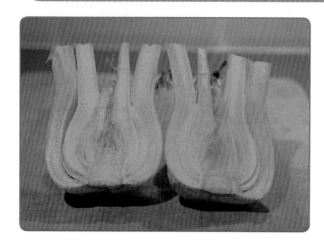

Florence fennel, not to be confused with the herb fennel to which it is closely related, is grown for its crisp bulbs with their distinctive aniseed flavour. The foliage and young stems are also edible and the seeds can be saved for use in recipes where they also impart a strong flavour of aniseed and a lovely fresh aroma.

Plants are highly decorative and all types of fennel are ideal subjects for the ornamental garden.

Growing

This is not the easiest crop to grow since it will bolt (run to seed) if growth is checked due to cold, dryness or root disturbance. Although the bulbs will not then be produced, all parts of the plant can be eaten.

Dryness is the biggest cause of failure, so dig in plenty of well-rotted organic matter in the autumn before sowing. Scatter 28–56g (1–2oz) of general fertiliser over the soil and rake in 7–10 days before sowing.

Propagation

Plants can be grown in trays and transplanted before seedlings become pot bound. They need careful handling to prevent bolting and many gardeners prefer to sow direct into the soil.

Do not sow outdoors until the soil has warmed sufficiently (May–June). The process can be speeded up by covering the area with polythene or cloches for a few weeks before sowing.

Sow thinly in rows to prevent the need for too much thinning. Seeds should be sown 13mm (½in) deep and the rows 45cm (18in) apart. Thin gradually until plants are 23–30cm (9–12in) apart; the thinnings are delicious in stir-fries.

Sow every 3–4 weeks to produce a succession of cropping through the summer.

Growing on

Never allow the seedlings to dry out; mulching can also help to maintain moisture levels. As the bulbs form, draw soil around them (earth up) to help blanch the white leaf bases. This improves the flavour by making them taste sweeter. Weed around the bulbs regularly to prevent competition.

Harvesting

Simply harvest bulbs as required when they are large enough and before they run to seed, removing the leaves and roots. However, all parts of the plant, including the leaves are edible. Allow a few plants to run to seed and collect the seeds for use in the kitchen.

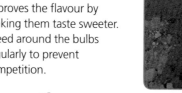

Pests and diseases

Slugs and snails Apply pellets, barriers or traps as soon as the seedlings emerge.

Varieties

'Orion': large, thick, rounded bulbs.
'Fennel di Firenze': large, crisp bulbs delicious raw or cooked.
'Amigo F1': good resistance to bolting.
'Mantovano': large, round, white bulbs.
'Victoria F1': round, pure white bulbs. Good bolting resistance.

Florence fennel												X = ok XX = ideal
Month	J	F	M	A	M	J	J	A	S	O	N	D
Sow/plant					XX	XX	XX					
Harvest								X	XX	XX	X	

NUTRITIONAL INFORMATION
Good range of nutrients, including phosphorus, potassium, folate and vitamin C.

Kohl Rabi

Prevent damage from birds by covering with netting

The bulbs (swollen stems) of this strange looking vegetable are at their best when between golf-ball and tennis-ball-size when they can be eaten raw grated in salads or cooked. They grow very quickly (sowing to harvest in 8–12 weeks) so should be sown in succession for a continuous summer supply.

Growing

Give plants a sunny spot and incorporate plenty of organic matter in the autumn before sowing, although this crop is not too fussy and is a little more tolerant of dry conditions than turnips, which tend to bolt if allowed to dry out. If allowed to become too dry, or if grown on very well-drained soil, kohl rabi has a tendency to become tough and woody.

As with other brassicas (include it with cabbages in your crop rotation), firm the soil before sowing or planting by tamping down the seedbed with the back of a rake or treading with your feet.

Propagation

Plants can be sown in cell trays for early crops, planting out in May once the soil has warmed slightly. Sow in a heated propagator set to 10–15°C (55–65°F). Germination is rapid, usually taking 7–10 days. Harden off well before planting out.

In the soil sow thinly in drills with rows about 30cm (12in) apart from May onwards. Warm the soil a week or two before sowing by covering with polythene or cloches.

Growing on

Thin seedlings in stages until plants are 10–15cm (4–6in) apart. Continue to water and weed carefully to avoid damage to the thin stem, which forms below the swollen 'bulb'. Early crops should be covered with cloches to prevent chilling or plants may bolt.

Pests and diseases

Cabbage root fly Reduce damage by placing cabbage collars around the stems once final thinning has taken place, or after planting out module-raised plants.

Take precautions against birds.

Harvesting and storing

Kohl rabi should be harvested as required when small to be enjoyed at its best. Simply lift the roots and remove the stem below the swollen bulb. Snap off the leaves. Peel older bulbs before grating raw in salads, stir-fries or boiling. Young roots can be boiled whole, while larger roots should be sliced.

It is possible to store roots whole with the outer leaves removed for a short time in boxes of sand or peat.

Varieties

'*Kolibri F1*': deep purple bulbs with white flesh.
'*Olivia F1*': green bulbs with good disease resistance. Suitable for harvesting later than most.
'*Lanro*': good green variety for soups, salads and coleslaw.

'Kolibri F1'

'Olivia F1'

Kohl rabi												X = ok XX = ideal
Month	J	F	M	A	M	J	J	A	S	O	N	D
Sow/plant				X	XX	XX						
Harvest							X	XX	XX	X		

NUTRITIONAL INFORMATION
Rich in vitamin C, fibre and potassium.

Lettuces

Lettuces are easy to grow, great value and nutritious. There is a range of types, many with interesting leaf shapes and colours and some are decorative enough to be grown in the ornamental garden.

For many years they have formed the basis of a green salad, but today they are the ideal complement to the many 'new' salad leaves that we love to eat in the UK.

Growing

Lettuces like a reasonably sunny spot in a well-drained, but moisture retentive soil and being leafy, fast-growing crops require reasonable levels of fertility. Ideally the soil should have a pH in the range of 6.5–7.5.

Dig in plenty of well-rotted organic matter in the autumn before planting to increase both soil fertility and its water-holding capacity during the summer. A week or two before sowing incorporate 56g (2oz) of general fertiliser such as Growmore or pelleted chicken manure.

Propagation

Lettuces can be sown direct into the soil in which they are to grow. However, it helps to avoid pests, such as slugs and snails as well as birds, if they are sown and established in cell trays before planting. As an alternative, many garden centres and specialists produce lettuce plants at the ideal stage for planting in spring and early summer.

Indoors, sow one seed per cell using a good quality multi-purpose or sowing compost. Cover the seeds lightly with compost or a light dusting of vermiculite. Water well and maintain at a temperature of 15°C (60°F).

Outside, sow from March onwards in shallow drills, 13mm (½in) deep and 30cm (12in) apart, and cover early crops with cloches.

Germination is generally rapid, taking from 7–10 days. Indoors, as soon as the majority of seedlings are through, the propagator lid should be removed and the young plants moved to the greenhouse bench.

Lettuces do not germinate well in hot conditions, so it is best to avoid sowing in July and early August. They are also ideal as a salad leaf crop (see page 148). Sow in succession every three weeks for a continual supply.

Growing on

Lettuce sown indoors should be planted out once they have produced three true leaves, allowing 7.5–10cm (3–4in) between plants. Scatter slug pellets or install traps and net

Sowing lettuces

1 Fill a 15-cell tray with fresh sowing compost.

2 Water the compost thoroughly.

3 Dig shallow holes 6–13mm (¼–½in) deep in the top of the compost.

4 Moisten the end of a dibber. With practice you can use it to pick up one seed.

5 Having transferred a seed into the hole in the top of each cell, cover with vermiculite or sieved compost.

6 Water and label your tray. Add a copper-based fungicide to the water to protect against damping off if you wish.

Protect early plantings with cloches or fleece

against birds. Keep well watered during dry spells and if your soil is lacking in nutrients, give it a liquid feed every 10–14 days.

'Salad Bowl' lettuces, which are grown for their cut-and-come-again leaf rather than a distinct heart, should be given a little more space as they have a spreading habit.

Thin every other plant once the leaves begin to touch and use the thinnings in the kitchen, allowing the remaining plants to reach full size.

Outdoor-sown plants are treated in a similar way, thinning in stages and using the thinnings as a baby leaf to mix with other salads or to add to sandwiches.

Harvesting

Cut hearting lettuces once the heart in the centre is firm, although plants can be eaten at any stage. Strip away any damaged outer leaves and wash the rest thoroughly before eating to remove dirt and insects.

'Salad Bowl' types can be harvested as whole plants or individual leaves can be removed for a cut-and-come-again harvest, which can go on until the plants run to seed.

Pests and diseases

Downy mildew causes angular yellow patches to appear on the upper surface of the leaves and these later become brown and may be infected with botrytis (grey mould). The corresponding patch on the underside of the leaf may become covered with a white mould in damp conditions. Thin plants to prevent overcrowding and sow disease-resistant varieties where possible. Spray with Bayer Dithane 945 at the first sign of attack.

Aphids (greenfly) attack the leaves of lettuces causing puckering and also spread viruses. Root aphids, attack the root of the plant causing collapse. Some resistant varieties are available. Thorough cultivation will kill over-wintering pests and expose them to predators and the weather. Remove infested plants immediately and do not replant the soil with lettuce for a year.

Slugs and snails Use your favoured form of slug and snail control through the life of the crop.

Bolting Water thoroughly and avoid growth checks.
Viruses Most viruses are spread by aphids and controlling this pest also helps to reduce the risk of virus. Affected plants become distorted, stunted and discoloured and should be removed.

Varieties

Non-hearting, cut-and-come-again
'Lollo Rossa': highly attractive frilled leaves with a strong red tint. Good in the salad bowl and in the flower border.
'Salad Bowl' and 'Red Salad Bowl': attractive frilly leaves in red or green.

Cos type
'Counter': long, sweet leaves. Good resistance to bolting, tip burn and downy mildew.
'Little Gem': the best-known cos type and still very popular.
'Marshall': unusual, deep red cos type. Grow as baby leaves or a hearted lettuce.
'Freckles': cos type with distinctive green leaves splashed with red. Slow to bolt and attractive in the flower border.
'Winter Density': a hardy type with a sweet flavour. Sown in succession, it can be harvested for much of the year.

Butterhead types
'All The Year Round': a good variety for year-round sowing and very hardy.
'Cassandra': large hearts with a full flavour. Resistant to downy mildew and virus.

Iceberg (crisphead) varieties
'Webb's Wonderful': crisp and tender; the best-known of the iceberg types.
'Triumph': medium heads. Tolerant of root aphids.
'Balmoral': dense, crisp heads. Tolerant of mildew and bolting.
'Sioux': medium-sized red variety. Highly attractive.

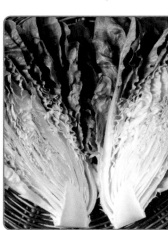

Lettuce												X = ok	XX = ideal
Month	J	F	M	A	M	J	J	A	S	O	N	D
Summer												
Sow/plant			XX	XX	XX	XX	X					
Harvest						X	X	XX	XX	XX	X	
Winter												
Sow/plant									XX	XX	X	
Harvest	XX	XX	X							X	XX	XX
Spring												
Sow/Plant									XX	XX	X	
Harvest				XX	XX							

NUTRITIONAL INFORMATION
Lettuces offer good levels of vitamins including A and K, plus a range of minerals.

Mushrooms

These days you can buy kits that allow you to grow all sorts of mushrooms from the standard white buttons to shiitake and lion's mane. All-inclusive kits contain spawn (usually consisting of grains such as wheat, or wooden dowels that have been inoculated or pre-infected with fungi), a sterile substrate usually consisting of compost, wood, straw or paper, and a container in which to grow your crop, or just the spawn. If you opt for the latter, you have to provide the substrate and this is often the most difficult bit to get right since the various types of fungi can be quite fussy about what they will and will not grow into.

Fungi facts

Since mushrooms are so different from any other crop you will grow, it can be helpful to know what a fungi is and therefore what conditions will make it grow happily.

■ Unlike the green plants we are all used to growing, fungi have no green chlorophyll – and no leaves to keep it in. Whereas green plants need sunlight to get their energy, fungi need no light at all. Instead they get all their energy from the substrate, usually dead or decaying matter, in which they are growing.

■ There are two parts to a fungus: the mushroom, which apart from being the tasty bit is the fruiting body of the fungus, and the thread-like mycelium, which is the bit that permeates the substrate, slowly digesting it.

■ Fungi are remarkable in that they can digest even the toughest materials such as fresh wood. Few other organisms can copy this trick and so fungi are often the first things that get to work on material, breaking it down to a degree that allows other things, such as insects, to get to work on it.

■ As well as something to feed on – and, as mentioned, this can be very specific depending on the species – they generally need some degree of warmth and moisture.

■ Although fungi will generally fruit of their own accord, a shock to their system will often trigger them into fruiting. In most cases this involves a sudden cold snap and is why autumn for most fungi heralds the best time for picking them in the wild.

Preparing the soil

To grow mushrooms it is essential that the substrate on which you wish to grow them is as sterile as possible. Ensure that only the mushrooms you want to eat colonise it and that pests, particularly little black mushroom flies, do not appear to ruin your crop. Logs should be freshly cut, and straw and compost must be sterilised with boiling water.

Traditionally, mushrooms are grown commercially using horse manure, preferably containing a high proportion of straw. It is sterilised during the thorough composting process that heats it, so killing pests, weeds and any fungal spores which may compete with and contaminate the crop.

Growing a crop

Your choice of substrate will depend largely on which fungi you decide to grow. Oyster mushroom kits can be purchased and these include some straw and polythene bags. To nemeko, or slime mushrooms, the cellulose found in paper is high dining and they can be grown on nothing more than a toilet roll, placed into a polythene bag, sterilised and moistened with boiling water. The spawn is simply dropped into the tube in the middle and the bag sealed until the mushrooms start to appear.

CULTIVATING ON LOGS

Logs offer another food source for fungi such as shiitake, oyster and lion's mane. Here again there are some strict rules to follow. Logs should be freshly cut, preferably when trees were dormant, around 10–15cm (4–6in) in diameter and used as soon as possible to avoid contamination from unwanted, possibly inedible or even poisonous species. The best are oak, ash, beech and birch.

If you cannot find suitable logs it is possible to buy them

from specialists ready inoculated (for a price). You can also buy mushroom growing boards from seed company D.T. Brown (tel: 0845 3710532) or via local stockists. These consist of chopped and sterilised poplar wood and can be used for growing shiitake and oyster mushrooms.

Having found your log, inoculating it is relatively easy. Drill holes in the wood just large enough to take the inoculated dowels, then knock them in firmly with a hammer. Alternatively, inoculated grain can be poured into each hole. To prevent contamination, some suppliers recommend sealing the holes with wax.

Keep your logs somewhere shady and moist. They can be wrapped in sacking and placed in a sheltered spot, such as under shrubs in a north-facing border, or the ends buried to keep them upright and the whole batch covered with sacking or polythene to keep them warm and damp.

Inoculated logs should start to crop after about 10 months (sometimes sooner) and may continue for up to five years according to some suppliers.

Pests and diseases

Mushroom flies are small black flies that live in unsterilised compost and will attack the developing mushrooms. Thorough compost sterilisation and good hygiene will keep them at bay.

Harvesting

Cut the mushrooms as low down the stem as possible using a sharp knife. They will keep in the fridge in a paper bag for several days, but are best used as soon as possible.

Mushrooms												X = ok XX = ideal
Month	J	F	M	A	M	J	J	A	S	O	N	D
Sow	XX	XX	XX	XX	XX	XX	XX	XX	XX	XX	XX	XX
Harvest	XX	XX	XX	XX	XX	XX	XX	XX	XX	XX	XX	XX

NUTRITIONAL INFORMATION
Mushrooms contain a little vitamin C and iron, plus some fibre.

Growing mushrooms on paper

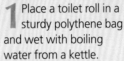

1 Place a toilet roll in a sturdy polythene bag and wet with boiling water from a kettle.

2 Pour the nemeko fungi spawn into the cardboard tube in the centre of the roll.

4 Watch progress adding more water if necessary (luke warm, not boiling).

5 When the fungi produce mushrooms harvest the mature ones and seal the bag again for a second crop.

3 Seal the top with a wire tie to keep in the moisture.

Onion Family

be higher. Large bulb onions also need a relatively long growing season and traditionally seeds are sown on Boxing Day, giving them the spring and summer to mature. Sets are especially good for areas with a short growing season and require less skill.

Onions are one of the most versatile and useful crops for the kitchen and are generally easy to grow either from seeds or sets (immature bulbs). The onion family includes bulb onions, shallots, garlic and leeks, all of which are described here. A combination of good storage properties and autumn as well as spring planting means we can have onions from the garden for much of the year.

Growing

Onions need a well-drained soil and plenty of sunshine to ripen the bulbs in the summer. They also require some shelter to prevent the leaves from being bent over prematurely and so reducing yield.

Although some gardeners use the same patch year after year to grow their onions, this can lead to problems such as white rot and eelworms and it is best therefore, to include them within a strict crop rotation (see page 48).

Dig in plenty of well-rotted manure before planting in the autumn and check the pH of the soil, which should be around pH 6.5. Rake in a general or onion fertiliser two weeks prior to sowing and just before sowing or planting tamp the soil down with the back of a rake to firm it.

Propagation

Raising onions from seeds offers the chance to grow a wider range of varieties and is cheaper than buying sets. However, it does require a suitable place to sow and losses are likely to

SOWING IN CELL TRAYS

Using cell trays removes the need to thin out the seedlings later and avoids root disturbance when planting. Alternatively, sow in seed trays, moving to small pots or cell trays when the seedlings are large enough to handle.

Place trays in a heated propagator set to 15°C (60°F) and maintain watering. Remove the propagator lid once most of the seedlings are through. Check watering regularly and once the seed leaf has straightened out (initially it loops over like a shepherd's crook) remove the trays and place them on the

greenhouse bench or a bright windowsill where they will receive as much light as possible. Maintain a temperature of 7–10°C (45–50°F) and harden off before planting out in April. If grown in large-celled trays, plants should not need to be moved on until planting out. If they were sown or pricked

out into small cells they may need to be potted on into 7.5–9cm (3–3½in) pots before planting out in the spring. Large types may also need a split cane and soft wire ring to support the leaves and prevent the top of the plant from bending over.

Leeks are sown in the same way, or sow direct into nursery rows and planted as described below.

SOWING IN THE SOIL

If sowing bulb onions, spring onions and leeks direct in the soil, prepare the soil as above and sow thinly in drills. The seedlings should be thinned as they grow and later thinnings

can be used in salads and stir-fries. Plants should eventually be 13mm–2.5cm (½–1in) apart in the rows. Larger bulb onions will require more space – 5–7.7cm (2–3in) for small bulbs, 10cm (4in) for larger bulbs.

ONIONS FROM SETS

Onion sets are ready-prepared immature bulbs. The best are heat-treated to kill the embryo flower bud in the centre of the bulb and this prevents bolting to which the crop is prone. These are planted in autumn or spring as described below.

OVER-WINTERING OR JAPANESE ONIONS

These varieties are selected for sowing in August as seeds following the techniques above, or planting in November as sets (see below).

Growing on

Once conditions allow, usually at the end of March/beginning of April, early-sown bulb onions can be planted out in rows 30–37cm (12–15in) apart and plants 10cm (4in) apart in the rows.

Onion sets, garlic cloves and shallots can be planted in March or in the autumn. Autumn planting allows the bulbs to produce a good root system before the onset of winter, giving them a head start in the spring.

To plant onion sets, form a drill with the edge of a hoe, rake or stick deep enough to just bury the top of the bulb beneath the soil. This avoids the problem of birds pulling at the top and uprooting it. Any very long 'tails' on the top of the bulbs can be carefully cut back with scissors before planting to help avoid the same problem.

Bulb onions should be planted during March and April depending on soil conditions, 10cm (4in) apart in the rows, allowing 25cm (10in) between the rows.

Shallots, which look similar when planted, actually split as they grow to form up to six small onions by the end of the season. They are planted from mid-February to mid-March and require a little more space between the bulbs – 15cm (6in) is ideal. Pop back any bulbs that are disturbed as soon as they are seen or consider covering with a crop protection net until rooted well and growing away.

Maintain watering initially during dry spells until the bulbs are well established; once they start to swell, water only during prolonged periods of drought. Weed regularly taking care not to disturb the roots or to damage the bulbs with the hoe.

GROWING LEEKS

Leeks are planted rather differently to encourage the longest possible blanched stem. Once seedlings are well established and about 20cm (8in) long and pencil-thick, lift them carefully, having watered them well the night before, or remove them from their cell trays or pots. Then make holes 15cm (6in) apart and 15cm (6in) deep with a large dibber and simply drop

a young leek into each hole. Rows should be spaced 23–30cm (9–12in) apart depending on the size of leek required. Baby leeks are delicious and require just 15cm (6in) between plants.

The young plants are simply watered in, the action of which washes a little soil down over the roots in the hole.

GROWING GARLIC

Garlic is planted in autumn or spring. As with onion sets, autumn planting is generally preferable as it allows the roots to establish over winter for an early start in the spring and gives the bulbs a longer growing season.

Split the bulbs up into their individual cloves, discarding

Planting leeks

1 Once your young plants are well established make final preparations to the soil, raking in some general fertiliser a week before sowing and raking the bed level.

2 Using a large dibber (the broken handle of a fork or spade is ideal, make hole 15cm (6in) deep in the soil at 10–15cm (4–6in) spacings.

3 Drop a plant into each hole before watering thoroughly. Do not fill in the hole after planting; the extra depth increases the length of blanched (white) stem.

Planting garlic

1 Unless buying elephant garlic which is sold by the clove, ordinary garlic comes as a complete bulb. Divide the cloves with your hands, discarding loose skin and debris.

2 Plant the cloves in well prepared soil, burying them 2.5cm (1in) deep.

3 Cover with soil and water in. A layer of netting will protect the cloves from birds and squirrels until they establish.

TOP TIP

TRIMMING LEEKS

When planting leeks, if the roots are very long they can be trimmed a little so that they fit the hole more easily. Some gardeners also like to trim the leaves back by a third to reduce water loss in the early stages, but trials have shown that this does not produce much, if any, tangible benefit.

TOP TIP

ONIONS FOR SMALL SPACES

Bulb onion seeds can be sown in small groups of four or five to a cell and grown on as a small clump. The plants will form small bulbs and are ideal for growing closely where space is limited.

wet weather is forecast. Some gardeners like to bend the leaves over and to point them along the rows to keep things neat, but this should not be attempted until the leaves bend naturally. Once the leaves begin to dry, use a fork to lever the bulb up and break the roots.

Leave the bulbs on the surface of the soil for a few more days before moving them to a sunny spot and placing them

any shrivelled cloves or loose skin. Prepare the soil, and plant as for onion sets, but burying the cloves 2.5cm (1in) deep and 10cm (4in) apart (deeper planting increases yield). Rows should be 15–20cm (6–8in) apart. Cover the cloves with soil and water well.

Contrary to popular belief, as well as plenty of sunshine, garlic needs lots of water to thrive, so maintain watering during dry spells throughout the growing season except when the bulbs begin to die back in August. Autumn-planted cloves should be given a dressing of sulphate of potash in February.

Weed regularly, taking care not to damage the developing bulbs.

Harvesting

By August, the foliage of bulb onions, shallots and garlic will have begun to yellow and bend over and at that point no further growth will take place. It is essential to allow the fleshy necks of the bulbs to dry naturally before lifting or they will rot in storage, so do not be in too much of a hurry to move them, unless

in open-bottomed trays raised off the ground on bricks, or make a simple rack from a piece of chicken wire supported by four short posts. Lay the onions on the rack in a single layer and leave them to dry in the sun. If rain is forecast, move the rack or trays under cover to continue the drying process.

Once they are completely dry, bulb onions and garlic can be woven into ropes using the leaves or string, or the leaves can be removed and the bulbs stored in paper or hessian sacks. Keep the bulbs in a cool, dark place until needed.

Single bulbs of garlic can be broken up into their individual cloves and stored in a ventilated garlic jar in the kitchen.

Leeks are simply lifted as required, trimmed (the roots and leaves removed), leaving about 10cm (4in) of green top and washed thoroughly.

Pests and diseases

White rot can lead to the total loss of a crop. Symptoms include poor growth and yellowing of the foliage, and when the bulb is lifted, rotting roots and a white fluffy mould can be seen underneath.

Black fruiting bodies of the disease may also be seen among the fluff and it is these that remain in the soil to infect future crops.

This soil-borne disease can remain in the ground for many years and because of this, crop rotation is not effective. Infected pockets of soil should not be used for growing onions or related crops and care should be taken not to move soil on boots or tools from infected to clean areas.

Growing onions in raised beds or pots might offer an alternative. Some gardeners do manage to grow crops in infected areas since the disease moves weakly through the soil, spreading mainly through contact between bulbs and roots. As soon as an infected patch is seen, the plants must be removed and the rest allowed to grow on, but this is a risky strategy.

Downy mildew is a disease of wet summers and causes the tips of the leaves to yellow and then turn brown or black. The affected area moves slowly down the leaf and in wet weather a grey fluffy mould appears. Growth is poor and the necks of the bulbs may become infected leading to rotting. The disease is often spread from over-wintered crops of Japanese onions to spring-planted crops. Sprays of Bayer Dithane 945 may help. Do not plant too closely together to allow air to move between the plants.

Onion fly Little white maggots attack the bulbs of onions and shallots and the stems of leeks causing plants to wilt and growth to be poor. Rotting often sets in as a result of the damage. Larvae over-winter in the soil and the flies emerge in May to breed. Up to four generations may be produced each year. Thorough cultivation, especially in the autumn, should help, and covering the crop with crop protection netting on clean ground should reduce attacks. Rotate crops to avoid a build-up of the pest.

Leek moth causes similar symptoms to onion fly, attacking the leaves and central growing point of the leek. Moths tunnel the leaves and stem, rendering them inedible and secondary rotting often occurs. Adult moths over-winter in plant debris, laying eggs on the crop in the spring. Up to six generations may occur each year. Clean away crop debris and spray the plants as soon as any damage is seen, repeating treatment as necessary.

Onion thrips cause a silvery flecking on the leaves and in severe cases growth may be greatly reduced. This tiny pest will attack other unrelated crops, such as greenhouse crops, tomatoes and brassicas, and spread viruses as they feed. Spray as necessary.

Rots The onion family suffers from various rots both when growing and in storage. Neck rots are the most common in bulb onions, especially in wet seasons or where the leaves are bent over while still green or bulbs are not properly dried off before storing. Check stored crops regularly and remove any infected bulbs.

Leek rust mainly affects leeks, but is found on other onions, too. It causes small yellow marks on the leaves with orange centres and these may join up to form larger damaged areas. It is not too serious, though severe attacks can lead to poor crops. Do not apply too much nitrogen to the soil before planting onions or feed with nitrogen-rich liquid fertilisers. Sulphate of potash applied in early summer may make growth a little more resistant.

Bolting may occur on crops that receive a check in growth, such as a spell of cold weather soon after planting or very dry conditions. Heat-treated onion sets overcome this problem and should always be purchased as a preference.

Varieties

BULB ONIONS FROM SEED:

'*Bedfordshire Champion*': an old variety and very reliable, producing good-sized bulbs which store well.

'*Hi-Keeper F1*': sow in spring or autumn for quality bulbs up to 120g (4oz) in weight.

'*Red Baron*': one of the most popular red onions. Reliable with a good flavour; also available as sets.

'*Paris Silverskin*': one of the most popular varieties for pickling. Small, crunchy, round bulbs.

'*Long Red Florence*': red, elongated bulbs, ideal for slicing or

using whole in stews. Pull young as spring onions or allow to mature.

'Ailsa Craig': an old variety, once popular for exhibition and still a great garden variety. Mild flavour and good keeper.

BULB ONION SETS:

'Sturon': a popular and reliable maincrop onion that is slow to bolt and stores well.

'Setton': preferred by some to 'Sturon', as it is said to have improved keeping qualities. Slightly flattened bulbs.

'ABS 101': can be planted from January onwards and can be harvested as early as June – earlier than autumn planted crops. Reasonable keeping qualities.

'Senshyu': a popular variety for autumn planting. Produces flattened yellow-brown bulbs ready for harvest in late June.

'Shakespeare': brown-skinned bulbs of good size. Harvest from July onwards from an autumn planting.

'Hercules': round bulbs with attractive golden skins. Good resistance to bolting and good keeping qualities. Plant in spring.

SHALLOTS FROM SEED:

'Ambition F1': sow March–April. Good resistance to bolting, virus and nematodes (eelworms).

'Prisma F1': sow March–April. Seedlings produce one bulb rather than splitting as with set-raised plants. Stores well.

'Zebrune': long French type, ideal for slicing

SHALLOTS FROM SETS:

'Pikant': produces heavy yields of small bulbs which keep well.

'Topper': as above.

'Picasso': mild flavoured bulbs with a pink flesh. Great for pickling and good resistance to bolting.

'Jermor': a long French shallot that is very popular as an all-purpose onion for the kitchen.

SPRING OR BUNCHING ONIONS:

'Shimonita': can be harvested young as spring onions or allowed to mature as a small leek. In this way rows can be harvested over a long period.

'White Lisbon': a tried and trusted variety that can be sown for much of the year.

'Lilia': a red variety that can be harvested as a spring onion or allowed to form a bulb.

'North Holland Blood Red': mild-flavoured red stems that can be left to mature and form a bulb.

'Guardsman': long, straight stems that stand well in the soil over a long period.

LEEKS

'Musselburgh': an old favourite. Winter hardy with a good length of blanched stem.

'Neptune': harvest from November to January. Good winter hardiness and resistance to rust.

'Lyon 2 Prizetaker': an old variety producing thick stems that stand well on the plot for some months.

'Oarsman F1': early harvesting uniform stems with a long blanch and little bulbing. Good tolerance to rust and bolting.

GARLIC

'Albigensian Wight': good autumn planting variety for harvesting in June. Good yields and keeps well.

'Lautrec': firm, pink cloves, ideal for January/February planting if soil conditions allow, March if the season is wet or cold.

'Chesnock Wight': a purple variety from Ukraine. Slightly later cropping, ideal for extending the season.

'Purple Moldovan': as above. A reliable hard neck type that has been grown for hundreds of years.

'Early Purple Wight: the earliest of the autumn-planted varieties, cropping by the end of May.

Elephant garlic: More closely related to leeks, elephant garlic produces massive cloves with a very mild flavour. Ideal for roasting whole.

Onion Family												X = ok XX = ideal
Month	J	F	M	A	M	J	J	A	S	O	N	D
Onions/shallots												
Seed												
Sow/plant	XX	XX	XX	X								
Harvest							X	XX	XX	X		
Onion sets												
Plant	X	X	XX	XX								
Harvest							X	X	XX	XX		
Garlic												
Plant	XX	XX	XX								XX	
Harvest					X	XX	XX	X				
Leeks												
Sow/Plant	XX	XX	XX	XX								
Harvest	XX	XX	XX							XX	XX	XX	XX

NUTRITIONAL INFORMATION

Contain vitamin C, calcium and iron. Very powerful anti-bacterial and anti-asthma qualities. Can help to lower cholesterol levels.

Parsnips

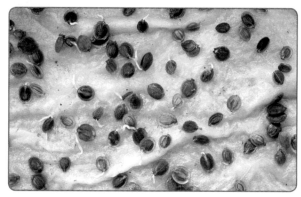

This crop needs a long growing season and as a result is often one of the first vegetables to be sown on the open plot each year. Its special flavour makes it well-worth dedicating the space to parsnips each year.

Preparing the soil

Parsnips need a similar soil to carrots (see page 110). The best roots come from a reasonably fertile, free-draining soil in a sunny or semi-shaded spot. The long roots need a deep root run to develop – large stones or hard layers in the soil will cause them to become misshapen – so dig thoroughly before sowing and add lime to bring the pH to 6.5 to 7. This reduces the risk of parsnip canker (see below).

As with carrots, manure should never be added the autumn prior to sowing or the roots will fork, so choose a spot that was manured for a previous crop, such as brassicas.

Propagation

February is the traditional month to sow in mild areas. Germination is poor in cold soils, so it is better to wait until March or even April if your soil is heavy or cold and wet.

Parsnip seed deteriorates rapidly so fresh seeds should be purchased each year and while they can be sown direct into the soil, the best way to start them off is by pre-chitting them. This involves sowing the seeds on to some moist kitchen towel in a lidded plastic box. Wet the paper thoroughly and then tip the box to allow surplus water to drain. Sow the seeds thinly on the surface, secure the lid and place the box in a warm place, out of direct sunshine – a windowsill or airing cupboard is fine. Remove the lid each day and if necessary rewet the paper, draining excess water each time. The seeds should swell within a few days as they absorb water and germinate within 10–14 days, the tiny root emerging from the seed coat.

Germination can be erratic, so allow as long as possible for the whole batch to germinate before sowing, while not letting the roots grow to more than 5mm (¼in) long.

The seeds can now be sown 13mm (½in) deep and 10–15cm (4–6in) apart in rows 30cm (12in) apart. Varieties intended to be grown as baby roots can be grown closer. Take great care not to damage the little roots when sowing. Any seeds that have failed to germinate are best discarded.

If sowing without pre-chitting, sow at the spacings above, but sow three seeds to each station, thinning to the healthiest seedling once they are large enough to handle.

Another way to improve germination and produce long, straight roots on heavy or stony soil is to prepare bore holes at each sowing station. To do this, make a tapered hole with a bar up to 60cm (24in) deep by knocking the bar into the soil and moving the end in a circular motion. Remove the bar and fill the hole with fresh seed compost before sowing two or three seeds on the top and covering with more compost.

Growing on

Water the seeds well after sowing and maintain even watering during dry spells to prevent the roots from splitting.

Weed regularly and ensure that plants are thinned so that each has room to develop. Remove thinnings or damaged leaves from the row to avoid the possibility of attracting carrot fly.

In areas where this pest is a problem, consider covering with crop protection netting after sowing.

Harvesting

Harvest from July onwards for small roots being used as baby veg. The bulk of the crop will be ready to lift as full-sized roots from September onwards. The flavour of parsnips improves after a period of frost when the starches held within the roots turn to sugar, making them even sweeter, so don't be in too much of a hurry to lift your crop.

The roots are very hardy and can be left in the soil until needed. If your soil is heavy and wet, roots can be lifted and stored in boxes of damp sand, peat or peat substitute, or frozen after first peeling, cubing and blanching in boiling water for three to four minutes.

Pests and diseases

Carrot fly can be a nuisance on parsnips, but tends to be less damaging than with carrots. Take precautions as for carrots (see page 110).

Parsnip canker is a damaging disease that causes rotting of the roots and is often worse around the crown. Patches turn purple, black or brown and a soft rot sets in. Rotate crops and choose a canker-resistant variety.

Varieties

'Javelin F1'

'Avonresister': a popular variety that has good resistance to canker. Can be grown at close spacings (as little as 7.5cm/3in).
'Gladiator F1': early maturing roots with a good flavour and canker resistance.
'Javelin F1': long, tapering smooth-skinned roots. Good canker resistance.

'Avonresister'

'Arrow': a variety well-suited to growing as mini veg at close spacings.
'Countess F1': high yields from this smooth-skinned variety. Good canker resistance.

Parsnips												X = ok XX = ideal
Month	J	F	M	A	M	J	J	A	S	O	N	D
Sow/plant		X	XX	XX	X							
Harvest	XX	X					X	X	X	XX	XX	XX

NUTRITIONAL INFORMATION
Contain vitamin C and potassium.

Peas

Raw peas, picked while still warm from the sun, are a delight that's hard to beat and children love them.

Unfortunately they are not the easiest crop to grow, but still well worth the effort. Pea shoots offer an easier and not any the less tasty harvest and are a great way to make use of spare seeds (see page 148).

Preparing the soil

Choose a reasonably sunny, sheltered spot where the tall plants will not become battered by drying winds. Early compact varieties can also be grown in large containers.

If the plants suffer drought, crops will be poor and powdery mildew will strike, so dig in plenty of well-rotted organic matter in the autumn. If necessary, adjust the pH to pH5.5–7. A week before sowing, rake in 28–56g per sq m (1–2oz per sq yd) of general fertiliser.

Propagation

Peas can be sown in the open ground, but often attract mice and birds so starting the crop off under cover can be an advantage. The earliest crops for harvesting in May/June are produced by sowing in February in small groups in 9cm (3½in) pots or deep cells, sweet pea pots or paper tubes.

Sow 2.5cm (1in) deep, one seed per cell or tube, or five per 9cm (3½in) pot.

Seeds can also be sown into household guttering, making the job of transplanting the young seedlings easier and avoiding root disturbance. Simply slide the seedlings out of the guttering and into a pre-prepared shallow depression in the soil as one long strip. If using this method, sow in three rows along the guttering allowing 5cm–7.5cm (2–3in) between seeds and staggering them in the rows.

Spring-sown peas will be ready to harvest in as little as 12 weeks from sowing, rising to 16 weeks for maincrop varieties. For maximum harvests, sow three batches from February, using an early variety for the first sowing (Feb), changing to a maincrop for an April sowing and back to an early type for a sowing in June/July for harvesting in the autumn.

When sowing outdoors, make a 25cm (10in) wide, 5cm (2in) deep, flat-bottomed drill with a hoe. Seeds are sown in three staggered rows (seeds alternated) 7.5cm (3in) apart. Cover with soil and water well. Space these triple rows at a distance to match the mature height of the crop.

Cover early sowings with cloches, sealed at the ends to deter mice and birds as well as to warm the crop. Later sowings should be protected from attack immediately after sowing with wire netting. Supports can be put in place either after sowing or soon after the shoots emerge. Use woody prunings such as hazel or stretch pea netting between the rows.

DID YOU KNOW?

Peas are capable of making nitrogen for themselves thanks to their root nodules, which are home to a bacteria called rhizobium. In return for a safe haven, the peas get a steady supply of nitrogen, fixed from the surrounding air.

Growing on

Maintain watering during dry spells to maintain growth and deter powdery mildew. This is particularly important for late varieties. Spray with a fungicide as necessary. Weed the rows to prevent competition to the plants, taking care not to damage the young shoots.

Harvesting and storing

Pick regularly and while still young and tender, as this not only ensures the best-flavoured peas, but keeps the plants cropping. This is especially true of mangetout and asparagus peas, where the whole pod is eaten, but also the sweet petit pois.

Pick as required or freeze while still young and sweet: simply pod, blanch in boiling water for one minute, drain, cool and freeze in labelled freezer bags or containers. They will keep for a year.

Pests and diseases

Pea moths emerge from early June to lay their eggs near the flowers from where they hatch and the larvae eat into the developing pods. After feeding they leave the plants and fall to the soil where they pupate. Avoid sowing in March as the resulting plants will flower during June/July when the pests are most active.

Powdery mildew is very common, especially on late crops. It can be kept at bay with regular watering and there are lots of fungicides available to help eradicate the disease. Choose a resistant variety where possible.

Pea thrips are tiny insects that suck the sap from the leaves and pods causing flecking and distortion. Damage is at its worst during June and July. Spray with a suitable insecticide.

Varieties

Early

'Feltham First': a popular variety for spring and autumn sowing.
'Kelvedon Wonder': as above.

'Canoe'

Second early

'Early Onward': heavy crops of short pods on compact plants.
'Canoe': long pods producing a heavy crop. Virtually self-supporting if planted in a block.

Maincrop

'Greensage': an early maincrop, up to 10 peas per pod.
'Cavalier': vigorous, heavy-cropping variety with good resistance to mildew.
'Ambassador': eight to nine seeds per pod. Good resistance to powdery mildew.
'Half Pint': dwarf plants, ideal for producing a small crop in pots and containers.

MANGETOUT AND SUGAR SNAP:

'Carouby de Maussane': purple flowers and heavy crops of flat, tender pods.
'Sugar Snap': to eat as mangetout, allow to mature and boil whole as French beans, or leave a little longer and shell as peas.

'Carouby de Maussane'

PETIT POIS:

'Waverex': heavy crops of little, sweet peas. Eat raw or cooked.
'Calibra': three or four well-filled pods produced in clusters.

ASPARAGUS PEA:

Attractive red flowers and winged pods. Little or no support required.

Peas												X = ok XX = ideal
Month	J	F	M	A	M	J	J	A	S	O	N	D
Early												
Sow		XX	XX							XX	XX	
Harvest					XX	XX						
Second early												
Sow			XX	XX								
Harvest						X	XX					
Maincrop												
Sow				XX	XX							
Harvest								XX	XX	XX		
Late maincrop												
Sow						XX	X					
Harvest									XX	X		
Mangetout/petit pois												
Sow				X	XX	XX	X					
Harvest									X	XX	X	
Asparagus pea												
Sow					XX							
Harvest									X	XX	XX	X

NUTRITIONAL INFORMATION

Good source of vitamins A, C, K, B1 and folic acid as well as potassium and phosphates.

Peppers

Peppers are easy to grow, versatile in the kitchen and expensive in the shops. Usually grown under cover in a greenhouse or polytunnel, they can be produced outdoors in mild areas where they add a splash of colour to the plot, pots or garden borders. Part of their fascination is the enormous range of varieties, both of sweet and chilli peppers. The latter range from mild to atomic in flavour – the smaller the fruit, the hotter they will be.

Growing

Peppers are mainly grown in pots, but if you intend to grow them outside choose a sunny, sheltered spot and prepare the soil as for tomatoes (see page 159).

Propagation

Sow thinly into trays or sow one seed per cell in a cell tray (module). Cover to a depth of 6–13mm (¼–½in) and water well before placing in a heated propagator set to 21°C (70°F) until the seeds germinate, usually within 7–10 days. Remove the cover once most of the seeds have germinated to prevent stretching and gradually reduce the heat, growing on at 15°C (60°F).

Growing on

Once the seedlings in cell trays have filled the compost, pot into 9–10cm (3½–4in) pots. Seedlings grown in seed trays are pricked out when large enough to handle and moved into modules or small pots. The seed leaves should be placed just above the level of the compost, burying any stretched stems.

Once plants have filled the pots with roots and are well

established, pot on into 15–20cm (8–10in) pots using good potting compost; loam-based composts give plants more stability in the pot later on. Alternatively, plant in growing-bags as for tomatoes.

If growing outdoors, plant out once the soil has warmed up – towards the middle of June in most areas – and cover with cloches for as long as possible, or grow in a mini greenhouse against a sunny wall. If planting in rows, allow 60cm (2ft) between plants.

Peppers tend to be self-branching, but can become rather tall and thin if left to their own devices. Pinching once when they reach 30cm (12in) tall is usually all that is necessary.

Plants do tend to become top heavy as they mature, particularly sweet peppers, and will require staking from an early age to keep them upright. Use a split cane and soft wire rings or string at first, and a short bamboo cane when potting into final pots.

Dwarf varieties

are ideal for growing on a sunny windowsill indoors or in the centre of containers on the patio.

Keep the compost just moist, but not wet, and feed every week with a high potash tomato feed. Misting with water each day or tapping the canes can help the flowers to set, but is not essential. Ventilate the greenhouse or polytunnel on warm days, keeping the temperature above 15°C (60°F) and watch for greenfly, which attack the shoot tips and cause distortion.

Harvesting and storage

Peppers can be harvested green or left until fully ripe and coloured according to the variety. Chilli peppers become hotter as they ripen, sweet peppers, sweeter. Picking any peppers while green encourages more fruit.

Sweet peppers should be used as required and will store for a week or so in a polythene bag in the fridge, or they can be roasted and preserved in olive oil or sliced and frozen.

Chilli peppers can be picked and allowed to dry slowly in

the sunshine on the greenhouse bench or in a dry, warm shed; they can also be placed in the freezer. Dried chillies will store in airtight jars for up to a year.

Caution: Never dry chillies in the airing cupboard with your towels and flannels

as the capsaicin, the hot element in the pepper, will transfer to them and then to your eyes and skin when the towels are used. Always scrub hands thoroughly after handling chillies and never rub your eyes or lips until you have done so.

Pests and diseases

Aphids attack plants under cover from a very early stage and may continue through the growing season. Squash with the fingers or spray as necessary.

Red spider mite is a problem under cover in hot seasons. Misting over with water every day can help. Spray with an insecticide as necessary, or use the predatory mite, phytoseiulus.

Varieties

SWEET PEPPERS

'Gypsy F1': early cropping, red tapering fruit.
'Jumbo F1': giant red fruit, ideal for stuffing.
'Orange Bell': thick-walled, blocky fruit ripening to orange.
'Yellow Bell': as above, but ripening to yellow.
'Redskin F1': dwarf plants, ideal for containers. Red fruit.
'Sweet Chocolate': heavy yielding, ripening to deep maroon/chocolate brown.

CHILLI PEPPERS

'Prairie Fire': bushy, compact plants producing lots of small, hot fruits.
'Etna': compact plants, ideal for containers. Small red fruit, very hot.
'Jalopeno': thin, blunt-ended fruit. Slice very thinly as a pizza topping. Hot.

'Habanero': 'Scotch bonnet' type, ripening to yellow. Very hot.

STUFFING PEPPERS

'Corno di Torro Rosso: long, thin-walled red fruit with a sweet taste.
'Tasty Grill Red F1': early-ripening, 25cm (10in) red fruit.
'Tasty Grill Yellow': as above, but ripening to yellow.

Peppers												X = ok · XX = ideal
Month	J	F	M	A	M	J	J	A	S	O	N	D
Sow*		XX	XX									
Sow**				XX								
Harvest								X	XX	XX	X	

*Indoor planting. **Outdoor planting*

NUTRITIONAL INFORMATION

Good source of folate, vitamin C, also vitamin A when ripe. Increases blood flow and helps to alleviate chest infections.

Potatoes

Newly lifted potatoes fresh from the garden are a delight not to be missed and since small crops can even be grown in containers, there is no reason why anyone cannot grow them for themselves.

Preparing the soil

Potatoes are vigorous, deep-rooted plants, producing lots of leafy cover. They are capable of competing with any weeds and so are a brilliant crop for clearing new ground or stifling perennials that may have established.

Potatoes will grow in most soils, but the best tubers come from deep, well-drained, fertile sites. The shoots are liable to damage by frost so choose a reasonably sheltered spot and avoid frost pockets. Very alkaline soils will tend to encourage scab – a common disease of potatoes – and so the pH of the soil should ideally be in the range of pH5–6.

Dig in plenty of well-rotted organic matter in the autumn prior to planting and then 7–10 days before planting rake in 90–120g (3–4oz) of general or potato fertiliser.

Propagation

Potatoes are purchased as small tubers known as seed potatoes. It is essential to buy tubers that are certified as virus free and these will be found in all good garden centres and mail order catalogues.

Early and second early varieties are chitted about six weeks before planting. Chitting involves placing the tubers in a single layer in seed trays or old egg boxes to shoot prior to planting. Place the rose end of the tuber (the end with the most eyes or embryo shoots facing upwards) and put the tubers in a light, frost-free place such as in a greenhouse or polytunnel and leave them. Small shoots will slowly develop and when they are about 2.5cm (1in) long, the tubers are ready for planting.

Recent research has shown that chitting is not absolutely necessary and that if you order or receive your tubers late for any reason, planting without chitting will not greatly reduce the eventual crop. It is not necessary to chit maincrop varieties.

Laboratory-raised, disease-free microplants and mini-tubers are available from a few specialists of some of the many old heritage varieties that were once popular but had slipped out of production.

Growing on

Once the tubers are ready for planting, either dig a trench 7.5–12.5cm (3–5in) deep according to the size of the tuber and 60cm (2ft) apart for early varieties, 75cm (30in) for maincrops, or dig individual holes.

If your soil is a little alkaline, lining the trench with a layer of grass clippings, or

popping a handful into each hole, can help to acidify the immediate area as the grass rots.

Tubers should be spaced 30cm (12in) apart for earlies and 37.5cm (15in) apart for maincrops. Cover the tubers by raking soil back over the top. In the case of early and second early varieties, where frost is likely to strike after planting, the shoots should be covered with soil again as they emerge to protect them. Alternatively, cover with several layers of crop protection fleece.

Once the shoots are about 23cm (9in) tall they should be earthed up. Potato tubers are produced on the stem of the plant rather than the roots. Therefore the longer the stem, the more tubers will be produced. Earthing up extends the length of stem and encourages a bigger crop. Use soil from between the rows and draw it up with a rake or hoe.

It takes lots of water to swell the tubers; give them a good soaking once or twice a week as the plants begin to flower if the weather is dry.

NO-DIG PLANTING

If you wish to follow a no-dig policy on your plot, there is an alternative to the method described above. Remove weeds and if the soil is very compacted lightly prick over with a fork and at the same time lightly rake in some general fertiliser.

Cover the soil with a layer of well-rotted organic matter and place the tubers on the surface in rows, spacing in the row as described above.

Cover the tubers with a 5–7.5cm (2–3in)

layer of straw and as the shoots grow, top up the straw mulch until it is 15cm (6in) deep. Then, switch to grass clippings, covering the area around the shoots with a 5cm (2in) layer. This will prevent light from reaching the developing tubers beneath the mulch layer and turning them green. If any hint of tuber shows through, keep adding grass clippings. When the time comes to harvest the potatoes, simply pull back the mulch and remove them as required, carefully covering up the remainder.

CONTAINER GROWING

Potatoes lend themselves to growing in containers, which is great if you are short of space. It is also a useful way of growing a small crop out of season for harvesting around Christmas, or for growing a few heritage varieties.

Any container will do providing it is no less than 30cm (12in) wide and deep and will exclude light from the developing crop. It is possible to buy potato planters from

many mail order catalogues and these often incorporate a means of harvesting, such as a door, in the design. However, large polythene pots, old compost sacks or a plastic dustbin are all suitable. If using old compost sacks, make a few holes in the base for drainage.

Add a 15cm (6in) layer of garden soil or compost to the base of the container and evenly space two or three tubers on top. Cover with a 15cm (6in) layer of compost – multi-purpose or second-hand compost from your pots or planters can also be used.

As the shoots grow earth them up, leaving the tips and a few uppermost leaves showing, and continue to do this until your container is full.

Water regularly adding a liquid tomato food to the water at half strength each time.

Harvesting and storing

Early and second early potatoes are eaten straight away, but maincrop tubers can be stored for winter use.

In the case of earlies, tubers are usually ready when the flowers open, but you should be able to tell from an experimental dig around the roots of one plant.

Maincrops are ready once the tops (haulms) have largely died back. They can be left in the soil and harvested as

needed at first, but if slugs are a problem, or if the season is very wet, they are best lifted and stored.

Lift carefully with a fork, pushing it into the soil well away from the base of the haulms so as to avoid spearing the tubers.

Rub off as much soil as possible and allow the tubers to dry for an hour or two before placing sound, undamaged examples in boxes, trays or hessian sacks and storing in a cool, but frost-free, dark place. Check regularly for any signs of rotting tubers.

Pests and diseases

Potato blight is the most damaging disease of potatoes and the cause of the Irish Potato Famine in the 1840s. Leaves develop brown spots and brown patches often appear on the leaf tips; soon afterwards the haulms collapse completely. The spores of the disease are then washed down into the soil to infect the tubers. Infection here may not be obvious at first, apparently sound tubers quickly rotting when stored.

Early crops should mature before the onset of the disease from midsummer onwards. Choose resistant varieties where possible – the Sarpo varieties are currently the best.

As soon as the leaf infection is spotted, remove the haulms and destroy them, preferably by burning. Never put infected tubers on the compost heap and take care to remove all small tubers from the soil when harvesting as these can act as a source of the disease, carrying it over winter to infect new crops.

Viruses attack potatoes causing distortion, mottling and rolling of the leaves, reducing yields. Always buy virus-free seed potatoes and control greenfly when seen.

Eelworm Several races of potato cyst eelworm are common. They live in the soil and infest the roots of potatoes and tomatoes, forming brown cysts filled with eggs on the outer surface. These overwinter in the soil to infect new crops. Infection often causes patches of potatoes to collapse and die. Choose resistant varieties and use crop rotation, remembering not to grow tomatoes or related crops on the same site as a previous potato patch.

Black leg This is a bacterial disease causing the base of the stem to blacken, become slimy and collapse. The upper leaves may roll and wilt and the foliage generally becomes yellow. Buy disease-free tubers and improve drainage.

Scab disease This takes two forms: common scab consists of scab-like patches on the skin that can be peeled off, although leading to extra waste and powdery scab, which causes similar symptoms on the tubers, but also infects the roots. Common scab is very widespread; infection is worse on alkaline or over-limed soil or sandy soils. Powdery scab occurs more on poorly drained, heavy soils. Both may survive in the soil for many years. Choose resistant varieties and improve drainage. Take care not to over-lime, especially if trying to control clubroot on brassicas.

Varieties

There are hundreds of varieties on offer, both modern and heritage.

EARLY VARIETIES

'Rocket': smooth, white-skinned round to oval tubers.

'Rocket'

'Swift': as above. Very reliable.

'Arran Pilot': old variety, still popular with many. Oval white tubers. Good drought and scab resistance.

'Red Duke of York'

'Red Duke of York': oval, red-skinned tubers with yellow flesh.

'Pentland Javelin': smooth, white potatoes with good disease resistance.

SECOND EARLY VARIETIES

'Kestrel': long, white-skinned tubers with attractive purple eyes. Good resistance to eelworm, slugs and blackleg disease.

'Kestrel'

'Charlotte': yellow-skinned waxy tubers, delicious hot or cold. Good scab resistance.

'Foremost': firm, white, delicious tubers with good resistance to scab.

EARLY MAINCROP

'Desiree': one of the best-known maincrop varieties. Red-skinned, white-fleshed tubers. Waxy flesh.

'Maris Piper': popular white variety, floury flesh great for mashing, chips, roasting or baking.

'Lady Balfour': white tubers with pink splashes, good flavour and resistance to eelworm and blight. Stores well.

'Sarpo Axona'

'Sarpo Mira': tasty, floury-fleshed red tubers with great blight resistance.

'Sarpo Axona': as above, but with more regular-shaped tubers.

'Sarpo Una': pink-skinned, oval tubers with white flesh and excellent blight resistance.

LATE MAINCROP

'Cara': popular white variety with

'Cara'

shallow red eyes. Smooth-skinned round tubers with good resistance to eelworm, blight and viruses.

'Druid': pink/red tubers with a good flavour and firm flesh. Resistant to scab, blight and eelworm.

SALAD POTATOES

'Lady Christl': smooth-skinned long white tubers with good disease resistance. Early.

'Lady Christl'

'International Kidney': also known as 'Jersey Royal', considered by many to have the best 'new potato' taste. Second early.

'Pink Fir Apple': an old variety (1850) and more popular than ever. Eat hot or cold, steam or boil in its skin. Maincrop.

'Belle de Fontenay': waxy texture, delicious hot or cold. Long, white, slightly curved tubers. Maincrop.

Potatoes												X = ok XX = ideal
Month	J	F	M	A	M	J	J	A	S	O	N	D
Earlies												
Plant			XX									
Harvest						XX	XX					
Second Earlies												
Plant				XX								
Harvest							XX	XX				
Maincrop												
Plant				XX								
Harvest										XX	XX	

NUTRITIONAL INFORMATION

Rich in potassium, phosphorus and magnesium. Vitamin C, A, K and folate.

Radishes

So easy to grow, summer radishes are the ideal crop for beginners and to get the kids into growing their own. By combining summer and winter types you can be eating these delicious roots for much of the year.

Preparing the soil

Summer radishes can be grown in virtually any soil and are also ideal for container-growing. To get the best from them and to produce the tenderest roots, choose a reasonably sunny site and use soil which was manured for a previous crop. Rake in 28–56g (1–2oz) of general fertiliser 7–10 days before sowing.

Japanese radishes are also grown for summer use, but since the roots may grow to 30cm (12in) or more the soil needs to be dug more deeply and very stony soils should be avoided, or the roots grown in bore holes as for parsnips.

Propagation

Sow seeds thinly in drills about 13mm (½in) deep and 15cm (6in) apart (summer varieties), or 23cm (9in) apart for winter types. Cover with soil and water well. The earliest sowings can be made under cover in a polytunnel or unheated greenhouse, or should be covered with cloches.

Radishes mature in as little as a month during the summer and do not stand in the soil for very long before becoming woody or bolting. It is a good idea to sow a short row every two or three weeks to produce a continual supply of tender roots.

Avoid sowing in July and August as plants are likely to bolt (flower) prematurely.

Growing on

Seeds germinate within 7–10 days and the young plants should be thinned out as soon as they are large enough, allowing 2.5cm (1in) between plants for the summer types. Thin mooli and winter varieties in stages to leave a final spacing of 15cm (6in).

Maintain even watering to prevent the roots from

TOP TIP

A GOOD CATCH

Since summer radishes grow so quickly they make an ideal catch crop to grow among other, slower veg, or can be used as 'marker' crops when sown with parsnips or carrots to mark the rows.

splitting or becoming spongy if they dry out. Protect the plants from slugs as soon as the seeds are sown.

Harvesting and storing

Harvest summer radishes while they are young and tender. Summer varieties will not store, other than for a week or so in the fridge in a polythene bag after lifting and trimming.

Japanese radishes are harvested from 15cm (6in) long, when they are at their most tender, but can be left to mature.

The longer, larger roots of winter varieties are hardier; they can be left in the soil during mild winters and harvested as required. Simply cover with fleece, straw or bracken to

keep off the worst of the frost or lift and store in boxes of damp sand in a frost-free place.

The varieties 'Munchen Bier' and 'Rat's Tail' are grown as summer radishes, but it is the tasty seed pods that are harvested and eaten rather than the roots. They can be steamed or eaten raw if harvested young.

Pests and diseases

Slugs love to nibble the developing fleshy roots, but will also attack the leaves. Use a biological control that gets into the soil to reach the pests. Back this up with some organic slug pellets.

Flea beetles cause the biggest problem on seedlings and

young plants. Protecting the plants with pest control fleece can help, as can dusting the leaves with fine, dry soil. Pest numbers can be reduced by moving a yellow sticky whitefly trap or piece of cardboard smeared with barrier glue over the top of the crop, barely touching the leaves.

Splitting The roots may split if plants experience a lack of water followed by a heavy watering. Maintain even watering at all times.

Bolting Plants run to seed if they experience a growth check or are sown in the height of summer. Avoid sowing in July and August.

Varieties

SUMMER

'French Breakfast'

'French Breakfast': the best-known of all summer radishes. The long red, white-tipped roots are quick to develop and have a mild flavour.

'Amethyst': a new variety with deep purple, round roots and crisp flesh.

'Munchen Bier': grown for its seed pods, which can be steamed, boiled or eaten raw.

'Rat's Tail': as above.

'Long White Icicle': mild-flavoured white, long roots.

JAPANESE (MOOLI) RADISH

'Mino Early' 'China Rose'

'April Cross F1': cylindrical white roots with a crisp, crunchy texture. Ideal for salads and stir-fries.

'Mino Early': long, white mild roots. Use as above or grate in salads.

WINTER

'China Rose': rose red skins and pure white flesh. Roots grow to 15cm (5in) long and 5cm (2in) wide. Good for winter salads and stir-fries.

'Mantanghong F1'

'Mantanghong F1': round, tennis-ball-sized roots with greenish-white skins and red flesh.

'Black Spanish Long': long tapered roots with brown skin and white, crisp flesh.

Radishes												X = ok XX = ideal
Month	J	F	M	A	M	J	J	A	S	O	N	D
Summer/mooli												
Sow/plant	X	X	XX	XX	XX	XX	X		X			
Harvest							X	XX	XX	X		
Winter												
Sow							XX	XX				
Harvest	X	X								X	XX	XX

NUTRITIONAL INFORMATION

Rich in vitamins C, A and K, folates and potassium

Rhubarb

Rhubarb is not thought of as a vegetable as it is used as an ingredient for desserts, but because it is the fleshy leaf stalks that are harvested and not a fruit, and since the crop is grown on so many allotments, it has been included here.

One of the first crops to provide a harvest each year, rhubarb requires very little attention, but to get the best from it year after year there are a few simple rules to follow.

Preparing the ground

Rhubarb loves plenty of moisture, but the crown itself should not become over wet or it may rot during the winter. Choose a sunny spot and dig in lots of well-rotted organic matter in the autumn before planting.

Rake in a little general fertiliser such as chicken manure or Growmore prior to planting.

Propagation

Rhubarb can be grown from seed, but the quickest and easiest way to a harvest is to buy in a named variety in the form of an established crown.

If you do decide to raise your own plants from seeds choose a good variety such as 'Glaskin's Perpetual' and sow in drills 2.5cm (1in) deep and 30cm (12in) apart. Allow to

establish, thinning to 15cm (6in) apart and move to permanent growing sites in the autumn or spring.

Crowns are planted from late winter to early spring. Dig a hole in the prepared soil large enough to take the rootball and fork over the base to improve drainage. Add a little well-rotted organic matter and plant the crown so that it is at the same height as in its original pot (assuming it is pot-grown). Bare-rooted plants should be planted so that the buds are just above the soil surface. Firm gently and water well.

Lift and divide crowns every four years in late winter, removing the young shoots with plenty of root and at least one bud. The old central part of the plant can be discarded.

Growing on

Mulch with well-rotted organic matter, such as garden compost or manure, each winter and water well during dry spells in the summer. Remove flower spikes as they appear.

Crowns can be forced for earlier crops by simply covering with a bucket,

large pot or rhubarb forcer to draw up the shoots. For very early sticks, plants should be lifted in late autumn and allowed to sit on the soil surface to be frosted a few times before potting into a pot just large enough to take the rootball. Place under the greenhouse staging or put in a dark shed and cover with a bucket or pot to completely exclude light. Water well. Once the sticks have been harvested throw the exhausted crown away.

Harvesting and storage

Sticks can be harvested from crowns once they have been in situ for 12–18 months. Remove the sticks by sliding the hand down the leaf stalk towards the crown as far as possible and gently pulling. Try to avoid leaving a stub as this may lead to rotting.

Sticks can be harvested as soon as they are large enough

in late spring/early summer and can continue to be pulled until July when the leaves should be allowed to develop fully to feed the crown for next year.

Sticks will store in the fridge, chopped and bagged, for

up to a week. They can be kept in the freezer for up to a year if they are first chopped and frozen in a layer on a tray, then bagged into convenient portions.

Pests and diseases

Crown rot The central parts of the plant may rot if the soil is very heavy or waterlogged during the winter. In heavy soils, plant on ridges to improve drainage.

Varieties

SEED

Glaskin's Perpetual': the most freely available variety and said to mature quickly for harvesting 12 months after sowing. Early cropping. Also available as crowns.
'Victoria': long, thin juicy stems with a good tart flavour. Late cropping. Also available as crowns.

CROWNS

'Timperley early': good for forcing. Very early cropping and reliable.
'Early Champagne': long, thick stalks. Good for making wine.
'Strawberry': long, red sticks. A late variety, good for extending the season. Can be harvested up to September.

> ## TOP TIP
>
> The leaves of rhubarb contain oxalic acid and are poisonous. However, they are safe to add to your compost heap as once completely rotted down they are harmless.

Rhubarb												X = ok XX = ideal
Month	J	F	M	A	M	J	J	A	S	O	N	D
Sow		XX	XX	X								
Plant	X	X	XX								X	X
Harvest	X	X	X	XX	XX	XX	X					

NUTRITIONAL INFORMATION
Contains vitamin C, folates and potassium.

Salad Leaves

For many, salad leaves have replaced our traditional, British green salad. The mixture of tastes, some mild, some hot and spicy, makes for a much more interesting meal or side dish. Salad leaves can be grown almost anywhere, even in a small container. Given some protection from a cloche, polytunnel or mini greenhouse during the winter, fresh leaves can be picked for much of the year, saving a fortune on supermarket 'pillow-packs'.

Avoid sowing in July/August as plants will tend to run to seed (bolt) before they have a chance to produce a good crop.

Preparing the ground

Any soils will do provided they are not waterlogged or very dry. These fast-growing crops can be grown in rows on the veg plot, but for convenience and to save space and reduce pest damage, many gardeners prefer to grow them in containers, perhaps close to the kitchen door for ease of harvesting.

Propagation

If growing in containers, choose a fresh multi-purpose or seed compost and sow seeds thinly over the surface in large pots, deep trays or window boxes. The container should be at least 7.5cm (3in) deep to sustain the plants for the whole of their lives.

Cover the seeds with their own depth of compost and water well. Very early sowings will benefit from the protection of a cloche, both to aid germination and to protect the leaves from the weather.

Growing on

Allow the seedlings to establish, thinning as necessary. The thinnings can be used whole in salads. Watch out for pests. In the open ground where you have sown mixtures containing mustard, rocket or any other members of the brassica family, you may also have to contend with flea beetle (see page 145).

Maintain watering during dry spells and as harvesting commences it may be necessary to feed the plants to help them to recover and produce another crop of tasty leaves. In this case a high nitrogen liquid fertiliser is best, applied every 7–10 days.

Harvesting and storage

Pick off single leaves or cut off with scissors as required. Alternatively, allow plants to grow and harvest the whole crown while still young and tender. Picking as a cut-and-come again crop, trays or containers can continue to produce leaves for many weeks, if not months, before they need replacing or run to seed.

Leaves will remain in good condition in the refrigerator for three or four days in a polythene bag.

Pests and diseases

Flea beetle (see page 145). Maintain watering as the pest is more of a problem in hot, dry weather.

Aphids Greenfly may be a problem from early spring onwards. Spray as necessary or rub off with finger and thumb.

Slugs and snails Pick off pests as seen and protect plants with your favoured form of slug control from sowing.

Capsids and leafhoppers are sap-sucking pests that mark the leaves as they feed. Control as for aphids, above.

Powdery mildew is often a problem later in the season or during hot, dry summers. Maintain watering and spray with a suitable fungicide as necessary.

Barriers of crop protection fleece can help to keep flea beetle at bay

Varieties

Salad leaves can be grown as single varieties or as themed mixtures (i.e. tangy, mild, spicy, stir-fry) and the selection to be found in seed catalogues is growing every year.

Rocket Available as wild rocket or cultivated forms. All have a very distinctive peppery taste. Great in salads, soups or stir-fries.

Wild rocket

Lettuce Loose-leaf lettuce such as red or green 'Salad Bowl' or the oak-leaf type 'Catalogna Cerbiatta' are best as a cut-and-come-again crop, although virtually any can be used.

Lettuce

Spinach Tasty leaves containing a good range of nutrients including iron.

Spinach

Chard

Chard 'Bright Lights': colourful stems and tasty leaves add interest and flavour to any salad. Can also be allowed to fully mature and the stems can be chopped into sections and steamed.

Beet 'Bull's Blood': dark red leaves add intense colour to salad dishes or can be allowed to mature when they are delicious steamed.

Beet 'Bull's Blood'

Endive This tangy lettuce-like vegetable (see page 114) is a little sweeter when harvested young, but still adds piquancy to any salad.

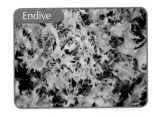

Endive

Mizuna/mibuna Oriental salad leaves that are easy to grow. The tangy, finely cut foliage looks attractive on the plate.

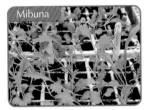

Mibuna

Oriental mustards A mixture of peppery and hot leaves. Some, such as red mustard, have colourful leaves. The older the leaves when harvested, the hotter they become.

Oriental mustard

Sorrel 'Blood Veined': Sharp, tasty leaves that add a splash of colour to salads. Also good in soups.

Land cress Peppery leaves that make an easy-to-grow substitute for watercress.

Sorrel 'Blood Veined'

Land cress

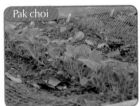

Pak choi

Pea shoots

Pak choi Mild foliage, great as a salad leaf or in stir-fries. Easy to grow, but prone to flea beetle.

Peas An ideal way to use up left-over seeds at the end of the season. Young pea shoots are delicious and can be harvested over many weeks.

Salad leaves												X = ok XX = ideal
Month	J	F	M	A	M	J	J	A	S	O	N	D
Sow		X	X	XX	XX	X		X	XX	X		
Harvest	XX	XX	X	X	X	XX	XX	XX	X	XX	XX	XX

NUTRITIONAL INFORMATION
Varies on the type grown, but most contain a good range of vitamins and antioxidants.

Salsify and Scorzonera

These unusual root vegetables are an acquired taste and something to experiment with once you have mastered your favourites. They are easy to grow, ornamental as well as edible, and considered by some to be a delicacy.

The white, thin parsnip-like roots of salsify are said to have a taste reminiscent of asparagus or oysters. The dandelion-like purple flowers are attractive, but seed freely – once you grow it you are unlikely to be without it.

The roots of scorzonera have a similar, but milder flavour and are brown or black. They are said to help deter carrot fly, making this a good companion crop for carrots. The yellow flowers of scorzonera are also attractive.

Preparing the ground

Both crops prefer an open, free-draining soil in a sunny position. Like carrots and other roots, they tend to fork if grown in recently manured or stony soil, so choose a spot that was manured for a previous crop and grow them alongside other roots in your crop rotation plan so that they receive the same treatment.

A pH of 6–7.5 is ideal, so check this in the autumn before sowing and correct if necessary. Add a little general fertiliser 7–10 days before sowing.

Propagation

Sow in rows 30cm (12in) apart and 13mm (½in) deep. Always use fresh seeds as, like carrots and parsnips, seeds quickly deteriorate after harvesting. Germination can be erratic unless conditions are ideal; sowing three seeds per station, with stations 15cm (6in) apart, and thinning to the strongest seedling helps to overcome any problems with poor emergence. Water well after sowing.

Growing on

Maintain watering during dry spells to reduce the risk of bolting and root splitting. Mulching around the plants with well-rotted organic matter can help to retain moisture and also deter weeds. Keep competing weeds at bay by hoeing regularly or pulling by hand.

Harvesting and storing

Harvest roots as required once they reach a good size – usually from October onwards. The roots are thin and easily

damaged when lifting; if the ground is likely to be frozen when the roots are required, lift some and store in boxes of peat, peat substitute or sand, or heel some roots in, as for parsnips, in a sheltered spot in the garden where the soil is unlikely to become solid.

Boil or steam the roots, skin and serve with a squeeze of fresh lemon juice. The young leaves are also edible.

Pests and diseases

White blister A disease that is also common on brassicas. Raised bumps appear on the leaves, which later turn yellow and then white as the disease produces spores. Pick off and destroy infected leaves.

Varieties

'Sandwich Island'

SALSIFY

'Sandwich Island': this is the variety most commonly offered and stands well through the winter.
'Mammoth': an old variety with long, tapering roots.

SCORZONERA

'Duplex': long taproots with good flavour.
'Russian Giant': a popular variety with long, black roots of good flavour.

'Russian Giant'

Salsify/scorzonera												X = ok XX = ideal
Month	J	F	M	A	M	J	J	A	S	O	N	D
Sow				XX	XX							
Harvest	XX	XX	X	X						X	XX	XX

NUTRITIONAL INFORMATION

A good source of calcium and potassium.

Spinach

Spinach is becoming popular as a healthy salad leaf as well as a cooked vegetable in stir-fries, soups and other recipes. It is easy to grow in the open ground or in containers and suffers from few pests and diseases. Like other salad leaves it is prone to bolting in hot, dry weather and requires regular watering during the summer. Easier still is perennial perpetual spinach and leaf beet or chard (see page 162).

Preparing the ground

Summer spinach is not fussy with regard to ground, but a reasonably fertile, well-drained soil in a sheltered spot that receives some sunshine each day is preferred, but a very hot spot should be avoided.

Digging in plenty of well-rotted organic matter helps to improve the water-holding properties of the soil and so alleviates bolting during the summer months. Early sowings benefit from covering with cloches or growing in the base of a cold frame.

If growing summer spinach in containers, a loam-based compost offers the benefit of not drying out quite so quickly and therefore helps to reduce the problem of bolting in hot weather.

TOP TIP

PLANTING COMPANIONS

Grow summer spinach between rows of slow-growing crops such as brassicas, sweetcorn or parsnips to make best use of space. The shade offered by these crops will also help reduce the risk of bolting.

Propagation

In the open plot, sow summer spinach thinly in rows 30cm (12in) apart and 13mm (½in) deep. Thin to the strongest seedling once the plants are well established.

Water well after sowing and remove competing weeds carefully with a hoe or by hand. Sow small batches in succession every three to four weeks to produce a continual supply of young leaves. By combining summer and winter types it is possible to be harvesting this crop for much of the year.

Right: Spinach can also be sown in cell trays, planting out when well established

Spinach can be grown in containers

Growing on

Protect the seedlings from slugs as soon as they emerge by applying wildlife friendly slug pellets or by using traps or a biological control once the soil has warmed sufficiently. Mulch lightly around the rows to help conserve moisture as the plants develop.

Thin plants as they grow – the thinnings can be used in stir-fries or salads. Maintain watering and if growing the crop as a cut-and-come-again salad leaf, feed every 7–10 days with a high nitrogen liquid feed to maintain vigour.

Continue to weed as necessary to remove competition and also to stave off pests and diseases such as aphids and powdery mildew.

Harvesting and storage

Summer types can be harvested by pinching or cutting off the outer leaves while they are still young and tender, allowing the central leaves to continue to develop. Alternatively, harvest whole plants.

Leaves will store in the fridge for three or four days in a polythene bag. To freeze, first remove the tough stems of summer spinach, blanch the remainder of the leaf in boiling water for one minute, then plunge into cold water, dry and seal in bags in convenient portions.

Pests and diseases

Aphids Spray as seen or rub off with the fingers.
Downy mildew A problem during wet seasons, this causes yellow patches on the leaves, often with corresponding patches of grey mould on the undersides. Choose a resistant variety where possible.

Slugs and snails More of a problem in summer types. Take precautions against these pests as soon as seeds are sown.
Caterpillars An occasional problem on perennial types. Pick off or spray as the pests are seen.
Bolting Choose a resistant variety where available. Water regularly and mulch perpetual types and chard.

Varieties
SUMMER TYPES

'Bordeaux F1': attractive red stems and spear-shaped leaves. Resistant to mildew. Tasty and reliable.
'Oriento F1': upright habit and deep green leaves. Good in stir-fries, salads or steamed.
'Lazio F1': round, dark green leaves. Good resistance to downy mildew and bolting.
'Barbados F1': smooth, round leaves. Good resistance to mildew.
'Bella F1': bred for spring, autumn and winter use. Slow to bolt.
'Triathlon': An early variety with excellent mildew resistance.

'Bordeaux F1'

'Triathlon'

NEW ZEALAND SPINACH

Not a true spinach, but grown and used in a similar way to summer spinach. Dwarf, trailing plants; pinch growing tips to encourage bushy growth – use these and young shoots to eat. Sow May to August.

New Zealand spinach

Spinach												X = ok XX = ideal
Month	J	F	M	A	M	J	J	A	S	O	N	D
Summer												
Sow			X	XX	XX	X		XX	XX			
Harvest	XX	XX			X	XX	X		X	XX	XX	XX
New Zealand												
Sow					XX	XX	XX	XX				
Harvest							XX	XX	XX	XX	XX	

NUTRITIONAL INFORMATION

Rich in vitamins A and C, plus antioxidants and useful levels of iron.

Sprouting Seeds

Being so easy to grow, sprouting seeds and micro-greens offer a great way for anyone – even those without a garden – to produce their own crops and they are ideal for introducing children to the joys of gardening and eating healthy food.

Sprouting seeds are simply sown on to damp kitchen paper in a plastic container, or into a seed sprouter or jam jar, and allowed to germinate and produce a shoot at which point they are harvested.

Micro-greens are similar to sprouting seeds, but allowed to develop a little further – if you have ever grown mustard and cress or bought a small container from the supermarket, you will have experienced micro-greens, too. Many gardeners have discovered the joy of growing micro-greens at home and as with sprouting seeds this is something that can be done all year round on a windowsill.

Preparing the ground

For sprouting seeds, a jam jar, piece of muslin and an elastic band is all you need. Once you become more serious about growing your seeds you may want to invest in a seed sprouter, a tiered container that allows you to grow several batches of different seeds at once and to water and drain them easily (see left). Most seed companies offer seed sprouters in their catalogues.

Micro-greens can be grown in half

seed trays, but you can also recycle any suitable plastic container providing you make a few drainage holes in the base. The base of the tray can be three-quarters filled with a layer of compost, but to prevent contamination from pests and diseases and the compost itself, vermiculite, which is naturally sterile, is a better option.

Propagation

If using a jam jar to sprout your seeds, place two or three tablespoons of seeds in the bottom, half fill the jar with water and cover the top with a piece of muslin secured with an elastic band. Shake the jar gently for a minute or two and then allow the water to drain out of the jar through the

Growing sprouting seeds

NOTE: *We have used a special sprouting jar, but a jam jar and muslin cover is just as good!*

1 Measure your seeds into the jar.

2 Cover the seeds with water and allow to soak overnight in a warm place.

3 Empty the water from the jar through the muslin or lid.

4 Rinse and drain the seeds at least once a day.

5 Harvest the sprouted seeds as soon as they have developed.

muslin covering. This process should be repeated at least once every day.

If using a seed sprouter, place a layer of wet kitchen towel in the base of each tray in the stack (there are usually three or four) and scatter seeds over the base of each tray in a single, reasonably thick layer. Gently trickle water into the top tray allowing it to slowly percolate through all the layers and into the sump at the bottom. Once the trays have drained the sump can be emptied. This process must be repeated at least once per day to ensure that the germinating seeds do not dry out and that moulds do not develop.

Some gardeners like to soak seeds overnight to encourage rapid germination. If you wish to do this, add your measured seeds to a jam jar, half fill it with water and shake gently, then stand on a warm windowsill or place in an airing cupboard overnight, without draining. Drain through the muslin covering, as above. To help you to judge how many seeds to pre-soak when using a sprouter, scatter your seeds into the tray before transferring them into a jar to soak, returning them to the tray after draining through the muslin as above. Never soak the seeds for longer than 12 hours or they will drown.

The ideal temperature for growing your sprouting seeds is 15–21°C (60–70°F) and seed sprouts can be placed either on the windowsill or in an airing cupboard. If in the light of a window, the sprouts will be green and if in a dark airing cupboard they will remain white.

Microgreens are sown reasonably thickly on to the surface of the vermiculite and the tray is placed in a shallow tray of water to allow the vermiculite to soak. Once it is thoroughly soaked, allow it to drain and pop the tray into a propagator or polythene bag to prevent it drying out.

Growing on

Whether using a jam jar or a seed sprouter, your seeds must be flushed with clean water twice a day to maintain the film of moisture around them, but also to wash away any unwanted fungi spores or toxins which might otherwise build up.

Black sunflower microgreens

Micro-greens need to be checked each day and watered if necessary.

Harvesting and storing

Most sprouting seeds should be ready to harvest within 7–10 days and after a final rinsing the whole plant – sprout and seed – can be eaten.

Micro-greens are harvested by cutting them off at the base of the stem with a sharp pair of scissors.

Both will store in a polythene bag in the salad drawer of the fridge for a few days, but are best eaten immediately after harvesting.

Pests and diseases

Sprouting seeds and micro-greens are generally trouble free, but must not be allowed to dry out or to linger in the trays or jars for too long or fungal diseases may occur.

Varieties

Most varieties can be used as both sprouts and micro-greens.

Mung beans: large, crunchy sprouts, perfect for stir-fries and salads.

Fenugreek: aromatic sprouts with a tangy bite.

Oriental mustard: tasty shoots with a hot bite – great for curries and sandwiches.

Black sunflower: nutritious large shoots, great with salads and cheese.

Rocket: peppery shoots bring a unique flavour to many dishes.

Radish: colourful, hot sprouts and seedlings.

Red mustard: use sparingly as these delicious sprouts and seedlings have a real bite.

Amaranth: red shoots add colour and a mild flavour to mixed salads.

Onions: any spare onion seeds can be sprouted to produce delicious seed sprouts or seedlings.

Peas: as above.

Beet: colourful seedlings with a pleasant taste.

Mung beans

Seed sprouts/microgreens												X = ok XX = ideal
Month	J	F	M	A	M	J	J	A	S	O	N	D
Plant	XX	XX	XX	XX	XX	XX	XX	XX	XX	XX	XX	XX
Harvest	XX	XX	XX	XX	XX	XX	XX	XX	XX	XX	XX	XX

NUTRITIONAL INFORMATION

Varies depending on the variety grown, but most contain a good range of vitamins and minerals.

Swedes and Turnips

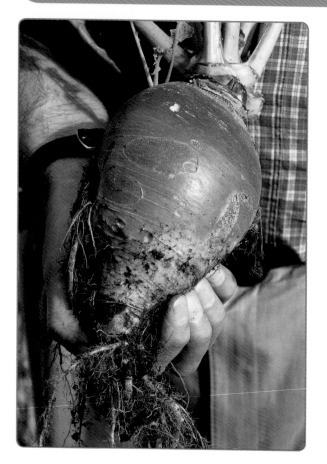

These traditional vegetables have lots to offer and deserve to be more widely grown. Both supply a good harvest when other fresh produce is hard to come by. Swedes are a great winter staple and thanks to improved varieties and the attention of gourmet chefs, turnips have shrugged off their image as a second-rate vegetable.

Growing

Choose a sunny site for your swedes and turnips. Well-drained, but moisture-retentive fertile soil is best. Both belong to the cabbage family and the ground should be prepared in the same way. Dig in the autumn to break up the soil from the previous crop and at the same time mix in plenty of well-rotted organic matter, following this in the spring with a dressing of general fertiliser 10–14 days before sowing. Then rake level and allow the soil to settle and the surface to become firm. To firm the ground still further before sowing it can be trodden lightly or a board placed over the soil where the row is to be and walked on.

Like cabbages, these crops prefer pH5.5–7; lime very acid soils as part of your crop rotation programme (see page 48).

Propagation

Swedes are slow-growing plants and need a long season in order to produce the large roots offered for sale in supermarkets. Turnips can be allowed to form large roots, but are at their best when young and tender – from golf-ball to tennis-ball size. They grow quite quickly and in order to have a long harvest, it is necessary to make successional sowings from spring and through the summer months.

Sow swedes thinly in rows 38cm (15in) apart and 13mm (½in) deep. Allow 30cm (12in) between turnips, but early sowings for the smallest roots can be spaced closer still at 23cm (9in). Sow turnips thinly, too, unless the plants are wanted for their tender tops rather than their roots, in which case the plants can be grown just 7.5cm (3in) apart. Cover with soil and water well. Cover crops after sowing with a crop protection fleece to reduce damage from flea beetles.

Tender baby turnips

Growing on

Thin out plants until they are 23cm (9in) apart if wanted as large maincrop roots, such as those for winter use. If turnips are wanted as young roots, thin to allow 13cm (5in) between plants; the young thinnings can be used as a salad leaf.

Maintain watering throughout the life of the crop as dryness can lead to bolting (running to seed), splitting and woody roots.

Remove weeds as they appear by hoeing or hand pulling and watch for pests and diseases as the crops develop.

Growing plants in deep cells prior to planting helps to protect them from pests

Harvesting and storing

SWEDES

Swedes are very hardy and are generally left in the ground until required. They can be lifted from late summer/early autumn if they are large enough and the remainder allowed to develop fully.

If your soil tends to become very cold and wet during the winter it may be best to lift the roots, twist off the tops and store them in boxes of dry sand, peat or peat substitute in a cool shed for the winter.

Swede 'Invitation'

TURNIPS

Early- to mid-season sowings of turnips are harvested when young and tender, lifting the largest roots and leaving the others in the row to grow on. Later sowings can be left to grow a little larger and treated as swedes (above).

Cut turnip tops in the spring as an alternative to greens. Plants should go on to produce several tasty harvests.

Turnip 'Snowball'

Pests and diseases

As brassicas, including swedes and turnips, suffer from the same range of problems (see page 106). The main problems are:

Flea beetle especially in the seedling stages. Protect with a sprinkling of fine dust or spray with

Cover with fleece to deter flea beetles and birds

a suitable insecticide. Use a sticky yellow whitefly trap to catch a few by drawing it over the leaves.

Splitting caused by uneven watering or wet weather after a prolonged dry spell. Water regularly (this will also help to control powdery mildew).

Slugs and snails will nibble the foliage and young roots, especially in wet seasons. Control using your favoured form of slug and snail killer.

Varieties

SWEDES

'*Invitation*': good resistance to club root and powdery mildew. Large, tasty roots.

'*Marian*': purple tops and pale yellow flesh. Also club root and mildew resistant.

'*Angela*': early cropping, dark purple roots.

'*Magres*': sweet-fleshed, purple-topped roots.

Swede 'Marian'

Turnip 'Oasis F1'

TURNIPS

'*Oasis F1*': sweet, juicy young roots said to have a melon-like flavour.

'*Milan Purple Top*': attractive flat roots with a purple top and white base. Good for early sowing.

'*Market Express F1*': fast-growing – harvest in as little as 50 days from sowing. Round, white roots.

'*Snowball*': quick-maturing round, white roots with a mild flavour.

Swedes/turnips												X = ok XX = ideal
Month	J	F	M	A	M	J	J	A	S	O	N	D
Swedes												
Sow					X	XX	XX					
Harvest	XX	XX	X						X	X	XX	XX
Turnips												
Sow			X	XX	XX	X	X	X	XX	X		
Harvest	X	X	TOPS	TOPS	X	X	X	X	X	X	XX	XX	XX

NUTRITIONAL INFORMATION

Rich in fibre and vitamin C.

Sweet Potatoes

Sweet potatoes are becoming a mainstream vegetable in Britain and can be found for sale in many supermarkets. It is possible to grow them in the UK, but they are not easy since they need a warm summer to crop well and sulk if the weather is cold and wet.

Sweet potatoes are not related to our familiar spud, but to a plant commonly thought of as a weed in the UK – bindweed – and also to the pretty annual climber, morning glory. However, there is no danger of sweet potatoes getting out of hand in your garden, thanks to our cold winters.

Left: The flowers of sweet potatoes betray the fact that they are distant cousins of our weed, bindweed

Right: Sweet potato slips

Preparing the ground

Sweet potatoes are best grown under cover in a polytunnel or greenhouse; they can be grown outside in mild districts and very sheltered, sunny spots. They require similar soils to our familiar potato: a free-draining, but moisture-retentive soil with pH5.5–6.5. Dig in plenty of well-rotted organic matter in the autumn before planting, but avoid too much nitrogen or the plants will produce masses of leaves and few edible tubers.

They can also be grown in pots either under cover or on a warm, south-facing patio. Containers should be well-drained and the compost not too rich in nitrogen – a sowing or multi-purpose compost is best.

Propagation

It is possible to take cuttings from shop-bought tubers that have been planted in trays, half-buried on the surface of moist sharp sand or compost and placed in a propagator set at 21°C (70F) or above to encourage shooting. Cuttings are taken when the shoots reach 23cm (9in) tall. Place four 5cm (2in) deep around the edge of a 15cm (6in) pot to root, covering at first with a polythene bag to increase humidity.

It is easier to buy rooted cuttings or slips from a reputable seed company, many of whom list them in their catalogues and usually deliver in May or June. These cuttings should be

potted up as above as soon as they arrive and grown on until the pot is full of roots (but not pot bound), at which stage the plants are planted out as one, without separating them, and the trailing stem from each plant trained in a different direction. Alternatively, pot up into the middle of a larger tub, or plant two or three pots of four cuttings in a growing-bag and train the shoots up bamboo canes. This has the advantage of keeping the shoots off the ground and prevents them from rooting.

Rooted cuttings can also be grown in rows and are often planted on ridges to ensure good drainage. Allow 25cm (10in) between plants and 75cm (30in) between ridges. Plant the rooted cuttings 5cm (2in) deep. Planting through a black polythene mulch helps to suppress weeds and prevents surface rooting, which otherwise diverts the plant's energy from the tubers.

Growing on

Water well after planting and keep the soil moist during dry spells throughout the life of the crop. Mist over the plants regularly to increase humidity and deter red spider mites,

particularly under cover. Lift trailing stems occasionally to prevent them from rooting into the soil.

Feed with a high potash fertiliser every 10–14 days during the growing season to maintain vigour and as stems grow pinch out the growing tips once they are 60cm (2ft) long to encourage bushy growth.

Harvesting and storage

Check the progress of tubers from 16–20 weeks after planting to see if they are swelling. They can be lifted carefully when large enough or left until the tops start to turn yellow and then lifted, taking care not to bruise the tubers.

Like the plants, the tubers are tender, so should be stored in a frost-free, dark place until needed. They will not maintain condition for very long and should be used within a week or two.

Pests and diseases

Aphids Greenfly feed on the young growing tips and spread viruses. The latter cause distortion and reduce yield. Spray as soon as the pests are seen.

Red spider mite A problem in hot summers and especially on plants under cover. Mist over regularly to discourage the pest from spreading. Spray with a suitable pesticide or introduce the predator, phytoseiulus.

Whitefly A problem under cover – spray as soon as the pest is seen or introduce a biological control early on.

Varieties

The choice is usually fairly limited in catalogues, but the varieties on offer will have been selected as those most likely to succeed in the UK climate.

'Beauregard Improved': found in most catalogues and popular for its good-sized tubers and tasty yellow flesh. Look for virus-free stock.

'T65': a variety with slightly larger tubers, selected to perform well in the UK.

'Beauregard Improved'

Sweet potatoes												X = ok XX = ideal
Month	J	F	M	A	M	J	J	A	S	O	N	D
Plant					XX	XX						
Harvest								X	XX	X		

NUTRITIONAL INFORMATION
Contains vitamins B and E, as well as beta-carotene, potassium and iron.

Sweetcorn

The sweetness of home-grown cobs is a delight and this is a crop that you should try and find space for if at all possible. It is not without its challenges; like sweet potatoes, it is a sun-lover that sulks in cold seasons and in colder northern regions, although modern supersweet varieties have largely overcome this problem.

Growing

Sweetcorn needs a sunny, sheltered spot with moisture-retentive, but free-draining soil. Dig in plenty of well-rotted organic matter in the autumn before planting. The pH should be in the range of 5.5–7.

Rake in a general fertiliser such as pelleted poultry manure or Growmore before planting.

Propagation

Seeds can be sown directly into the ground, but this tender crop gets off to a much better start if sown under cover and transplanted outside once all fear of frost has passed.

Sow one seed into each cell of a cell tray (module) or sow into individual deep pots such as sweet pea pots, Rootrainers or home-made paper pots. Old toilet roll tubes can also be recycled and used as containers.

Use fresh seed compost, burying the seeds 2.5cm (1in) deep. If sowing direct outside sow at the same depth in blocks, allowing 35cm (14in) between rows in the block and 35cm (14in) between sowing stations. Modern F1 varieties are more reliable and expensive and therefore sowing just

one seed per station should be all that is required, but you may wish to plant a few spares in pots to fill in any gaps that may result. Only attempt outdoor sowing in the far south or south-west of the UK.

Water well and maintain a temperature of 13°C (55°F) in a propagator or frost-free greenhouse. Once the seedlings are well established they should be hardened off thoroughly before planting out when the frosts are over.

Growing on

As a member of the grass family, sweetcorn is wind pollinated. Male and female flowers appear on different parts of the plant, with the males on the very top of the plant and the female 'tassels' or silks lower down in front of the embryo cobs.

Pollination is helped by planting in blocks rather than the rows used for most other vegetables.

Allow 35–45cm (14–18in) between the plants either way. Wider spacing allows you to grow another crop in between the plants, such as a low, fast-growing salad crop. Alternatively, the sturdy stems of sweetcorn can be used to support

climbing beans with a third crop, such as squashes or cucumbers, below. The sweetcorn provides support to the beans, shade to the squashes and, in turn, the squashes help to retain moisture and cool the soil thanks to their lush covering of foliage.

Water sweetcorn generously during dry spells and remove any competing weeds as they appear, taking care not to damage the shallow roots of the corn. Plants have a habit of producing roots on the stem just above soil level and these should be earthed up to encourage them to grow as they help to anchor and feed the tall plants.

Harvesting and storage

The cobs are ready to harvest when the silks turn brown and when the outer green husk covering them is peeled back a

little to expose the plump, yellow grains. Push your nail into a grain and if the liquid is clear, the cob needs a little longer to ripen; if it is milky the cob is ready for harvesting and can be twisted away from the main stem.

As soon as the cob is harvested the sugars in the grains begin to turn to starch and the cob starts to lose its sweetness. It should be eaten as soon as possible or, if you have a glut, frozen after blanching for four to six minutes. Cool in cold water, drain and freeze whole or cut in half, storing in labelled freezer bags for up to a year.

Pests and diseases

Mice and birds will nibble the young plants soon after planting. Cover with wire netting until established.
Slugs and snails also attack young plants. Install traps or scatter bird friendly slug pellets, topping up as necessary after prolonged rainfall.

Varieties

'Indian Summer'

'Equinox F1': exceptionally sweet, white grains on large cobs.
'Sweet Sensation F1': a supersweet variety. Early-cropping, producing cobs tightly packed with grains.
'Indian Summer F1': unusual cobs with multi-coloured grains. Very sweet.
'Northern Extra Sweet F1': early supersweet type bred for cooler climates.

'Mini Pop F1': mini cobs picked as the tassels appear, before the grains begin to swell, and eaten whole. Can be planted just 20cm (8in) apart.
'Lark F1': mid-season superweet type with well-filled rich yellow cobs.
'Sundance F1': recommended for cooler northern districts. Creamy-yellow grains on 18cm (7in) cobs.
'Sweetie Pie F1': early maturing and very sweet. Delicious raw or cooked.

'Mini Pop F1'

Sweetcorn												X = ok XX = ideal
Month	J	F	M	A	M	J	J	A	S	O	N	D
Plant				XX	XX	XX						
Harvest							X	XX	XX	X		

NUTRITIONAL INFORMATION
Rich source of fibre and vitamin B.

Swiss Chard (Leaf Beet)

Leaf beet and its cousin perpetual spinach are becoming popular as a nutritious alternative to spinach. Ruby and rainbow chard also add welcome colour to the veg plot.

Swiss chard is highly productive and includes the colourful ruby and rainbow chard with brightly coloured stems, which are ornamental enough to be grown in the flower border.

Perpetual spinach is not a spinach at all, but a leaf beet, and is related to beetroot and Swiss chard (leaf beet), but is used as a bolt-resistant form of spinach by many gardeners. It can be cropped for more than one season, but is best grown as an annual and replaced each year.

Perpetual spinach is useful for dry soils, where bolting is a problem for summer types, and for extending the season into the autumn and winter.

Preparing the soil

Leaf beet is not fussy, but prefers a fertile soil which has had some manure added in the autumn. Add a general fertiliser 14 days before sowing or planting and rake in. All types will tolerate some shade.

Propagation

Perpetual spinach and chard should be sown in stations 10cm (4in) apart and 2.5cm (1in) deep. Allow 38–45cm (15–18in) between rows.

All types can also be sown in cell trays and this is an advantage if growing rainbow chard since it allows you to select the colours more easily, ensuring you have a good range of red, yellow, white or orange-stalked plants. Avoid growth checks such as dryness or plants may bolt.

Growing on

Thin direct-sown seedlings until they are 30–38cm (12–15in) apart in the rows. The thinnings can be added raw to salads; larger plants can be steamed.

Plant cell-raised plants at their final spacings and water well. Cover with cloches from autumn to spring for winter harvests.

'Bright Lights'

'Swiss Chard'

Perpetual spinach

Harvesting

Sowing to harvesting takes as little as 12 weeks in the summer. In the case of Swiss and ruby chard, either lift whole plants or pick individual leaves while still young and tender, taking one or two off each plant. Perpetual or winter spinach is harvested in much the same way, but the leaves and stems are taken when larger.

The stems and leaves of chard and perpetual spinach should be chopped and blanched for 1½ minutes before plunging in cold water and again storing in bags or tubs.

Pests and diseases

Slugs and snails will damage seedlings. Take precautions soon after sowing.
Caterpillars attack mature plants in summer. Pick them off or spray as necessary.

Varieties

LEAF BEET

'Bright Lights': succulent, colourful stems. A colourful plant for growing in containers or the flower border.
'Ruby Chard': as above, with deep red stems.
Swiss chard: as above, but with white leaf stems.
Perpetual spinach: Good non-bolting substitute for spinach

Swiss chard/perpetual spinach												X = ok XX = ideal
Month	J	F	M	A	M	J	J	A	S	O	N	D
Sow			XX	XX	XX	X		XX	X			
Plant					XX	XX	XX	XX	X			
Harvest	X	X	X	X	X	X	XX	XX	XX	XX	X	X

NUTRITIONAL INFORMATION

Packed with vitamins A, E, C and K. Also good levels of iron, potassium and magnesium as well as a range of other nutrients.

Tomatoes

Tomatoes are perhaps the most popular crop in the UK among those who grow their own. There are varieties suitable for planting in almost any situation from an open plot to a hanging basket. Modern varieties are heavy cropping and many need no training at all. They are versatile in the kitchen, too, where they can be used for juices, soups, sauces, sandwiches, salads and much more.

Preparing the soil

Tomato varieties are usually suitable either for growing outdoors or indoors, though many are dual-purpose.

If growing outdoors, choose a sunny, sheltered spot. If growing in the ground, the soil should be reasonably fertile; dig in some well-rotted garden compost or manure in the autumn and add 56g (2oz) of general fertiliser two weeks before planting.

Alternatively, tomatoes lend themselves to growing in containers, including hanging baskets and patio tubs. Use well-drained containers and be prepared to water regularly as any shortages could lead to a disorder known as blossom end rot (see page 166). Use a good multi-purpose or potting compost and if you can't always be around to water consider adding some water-retaining gel to the compost before filling the containers.

Propagation

If growing indoors, the earliest crops are produced from late December/January-sown seeds. However, it is only worth attempting early sowings of you can provide both the heat and light necessary to keep your plants short and stocky. For most of us the cost is prohibitive and a March sowing is as early as we should attempt.

Seeds for outdoor or indoor crops should be sown in cell trays or small pots, or into seed trays. Cover with 6mm (¼in) of compost or sharp sand (the latter helps to pull the seed coat from the seed leaves as they come through the compost). Water before placing in a heated propagator set at

15–18°C (60–65°F) and cover until most of the seedlings have germinated. Ventilate and then remove the cover once 70 per cent are through to prevent any unnecessary stretching. In seed trays, as soon as the seedlings are large enough to handle prick them out into individual 7.5cm (3in) pots, burying the stems so that the seed leaves are just above the level of the compost.

Growing on

Reduce temperatures to 13–15°C (55–60°F), acclimatising plants to cooler conditions, but allowing them as much light

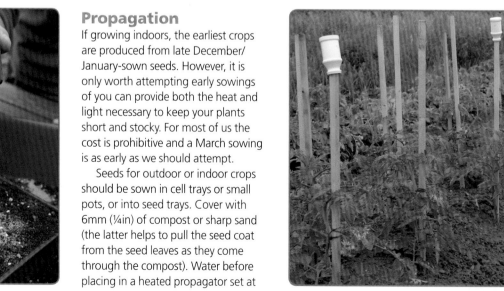

as possible. If growing on a windowsill, turn plants every day to encourage even growth. In the greenhouse, make sure that the glass is spotless.

Harden off plants if intending to grow in the open so that by the time of the last frost they are ready to move outside. Outdoor plants should be planted in rows 75cm (30in) apart with 45cm (18in) between plants. Provide stout stakes and tie the plants to them immediately.

If growing inside, the greenhouse border can be used for planting, but over time this can lead to problems with pests and diseases and most gardeners prefer to grow in pots or growing-bags. Most growing-bags offer a limited rooting depth, so a better option is to use ring culture (see page 86). This offers your plants an increased volume of compost later in the season and a bigger reservoir of water and nutrients when they need it most.

TRAINING AND TRIMMING

Tomatoes, whether outdoor or indoor varieties, are either cordon (also known as indeterminate: grow on one straight stem) or determinate (bush). Cordons must have their side shoots removed as soon as they are large enough to handle. The bushy types need little training or support throughout their lives other than to remove yellow leaves.

Above: The sideshoots of cordon tomatoes are removed regularly

Left: Bush tomatoes do not require training

As cordon plants grow it is essential to tie the main stem to the stake regularly, taking care not to damage trusses by passing the string above and not below them. Another method to use in the greenhouse or polytunnel is to bury a string under the rootball of the plant when planting and tie the other end to the eaves. As the plant grows, and when the tip is still pliable, it can be wound gently around the string, making sure that it passes over any trusses.

As the trusses form and the fruit starts to ripen, the older leaves can be stripped from the base of the plant upwards to allow light to reach the truss. Only strip leaves to a point just above the lowest truss. Once that truss is picked, leaves can be removed up the stem until the next truss is reached since in very hot weather the shade provided by the leaves can be a good thing, preventing the fruit from becoming scorched – a condition known as green-back.

Once cordon-trained plants have formed four trusses outdoors and seven trusses indoors pinch out the growing tip two leaves above the last truss to concentrate the plant's energies on ripening the fruit.

FEEDING AND WATERING

It is essential to maintain even watering throughout the life of the crop to avoid both fruit splitting and blossom end rot, especially if growing in containers or under cover. Also, since tomatoes are such hungry plants, they require feeding once a week with a high potash tomato food; look for one that also contains magnesium, calcium and trace elements. If you prefer, you can mix the feed at half strength and feed at every watering.

If the weather becomes dull and cold, growth will slow and the compost will tend to become wet. Take care under these conditions not to over water, but to tailor applications accordingly.

Above: A simple irrigation system can help supply your plants' needs

Harvesting and storage

Harvest fruit regularly as it ripens to a colour typical of the variety and begins to soften. If the weather is dull, fruit can be encouraged to ripen by hanging banana skins among the trusses. These release ethylene and help to speed up the ripening process.

Below: Fruit splitting is caused by irregular watering

Towards the end of the season, fruit may have to be picked when green. Place on a sunny windowsill, especially with other ripening fruit such as windfall apples or bananas or their skins, to encourage ripening. Alternatively, partner them with fruit, but keep them in the confines of a drawer.

Another way of encouraging ripening and getting plants out of the way to allow greenhouses and polytunnels to be cleaned at the end of the season, is to sever the stems at ground level and hang the plants upside down on the back of a shed door or nail on the wall to continue the ripening process.

Tomatoes can be stored in the salad drawer of the fridge for up to a week, but if you produce a glut there are lots of ways of using them, whether ripe or not, including making sauces, ketchup, chutneys and pickles, or drying or freezing them.

Pests and diseases

Whitefly are little white flying insects which suck the sap from the leaves and together with the scales (immature whitefly) excrete honeydew. This is colonised by black sooty mould, which fouls the fruit and leaves and lowers yield. Spray as soon as the pests are seen, use sticky yellow traps to trap flying adults, or introduce the parasitic wasp encarsia.

Blossom end rot is a disorder caused by a lack of calcium in the fruit, usually due to water shortage – even for a few hours – when the affected fruit was forming. Maintain even watering.

Tomato blight (see potato blight, page 142). This is the same disease that appears first on potatoes and causes similar symptoms on this crop. The leaves turn brown, usually on the tips and around the edges, then quickly collapse. Brown spots appear on the fruit, which is rendered inedible and soon rots. Spray to protect plants before the disease strikes using Vitax Bordeaux Mixture or Murphy Traditional Copper Fungicide. Select a resistant variety such as 'Legend' or 'Ferline'.

Varieties

There are literally hundreds of varieties available, including some intriguing heritage types with names like 'Green Banana', 'Bloody Butcher', and 'Black Krim', which are available from specialists (see page 176). Below are a few reliable modern varieties to get you started. All are grown as cordons unless stated otherwise.

'Shirley F1'

'Sweet Million F1'

INDOORS

'Shirley F1': a popular greenhouse tomato producing medium red fruit of good flavour.

'Big Boy F1': very large fruit, the biggest over 450g (1lb) in weight. Good for sandwiches, grilling and soup.

'Vanessa F1': medium-sized red 'vine-ripening' fruit, which remain in good condition on the plant after ripening for up to two weeks. Good resistance to splitting.

'Ferline': vigorous plants, producing good yields of medium to large red fruit. Good resistance to blight, fusarium and verticillium wilt.

'Ferline'

OUTDOORS

'Super Marmande': a beefsteak type – fewer fruit, but very large and early. One slice can be enough for a sandwich.

'Roma': a typical Italian plum tomato, good for soups and sauces. Semi-bushy habit that does require some support.

'Tigerella': unusual red fruit, stripped with greeny-yellow. Good tangy flavour.

'Sub Arctic Plenty': bushy plants that set and ripen well even in poor seasons. Early, red small- to medium-sized fruit.

'Tigerella'

INDOORS OR OUTDOORS

'Alicante': a reliable old favourite, with a good flavour.

'Sungold F1': small- to medium-sized orange fruit with a sweet flavour.

'Sweet Million F1': a cherry tomato producing long trusses of little sweet tomatoes. Heavy cropping and vigorous.

'Tumbling Tom Red': another cherry type – ideal for hanging baskets or pots on the patio. Trailing, bushy habit. 'Tumbling Tom Yellow' is also available from many catalogues.

'Sweet Olive F1': delicious olive-shaped red fruit produced in large numbers.

'Legend': early-ripening beefsteak type with a bushy habit and good blight resistance.

'Sweet Olive F1'

Tomatoes												X = ok XX = ideal
Month	J	F	M	A	M	J	J	A	S	O	N	D
Greenhouse												
Sow	X	X	XX	XX	X							
Harvest				X	XX	X	XX	XX	XX	XX		
Outdoors												
Sow			XX	X								
Harvest								XX	XX	XX	XX	

NUTRITIONAL INFORMATION

Rich in vitamins A and C and antioxidants, including lycopene.

Herbs

Herbs are as much a part of the allotment or veg garden as the vegetables themselves. They have been grown for centuries, first as medicinal plants and now, too, as essential ingredients for so many sweet and savoury dishes.

The topic of herb growing deserves a book on its own and everyone will have their favourites. Here we mention a selection – those which few self-respecting chefs would want to be without and at the same time are easy to grow either on a veg plot or simply in a container on a sunny patio or even a warm windowsill.

Basil

Basil is a tender plant, best treated as an annual and grown in a greenhouse or polytunnel, or on a sunny windowsill. There are many varieties of basil available either as young plants from garden centres or specialists, or as seeds.

PREPARING THE GROUND

Basil can be grown in the ground during the summer in well-drained soil in a sunny, sheltered spot. Indeed, many varieties are highly decorative and can be grown in the ornamental garden or in containers outdoors in mild

areas. They are though more often grown in containers in the greenhouse and make a good companion plant for tomatoes since basil is said to deter whitefly as well as tasting delicious with them. It is also said to deter flies when grown on the kitchen windowsill.

PROPAGATION

Sow thinly in pots or a small pinch to each cell in a cell tray and maintain a temperature of 18–21°C (65–70°F) in a heated propagator. Check watering every day and soak any dry patches with a fine rose or mist spray. Do not over-water and uncover the seedlings once most are through the compost.

Sowing two or three batches during the spring and summer at four-week intervals ensures a continual supply for the kitchen. Sow a batch in July for growing on a sunny windowsill to provide leaves for winter dishes.

GROWING ON

Basil is prone to damping off diseases so watch the seedlings carefully and prick out as soon as they can be handled, keeping them in small clumps of three or four. Pot into 9cm (3½in) pots.

Grow plants on at a temperature of 15–18°C (60–65°F) and give them as much light as possible. Allow the surface of the compost to dry out between waterings to prevent stem and root rots and also botrytis (grey mould).

Shade pale-leaved varieties from very hot sunshine, as they are prone to scorching, and pick off flowers as they appear because they tend to reduce the quality of the foliage.

HARVESTING

Pick leaves or shoots as required. Taking off shoot tips also encourages the plant to branch and produce new growth. Feed occasionally to encourage plants to produce a new flush of leafy growth. Preserve leaves for winter use by freezing in ice cubes.

Chives

Chives are attractive, compact plants forming a grass-like clump of deep green leaves. These are topped with pompom-like purple flowers which, like the leaves, are edible.

As members of the onion family, chives require the same conditions to thrive as the other culinary types, including bulb onions, shallots and spring onions, although they will tolerate partial shade (see page 128).

In addition to the common chive with its typical tubular onion leaf and purple blooms, garlic chives with broader flat leaves and white flowers are also available and make a good mild garlic substitute.

PREPARING THE SOIL
Choose a sunny or partially shaded site in well-drained, moist soil. Chives will tolerate poor soils quite well.

PROPAGATION
Seeds can be sown in spring as for other onions (see page 128). A small pinch of up to half a dozen seeds in a cell, or a thin scattering in a small pot, can then be grown on as one plant once the seedlings are well established. Alternatively, divide clumps in autumn or spring and replant immediately. In autumn, pot up a clump to bring indoors and grow on the windowsill for winter use.

GROWING ON
Simply allow to grow, watering in very dry weather. The occasional liquid feed after a heavy cutting will encourage a new crop of leaves. Although the flowers are edible and highly attractive they are best picked off if you wish to maximise the yield of tasty leaves. Divide clumps every two or three years and replant to prevent overcrowding.

HARVESTING
Snip off whole leaves to within an inch of so of soil level when required. The leaves can be frozen in ice cubes, dried or used to make vinegars (see below).

Coriander
Also known as cilantro, coriander is a delicate herb producing attractive, deeply cut leaves and tiny white flowers. It is grown for its leaves, which have a distinctive flavour, and also its seeds, which are an essential ingredient of many recipes.

PREPARING THE SOIL
Only sow outdoors in mild areas, choosing a sheltered, sunny site in free-draining soil. Otherwise treat as a container plant and grow in any free-draining potting compost or growing-bag.

PROPAGATION
Coriander can be started in September for over-wintering in the greenhouse or polytunnel and picking the following year, but it is more usual to sow in the spring from April to June. Plants soon run to seed during the summer so are best sown in small batches a month or so apart.

In mild areas coriander can be sown in the open in shallow drills 13mm (½in) deep and 30–45cm (12–18in) apart. Alternatively, sow into the greenhouse border or very thinly over the surface of the pots in which they are to grow (transplanting tends to encourage bolting). Heat should not be necessary for germination.

GROWING ON
Thin seedlings to leave 20cm (8in) between plants; the thinnings can be used in salads and stir-fries. Water regularly to avoid growth checks, which may cause plants to bolt (run to seed) prematurely; this is especially important in pots and plants should never be allowed to wilt.

HARVESTING
Leaves can be picked as required or frozen in ice cubes. If it is the seeds that you require, allow the plants to run to seed and keep them watered. Once the seed pods are ripe, snip off the flower stem and hang them upside down inside a paper bag to dry before storing in glass jars or airtight plastic containers (see page 74).

Mint
There are many varieties of mint, each with subtle differences in scent and flavour. They are herbaceous plants (die back to soil level each year) and spread by means of creeping roots and stems which makes them very invasive if not kept in check.

PREPARING THE GROUND
Mint prefers a moisture-retentive, but free-draining soil which is reasonably fertile. To keep it in check it is a good idea to grow mint in a container, such as a large pot either filled with garden soil or compost, and to sink this into the ground with the lip of the pot protruding above the soil by about 2.5cm (1in).

PROPAGATING
Take softwood cuttings during the spring and summer or divide established plants in the spring (see page 56).

GROWING ON
After planting, water during dry spells and keep growth in check to prevent shoots from 'escaping' into the surrounding soil. To prolong the harvest plants can be lifted in their plunged pots and taken into the greenhouse or polytunnel in late summer to encourage a flush of new growth for use in the autumn. Similarly, they can be brought indoors in early spring to force shoots into growth a little earlier.

HARVESTING
Pick leaves or young shoot tips as required. Can also be dried, frozen in ice cubes or used to make vinegars, oils and butters.

Parsley
There are several forms of parsley and the most popular in the kitchen is the flat leaf type. Curled leaf parsley, being very hardy, is always useful to grow and is highly decorative both in the garden and on the plate as a garnish.

PREPARING THE SOIL
Since parsley is related to carrots and parsnips, its requirements are similar, except that parsley will tolerate some shade. Choose a reasonably fertile, moist soil.

PROPAGATION
Seeds are sown in March or April for summer pickings and August for winter use. Sow 13mm (½in) deep in rows, or a few seeds into each cell of a cell tray. Place in a propagator and maintain 21°C (70°F) until the seeds have germinated.

Germination is often poor in cold soil, so if sowing direct allow the soil to warm first, covering with black polythene or cloches in the spring to speed the process. Soak seeds overnight in tepid water and/or pour boiling water into the seed drill prior to sowing.

GROWING ON
Thin seedlings in stages to 23cm (9in) apart and maintain watering during dry spells. Remove thinnings from the area so as not to attract carrot fly. Cover against the pest with crop protection fleece if it is prevalent in your area.

Established cell-raised plants can be planted into pots and containers, hanging baskets or strawberry pots, and kept close to the house for ease of picking. Plants are biennial and will run to seed in their second year, so treat as an annual or allow a few plants to seed the following year and move seedlings while young.

HARVESTING
Pick off leaves as required. Leaves can be dried or chopped and frozen in ice cubes.

Rosemary
This woody shrub is easy to grow and highly decorative. It has many uses in the kitchen and also for summer barbeques when sprigs can be either wrapped in foil along with fish, pork or lamb, or simply thrown on the fire to release their essential oils to the air.

PREPARING THE SOIL
Rosemary prefers a sunny, sheltered spot in well-drained soil. It also does well in a tub on the patio provided it is given some shelter from frost and cold winds during the winter.

PROPAGATION
Rosemary can be grown from seeds sown in the spring, heel cuttings taken in spring, or semi-ripe cuttings taken in late summer (see page 62), but it is much easier to buy a small, ready-grown plant and to grow it on. The common rosemary is great for culinary purposes, but there are a number of decorative varieties, including some with coloured leaves.

GROWING ON
In the open soil or flower border this shrub largely grows itself. Cutting sprigs for the kitchen tends to keep plants pruned, but if they do need shaping they can be lightly trimmed in early summer after flowering. In pots, maintain watering during dry spells, but do not over-water, and feed occasionally or use a controlled release fertiliser to keep plants healthy and vigorous.

HARVESTING
Simply snip off shoots as required and use sparingly. Leaves can be dried.

Sage
Sage deserves a place in any ornamental garden, particularly the variegated (coloured-leaf) forms which are attractive at the front of the border or in pots on a sunny patio.

PREPARING THE GROUND
Sages love a sunny spot in well-drained, reasonably fertile, but not rich soil.

PROPAGATION

Common green sage, *Salvia officinalis*, can be grown from seeds sown in the spring in a heated propagator set at 15°C (60°F), but all sages are easy to increase from tip or heel cuttings taken in spring and summer (see page 62).

GROWING ON

Sages are short-lived perennials that tend to become woody and sparse after four or five years. Keep them productive for as long as possible by trimming to remove the flowers in the summer and also cutting back into old wood if necessary in April/May.

Thyme

This is a pretty plant and worth growing for its ornamental value alone. The perfumed, often variegated foliage and blue, white or pink flowers are a delight. There are many varieties available, but for culinary uses common thyme (*T. vulgaris*) is most often sold as seeds.

PREPARING THE GROUND

Thyme needs a sunny spot in well-drained soil to thrive. It is ideal for planting along paths, in rock gardens, even in the cracks in paving, and will often self-seed among stone chippings on hard areas. It grows well in containers filled with well-drained, gritty compost.

PROPAGATION

Trimmings produced in late summer when the plants are cut back to remove the old flowers can be used as cuttings, or semi-ripe shoots can be removed with a heel during the summer and rooted in a gritty compost. Plants can also be divided or shoots layered, but for large numbers of plants sowing seeds in the spring is the quickest and cheapest way of propagating common thyme. Sow a small pinch of the tiny seeds into each cell of a cell tray and grow as one plant.

GROWING ON

Plant out cell-raised plants 23–38cm (9–15in) apart in a sunny, well-drained spot or into containers on a sunny patio. Thyme is a woody plant and relatively short-lived, though a light trim in late summer will encourage new growth.

HARVESTING

Pick leaves and shoot tips as required at any time. Tips can be dried or used to make oils and vinegars.

Preserving

Many herbs can be preserved by freezing in ice cubes. Pick, wash and chop fresh leaves, place in an ice cube tray and fill with water. A cube or two can be dropped into a pan of boiling water when cooking.

Herb butters

To make herb butters using chives, sage, parsley or thyme, finely chop about three tablespoons of the fresh herb, and beat into 225g (8oz) of slightly softened butter. Add the juice of one lemon, a little salt and black pepper and mix thoroughly.

Chill before using or transfer to an ice cube tray and freeze. The cubes of butter can then be added to recipes as required.

Herbal oils

Fill a suitable glass container with fresh herbs (loose fill, rather than pack tightly), such as basil, mint, rosemary or thyme. Cover with best quality sunflower oil, seal, label and allow to steep for two weeks before use.

Herbal vinegars

Pick fresh herbs such as basil, mint, chives, rosemary or thyme, and bruise lightly. Use them to loosely fill a sterilised glass container as above and cover with warmed cider or wine vinegar. Seal and keep on a windowsill. Shake the container each day for two weeks. Taste and repeat with fresh herbs if you require a stronger flavour. When it is to your satisfaction strain through muslin and pour into a clean glass container, add a last sprig of the herb, label and seal.

Drying

This is a classic way to preserve most herbs. It must be done slowly, i.e. not in an oven, to preserve the essential oils. Tying sage, thyme and rosemary into bunches and hanging upside down in an airing cupboard or a dark dry shed, or similar, is ideal. Alternatively, lay the leaves or stems on clean muslin, which has been stretched over a wire rack, and place in an airing cupboard. Depending on the temperature, drying may take up to two weeks.

ESSENTIAL INFORMATION

Glossary

annual Plant that grows and flowers in a single season.

antioxidants Molecules that help to prevent the breakdown of chemicals, thus reducing the number of potentially harmful free radicals in the body. Free radicals may cause damage to the cells in the body, leading to the formation of cancers.

base dressing An application of organic matter or fertiliser, applied to the soil prior to planting or sowing.

beta carotene Plant pigment that gives orange carrots their distinctive colour. Leads to development of vitamin A, which protects against cancer and heart disease.

biennial Plant taking two years to complete its lifecycle.

blanch The practice of excluding light to produce sweeter tasting leaves and stems, e.g. endive. Also, to immerse in boiling water to soften or remove skins perhaps in preparation for freezing.

bolt To flower and produce seed prematurely.

brassica Member of the cabbage family (*Brassicaceae*).

broadcast To scatter granular substances such as seeds, fertiliser or pesticide evenly over an area of ground.

capping Crust forming on the surface of soil damaged by compaction, watering or rainfall.

cell tray (or module) Containers used for propagating and growing young plants.

chitting Pre-germination of seeds or seed potatoes before sowing.

cloche Small portable structure used to protect crops outdoors.

cold frame Small, unheated covered structure used to harden off young seedlings or grow tender crops.

compost Decomposed organic waste from the garden or kitchen used as a mulch or soil conditioner. Also, a potting or seed-sowing medium.

cultivar New plant variant produced as the result of intentionally crossing two parent plants.

damp down To wet the floors and benches in a greenhouse or polytunnel in order to increase humidity and lower high temperatures.

dormancy Ceasing of growth during the winter months.

earth up To pull soil around the base for support, to deter frost or to cover a plant for the purpose of blanching.

enzymes Proteins that speed up reactions and drive the living process in the body.

essential oil Volatile oil contained in many plants such as rosemary and basil.

evergreen Plants keeping their leaves throughout the year.

F1 Hybrid Plants obtained by crossing two selected pure-breeding parents to produce uniform, heavy cropping offspring.

fleece Insulating cover used to protect crops from cold and pests.

folic acid Water-soluble form of vitamin B9, often found in fruit and veg.

friable Soil with a crumbly, workable texture, capable of forming a tilth, such as in a seed-bed.

forking (or fanging) A term to describe the forking of a root vegetable.

fertiliser Material applied to the soil or plants to provide nutrition.

fungicide Chemical used for the control of fungal diseases.

germination Process of growth from dormant seed to young plant.

green manure Fast-growing crop grown for digging into the soil to improve its structure and nutrient levels.

growing-bag Bag of compost used as a growing medium for producing salads and herbs.

half-hardy Plants that grow in low temperatures but will not withstand frost.

harden off To accustom plants to lower temperatures before planting.

hardy Plants that can tolerate frost without protection.

haulm Top growth of plants such as potatoes.

heart up Stage at which leafy vegetables swell to form a central heart.

heavy soil Soil, such as a clay, which holds lots of water.

herbaceous Non-woody plants that die down at the end of the season, coming up again next year – e.g. asparagus.

herbicide Chemical used to kill weeds.

humus Organic decayed remains of plant material in soils that binds the particles together.

hybrid Plant resulting from the breeding of two distinct species or genera.

infusion Tea made by seeping leaves in boiling water.

inorganic Term used to describe fertilisers made from naturally occurring minerals, or artificial fertilisers.

insecticide Chemical used to kill insect pests.

John Innes compost Loam-based growing medium made to a standard recipe.

leaching Washing out and loss of soluble nutrients from topsoil.

leaf Plant organ containing the green pigment (chlorophyll) essential for photosynthesis.

leaf mould Peat-like material made from decaying leaves.

legume Pea and bean family.

lime Calcium used to raise the pH (alkalinity) of the soil.

loam Fertile soil of medium texture.

maincrop Biggest crop produced throughout the growing season.

minerals Natural compounds used in the body to help many processes and often associated with enzymes.

mulch Layer of material applied to the ground to control weeds, conserve moisture and protect the soil.

neutral Soil or compost with a pH value of 7 which is neither acid nor alkaline (see pH).

nutrients Minerals essential for plant growth.

organic Term used to describe substances that are derived from natural sources, e.g. plant waste. Also used to describe gardening without the use of chemicals.

pan Layer of compacted soil that prevents the movement of water and oxygen, impeding root development and drainage.

perennial Plant that lives for three or more years.

perlite and vermiculite Forms of expanded volcanic rock. Used in propagation and to improve drainage in potting composts.

pH Measure of acidity or alkalinity in the soil or compost based on a scale of 0 to 14. A pH below 7 is acid and above, alkaline.

pinch out To remove the growing tip of a plant to encourage branching.

pot on To move a plant into a larger pot as the roots develop.

potassium Mineral essential for our cells to ensure that they function correctly.

prick out To transfer seedlings, from a seedbed or tray, with the purpose of giving them room to grow.

propagation Process of increasing plant stocks by seed or vegetative means (cuttings or division).

radicle Root of a seedling.

rhizome Fleshy underground stem that acts as a storage organ.

root Part of the plant that absorbs water and nutrients and anchors the plant.

root crops Vegetables grown for their edible roots.

runner Trailing shoot that roots where it touches the ground, e.g. strawberry.

seed Dormant embryo, capable of forming a new plant.

seed leaves (cotyledons) First leaf or leaves produced by a seed following germination.

seedling Young plant grown from seed.

sets Small onions or shallots used for planting.

shoot Branch or stem.

side shoot Branch or stem growing from the main stem.

species Group of closely related plants with similar characteristics.

stamen Male pollen-producing part of the plant.

stem Main stem of a plant, from which sideshoots appear.

stigma Part of a pistil (the female organs of a flower) that receives pollen.

subsoil Layers of less fertile soil immediately below the topsoil, often lighter in colour.

sucker Stem originating below soil level, usually from the plant's roots or underground stem, as in raspberries.

systemic or translocated Term used to describe a chemical that is absorbed by a plant at one point and then circulated by the sap.

tap root Main anchoring root of a plant, usually growing straight down into the soil. Often a storage organ, e.g. carrot.

tender plants With little or no tolerance of frost.

thinning Uprooting of seedlings to improve the quality of those that remain. Also, the removal of fruit or shoots to prevent overcrowding.

tilth Surface layer of soil produced by cultivation.

top-dressing Application of fertilisers or bulky organic material to the soil surface or compost in a pot.

topsoil Upper, most fertile layer of soil.

transpiration Evaporation of moisture from plant leaves and stems via pores known as stomata.

transplant To move a plant from one growing position to another.

tuber Modified underground stem used to store moisture and nutrients.

variety Botanical classification used to describe a naturally occurring plant variant (see also cultivar).

vegetative Parts of a plant that are capable of growth.

vitamins Nutrients required in the body, essential for metabolism (the chemical reactions that take place in living cells to allow them, and therefore our bodies, to function). They are separate from the many minerals that are also essential to keep us healthy.

weathering Effect of rain and frost on the soil.

wind-rock Destabilising of plant roots by the wind especially after planting.

Useful addresses

Seeds and young plants

Alan Romans
tel 01 337 831060
www.alanromans.com

Association Kokopelli
tel 01227 731815
www.kokopelli-seeds.com

Chiltern Seeds
tel: 01229 581137
www.chilternseeds.co.uk

D.T. Brown & Co
tel 0845 1662275
www.dtbrownseeds.co.uk

Edwin Tucker & Sons
tel 01 364 652233
www.edwintucker.com

E.W. King & Co
tel 01 376 570000
www.kingsseeds.com

GoGrow
tel 0845 4300601
www.gogrow.co.uk

Heritage Seed Library
tel 02476 303517

Jekka's Herb Farm
tel 01454 41 8878
www.jekkasherbfarm.com

Medwyn's Seeds
tel 01248 714851
www.medwynsofanglesey.co.uk

Mr Fothergill's Seeds
tel 0845 1662511
www.mr-fothergills.co.uk

Moreveg
tel: 01 823 681302
www.moreveg.co.uk

Nicky's Nursery
tel 01 843 600972
www.nickys-nursery.co.uk

Samuel Dobie and Son
tel 01 803 696444
www.dobies.co.uk

Seeds-By-Size
tel 01442 251458
www.seeds-by-size.co.uk

Seeds of Italy
tel 0208 427 5020
www.seedsofitaly.com

Select Seeds
tel 01246 826011
www.selectseeds.co.uk

S.E. Marshall & Co
tel 01 480 443390
www.marshalls-seeds.co.uk

Shelley Seeds
tel 01244 317165
shelleyseeds@chesterl37.fsnet.co.uk

Simply Vegetables
tel 01 449 721720
www.plantsofdistinction.co.uk

Simpson's Seeds
tel 01985 845004
www.simpsonsseeds.co.uk

Suffolk Herbs
tel 01 376 572456
www.suffolkherbs.com

Suttons Seeds
tel 0870 220 2899
www.suttons-seeds.co.uk

Tamar Organics
tel 01 822 834887
tamarorganics@aol.com

Terwins Seeds
tel 01284 828255
www.terwinseeds.co.uk

The Herbary
tel 01985 844442
www.beansandherbs.co.uk

The Organic Gardening Catalogue
tel 0845 130 1304
www.OrganicCatalog.com (*also sundries*)

The Real Seed Catalogue (Vida Verde)
tel 01239 821107
www.realseeds.co.uk

Thomas Etty
tel 01460 57934
www.thomasetty.co.uk

Thompson & Morgan
tel 01473 688821
www.thompson-morgan.com

Wallis Seeds
tel 01245 360413

W. Robinson & Sons Ltd
tel 01524 791210
www.mammothonion.co.uk

Unwins Seeds
tel 01480 443395
www.unwinsdirect.co.uk

Sundries

Ferndale Lodge
tel 0844 314 1342
www.ferndale-lodge.co.uk
Garden Direct
tel 01992 890 770
www.gardendirect.co.uk
Haxnicks
tel: 0845 241 1555
www.haxnicks.co.uk
LBS Garden Warehouse
tel 01282 873370
www.lbsgardenwarehouse.co.uk
Two Wests & Elliott
Tel: 01246 451077
www.twowests.co.uk
Link-a-bord
tel 01773 590566
www.linkabord.co.uk

Wormeries

Original Organics
tel 0808 1209676
www.originalorganics.co.uk
Wiggly Wigglers
tel 01981 500391
www.wigglywigglers.co.uk

The Recycle Works
tel 0800 0320377
www.recycleworks.co.uk

Information

Garden Organic
tel: 024 7630 3517
www.gardenorganic.org.uk
Kitchen Garden Magazine
tel: 01507 529529
www.kitchengarden.co.uk
National Society of Allotment and Leisure Gardeners
tel: 01536 266576
www.nsalg.org.uk
National Vegetable Society
tel: 01382 580394
www.nvsuk.co.uk
Organic Gardening Magazine
tel: 01507 529529
www.organicgardening.co.uk
The British Beekeepers Association
www.britishbee.org.uk
The Royal Horticultural Society
tel: 0845 062 1111
www.rhs.org.uk
The Soil Association
tel 0117 314 5000
www.soilassociation.org

Tools

Bulldog Tools
tel 01279 401572
www.bulldogtools.co.uk
Fiskars Brands
www.fiskarsbrands.com
Spear & Jackson
tel 0114 281 4242
www.spear-and-jackson.com
Mantis
tel 0800 988 4828
www.mantis-uk.co.uk

Pest Control

Commonsense Gardening
www.garden-care.org.uk
(also links to major pesticide manufacturers)
Green Gardener
tel 01603 715096
www.greengardener.co.uk
Growing Success
tel 01622 717373
www.monrobrands.com/growingsuccess
Scarletts Plant care
tel 0845 0945 499
www.ladybirdplantcare.co.uk
Slug Rings
tel: 01225 851524
www.slugrings.co.uk

Index

January

SOW

Salad leaves
Tomatoes (heated crops)
Peppers

Aubergines
Summer cabbage

PLANT

Early potatoes (in pots)
Fruit trees and bushes

Rhubarb

HARVEST

Parsnips
Celeriac
Winter/Savoy cabbage
Jerusalem artichoke
Leaf beet
Brussels sprouts
Carrot
Celery
Chicory
Endive

Kale
Leek
Kohl rabi
Winter lettuce
Winter radish
Salsify/scorzonera
Spinach
Swedes
Turnips

Tips for January

■ Plant out shallots and garlic – If you planted garlic cloves in pots in the autumn, these should by now have produced some healthy shoots and can be planted out if the weather and soil conditions allow. Shallots can also be planted in milder areas of the country, but if the soil is too wet or frozen, delay until conditions improve. Cover with a cloche in the early stages.

■ Order seed potatoes – If you want the best choice of varieties order now to avoid disappointment.

■ Parsnips – if the ground is likely to become frozen, lift some roots and 'plant' in a sheltered spot so they are available when needed.

■ Brussels sprouts – remove the plants and compost them once the whole crop has been harvested.

February

SOW

Lettuce
Broad beans
Early peas
Onions
Summer cabbage

Chicory/endive
Parsnip (if conditions allow)
Radish (under cloches)
Turnip

PLANT

Onion sets
Shallots
Rhubarb

Chinese and Jerusalem artichoke

HARVEST

Winter and Savoy cabbage
Leeks
Kale
Jerusalem artichokes
Broccoli
Brussels sprouts
Parsnips
Cauliflowers

Celeriac
Celery
Chicory
Winter radish
Spinach
Salsify
Scorzonera
Forced rhubarb
Swedes

Tips for February

■ Check seed stocks to make sure you have everything you need. Sort them in month order of sowing, so nothing is forgotten.

■ Buy labels and a few good permanent pens.

■ Clean and replace any damaged propagator lids, cloches and cold frames.

■ Check stocks of paraffin and top up if necessary.

■ Repair and replace damaged tools.

■ Buy compost once fresh stocks hit the garden centres.

March

SOW

(under cloches where possible)

Lettuce	Leeks
Carrots	Beetroot
Outdoor tomatoes (sow with heat)	Radish
	Brussels sprouts
Parsnips	Summer cabbage
Onions	Celery
Shallots	Celeriac

PLANT

Early potatoes

HARVEST

Winter and Savoy cabbage	Celeriac
	Celery
Leeks	Chicory
Kale	Winter radish
Jerusalem artichokes	Spinach
Broccoli	Salsify
Brussels sprouts	Scorzonera
Parsnips	Forced rhubarb
Cauliflowers	Swedes

Tips for March

■ Keep on top of weeding, since weeds will soon outgrow your crops in the improved conditions of spring. This includes over-wintering crops such as onions and garlic and permanent plantings such as strawberries and asparagus.

■ Provide supports for early peas and buy your canes in preparation for growing climbers such as runner beans and climbing French beans, also taller-growing peas.

■ Apply fertiliser to the ground in preparation for sowing as the weather permits.

■ Feed over-wintered brassicas with a sprinkling of ammonium sulphate or other high nitrogen feed.

April

SOW

Broccoli	Kohl rabi
Summer cabbage	Spinach
Leeks	French bean (under cloches)
Onions	
Radish	Broad bean
Lettuce	Salsify
Tomatoes	Scorzonera
Brussels sprouts	Turnip
Peas	Swede
Beetroot	Leaf beet
Carrots	Parsnips (early in month)
Cauliflower	Runner bean (late in the month)
Kale	
Celery	Sweetcorn (late in the month)
Endive	

PLANT

Potatoes	Asparagus
Onion sets	Artichokes
Shallots	Summer cabbage

HARVEST

Parsnips	Baby salads
Celeriac	Kale
Jerusalem artichokes	Broccoli
Winter cauliflowers	Chicory
Winter cabbages	

Tips for April

■ Harvest parsnips before they make new growth.

■ Add fertiliser 10–14 days prior to sowing or planting.

■ In the south it is possible to sow French beans in April under cloches.

■ Sow cabbages that will be ready for harvesting during July and August. They can be sown into nursery beds in the plot, but can be more easily protected from pests such as pigeons if sown in cell trays and grown on in a cold greenhouse or cold frame until ready for planting.

■ Turnips are an underrated crop, but if harvested young are delicious and can even be eaten raw. Sow now, but as with radish (to which they are related) take precautions against flea beetle which can decimate the seedlings, turning the leaves to lace.

May

SOW

(get out there and get busy!)
Beetroot
Carrots
Lettuce
Spring onions
Radish
Spinach
Runner beans
French beans
Peas (second early/ maincrop)
Aubergine (early in the month)
Tomatoes (early in the month)
Broccoli
Summer cabbage
Summer cauliflower
Courgettes
Squashes
Cucumbers
Marrows
Endive
Radicchio
Salad leaves
Kale
Herbs
Florence fennel
Kohl rabi
Salsify
Scorzonera
Sweetcorn
Turnip
Swede

PLANT

Brussels sprouts
Cabbages
Globe artichoke
Calabrese
Broccoli
Maincrop potatoes (early in the month)

HARVEST

Spring cabbage
Radish
Lettuce
Salad leaves
Rhubarb

Tips for May

■ Cover tender crops with several layers of fleece on chilly nights and close the ventilation on cold frames by late afternoon to conserve heat.
■ Don't let the weeds take control at any stage or they will quickly crowd out your seedlings and encourage pests. Remove them, by hand if necessary while still small to keep root disturbance to your crops to a minimum.
■ Be prepared to thin seedlings regularly to give the remaining plants room and light to develop. This is best done in stages and the final seedlings to go can often be used as delicious mini veg.
■ Earth up potatoes as necessary to protect them from the frost.

June

SOW

Broccoli
Autumn cabbage
Winter cauliflower
Lettuce
Corn salad (early in month)
Salad leaves
Beetroot
Carrots
Runner beans
French beans
Broad beans (early June)
Swedes
Spinach
Endive
Radicchio
Florence fennel
Sweetcorn
Turnip
Cucumbers (outdoor)
Kale
Herbs
Kohl rabi
Parsley
Pak choi
Peas
Radish
Rocket
Perpetual spinach
Swiss chard
Salad onions

PLANT

Runner beans
French beans
Broad beans
Tomatoes
Sweetcorn
Squashes
Cucumbers
Cabbage
Cauliflowers
Marrows
Peppers (late June)
Courgettes
Kale
Florence fennel
Celery
Celeriac
Cabbages
Leeks
Lettuce

HARVEST

Asparagus
First early potatoes
Cabbage
Peas
Lettuce
Radish
Broad beans
Beetroot
Leaf beet
Tomatoes (indoor)
Swiss chard
Swedes
Turnips
Rocket
Salad leaves
Salad onions
Carrots
Corn salad

Tips for June

■ Collect water via all available means.
■ Apply mulches wherever possible.
■ Plant flowers among crops such as calendulas, limnanthes and nasturtiums to attract pollinating insects.

July

SOW

Dwarf beans
Broad beans
Leaf beet
Spring cabbage
Oriental cabbage
Carrots
Chicory
Endive/Radicchio
Corn salad

Kohl rabi
Lettuce
Salad leaves
Radish
Pak choi
Parsley
Peas
Turnip

PLANT

Kale
Winter cabbage
Brussels sprouts
Broccoli
Cardoon
Cauliflower

Cucumber (early in month)
Squash (early in month)
Lettuce
Radicchio
Leeks

HARVEST

Kale
Kohl rabi
Rocket
Rhubarb (last stalks)
Leaf beet
Swiss chard
Lettuce
Salad leaves
Radish
Spring onion
Garlic
Bulb onions
Parsley

Broccoli
Pak choi
Peppers
Tomatoes
Cucumbers
Endive
Beetroot
French beans
Runner beans
Carrots
Celery
Summer cabbage

Tips for July

■ If dry, make use of water by using on plants that need it like squashes, salads, turnips and swedes.

■ Squash the yellow eggs of cabbage white butterflies as they are seen. Cover the crop with Enviromesh to prevent further infestations.

■ Pollinate the female flowers of melons as they appear by picking off a mature male flower and placing the pollen bearing anthers close to the female pistil.

August

SOW

Winter/spring lettuce
Spring cabbage
Chinese cabbage
Pak choi
Carrots (if weather cool)
Endive

Kohl rabi
Radish
Spinach (in cool conditions)
Turnips

PLANT

Savoy and winter cabbage
Cauliflowers

Kale
Leeks (early in month)

HARVEST

Lettuce
Globe artichokes
Broad beans
Runner beans
French beans
Peppers
Onions
Beetroot
Leaf beet
Broccoli
Summer cabbage
Carrots
Summer cauliflowers

Early celery
Cucumbers
Endive
Kohl rabi
Marrow
Summer squash
Peas
Potatoes
Radish
Spinach
Sweetcorn
Tomatoes
Turnip

Tips for August

■ Continue to harvest early and second early potatoes. Try not to leave any stray tubers in the soil.

■ Water peas well during any dry spells. This should, help to keep powdery mildew at bay.

■ Place straw under developing pumpkins and other squashes to keep the fruit clean and pest free.

■ Harvest outdoor (ridge) cucumbers when they reach 15–20cm (6–8in) in length. If any plants show signs of virus (leaves blotchy and growth poor or distorted) they should be lifted and disposed of.

■ Begin harvesting sweetcorn as the cobs ripen. Pull back the sheath covering the cob and push your fingernail into one or two grains. If milky liquid comes out the corn is ripe, but if the liquid is clear, leave the cob for a few more days to ripen properly.

September

SOW

Salad leaves
Spinach
Spring cabbage (early in the month)
Endive

Lettuce (for spring harvesting)
Over-wintering onions
Turnips

PLANT

Spring cabbage

HARVEST

Globe artichokes
Aubergines
Peppers
Tomatoes
Broad beans
Runner beans
French beans
Drying beans
Leaf beet
Beetroot
Carrots
Broccoli
Brussels sprouts (late in the month)
Summer cabbage
Oriental cabbage
Cauliflowers
Celery
Celeriac

Outdoor cucumbers
Endive
Radicchio
Kohl rabi
Leeks
Lettuce
Courgette
Marrow
Summer squash
Onions
Peas
Maincrop potatoes
Radishes
Spinach
Salad leaves
Swedes
Turnips
Sweetcorn

Tips for September

■ Shred woody waste such as sweetcorn, tomato and brassica stems before adding to the compost heap.
■ This is a good time to install insect homes, hedgehog homes and to undertake other wildlife friendly projects so that they are there and ready for creatures looking for a haven for the winter.
■ Remove the growing tip from outdoor tomatoes if you haven't already done so once plants have produced four or five trusses to improve the quality of fruit left on the plant and to encourage ripening. Maintain watering and feeding until the final fruits are picked.

October

SOW

Rocket
Mibuna
Mizuna

Early peas
Winter lettuce

PLANT

Spring cabbages
Winter lettuces
Rhubarb

Onion sets (early in the month)
Garlic (early in the month)
Broad beans

HARVEST

Parsnips
Carrots
Beetroot
Chard
Lettuce
Radish
Salsify
Scorzonera
Potatoes
Spinach
Swedes
Celery

Celeriac
Cauliflowers
Winter cabbage
Oriental cabbage
Brussels sprouts
Broccoli
Sweetcorn (early in month)
Tomatoes (early in the month)
Turnips

Tips for October

■ When clearing the ground, lift all old leaves, stems and potato tubers.
■ Pull any weeds to prevent them from establishing over winter and from harbouring pests and other problems for next season's crops.
■ Newly lifted canes should be lifted and the ends dipped in a garden disinfectant before storing.
■ Pick up fallen leaves and compost them in a bin made from a 'cage' of chicken wire supported by four canes. Alternatively store them in black plastic sacks, each with a few holes stabbed in the side with a garden fork to allow some air to pass through.
■ Invest in or make some simple cloches and sow some salad leaves as soon as possible if the weather allows. Use cloches to cover late-sown carrots, early peas and broad beans, also late salads such as radishes which have yet to be harvested.

November

SOW

Field beans as a
green manure
Broad beans

Sprouting seeds
Peas

PLANT

Garlic cloves
Onion sets
Broad beans

Peas
Rhubarb

HARVEST

Spring onions
Salad leaves
Spinach
Celeriac
Carrots
Parsnips
Leeks
Lettuce
Endive
Radicchio
Jerusalem artichoke
Leaf beet

Kohl rabi
Salsify
Scorzonera
Radish
Broccoli
Brussels sprouts
Chinese cabbage
Winter cabbage
Autumn cauliflower
Celery
Chicory
Kale

Tips for November

- This is a good time to plant most garlic varieties for the best possible crop next year.
- Shred woody prunings as they are collected. They can be used to top up the covering on paths or stored separately and allowed to rot down.
- Go through overwintering crops such as brassicas and leeks, removing yellow leaves which otherwise act as a hiding place for overwintering pests such as slugs and diseases such as leek rust.
- Stake tall overwintering crops such as Brussels sprouts to protect them from the winter winds; firm around the base of the stem with your heel beforehand. Put some form of protection in place against pigeons which may become a nuisance as alternative sources of food become more scarce.

December

SOW

Broad beans
Early peas
Winter lettuce

Mizuna
Mibuna
Rocket

PLANT

Broad beans
Early peas

Winter lettuce

HARVEST

Winter cabbage
Savoy cabbage
Kale
Early broccoli
Brussels sprouts
Leeks
Carrots
Swedes
Celeriac

Celery
Jerusalem artichokes
Chinese artichokes
Chard
Winter cauliflowers (early in the month)
Parsnips
Salsify
Scorzonera

Tips for December

- If you have decided to try the no-dig method cover bare ground with well-rotted manure or compost to protect it from the rain and leave it for the worms to incorporate.
- Decided to stick with the spade (well it is a good winter work-out)? Then keep up the digging, but just a small patch at a time to avoid strain.
- This is a good time to assess the plot and to decide if the 'useful' things you have been hoarding all year are really worth keeping or are just a harbour for pests.
- Clean and oil those tools such as spades, hoes, shears and secateurs. Sharpen blades where appropriate or replace if too worn or notched.
- Order your seeds. If you've been keeping a crop diary through the year, use this to help you decide what to grow and what to avoid. If you've had any pest or disease problems this year, check the catalogues for resistant varieties.
- If you sowed a batch of broad beans or peas outside last month for cropping in May or June, check that cloches are still in place and that weeds are not threatening to take over. Ensure that mice are kept at bay, using traps if necessary.